War and Conflict in the Middle Ages

War and Conflict Through the Ages

Jeremy Black, *War in the Nineteenth Century*
Stephen Morillo, *War and Conflict in the Middle Ages*
Brian Sandberg, *War and Conflict in the Early Modern World*

WAR
AND
CONFLICT
IN THE
MIDDLE
AGES

A GLOBAL PERSPECTIVE

STEPHEN MORILLO

polity

First published in 2022 by Polity Press

Polity Press
65 Bridge Street
Cambridge CB2 1UR, UK

Polity Press
111 River Street
Hoboken, NJ 07030, USA

ISBN-13: 978-1-5095-2977-3
ISBN-13: 978-1-5095-2978-0 (pb)

A catalogue record for this book is available from the British Library.

Library of Congress Control Number: 2022930139

Typeset in 10.5 on 12 pt Plantin by
Cheshire Typesetting Ltd, Cuddington, Cheshire
Printed and bound in Great Britain by TJ Books Ltd, Padstow, Cornwall

The publisher has used its best endeavours to ensure that the URLs for external websites referred to in this book are correct and active at the time of going to press. However, the publisher has no responsibility for the websites and can make no guarantee that a site will remain live or that the content is or will remain appropriate.

Every effort has been made to trace all copyright holders, but if any have been overlooked the publisher will be pleased to include any necessary credits in any subsequent reprint or edition.

For further information on Polity, visit our website: politybooks.com

Contents

Preface

When my editor at Polity, Pascal Porcheron, asked me if I would be interested in writing a book about medieval warfare from a global perspective, I said "yes" because I figured I'd been researching this topic in one way or another for my whole career, so writing this book would be a simple process of mashing up some of my "greatest hits" with some standard general accounts. It was only after I signed to do the book that I took it seriously, and realized that the easy approach would not suffice.

The result is that this book represents my complete rethinking, from the ground up, of medieval warfare: how it worked, what it meant, and how to see all that from a global perspective. This turned out to be a far harder but also a far more rewarding task than I had anticipated. But I learned a great deal from the process of thinking through this topic anew, and I hope you, the reader, will also find new and valuable insights into the topic here.

Events also conspired to frame the project in a way that turned out to be more relevant to today than I could have anticipated. Having started with the discovery that I could plausibly define a "global Middle Ages" in terms of climate change and pandemics at both ends of the period, I saw our contemporary and increasingly critical problem with human-driven climate change suddenly get combined with a new global pandemic. And in addition to relevance, I also got time: much of this book was drafted under conditions of lockdown that removed many of the distractions that usually slow the writing of a book. I'm not going to "thank" COVID-19 for this, of course. No one wants "help" that deadly. Let's just say that context helped keep me focused.

The task was always going to be challenging anyway. Viewing medieval war and conflict from the ten-thousand-foot altitude demanded by a global perspective, so that patterns and commonalities could be discerned from above, while keeping in view the details that make the topic so interesting, is as difficult as the visual metaphor makes it sound. But it proved, as I have said, very rewarding, and I hope you find it so, too.

Acknowledgments

This book arose from a suggestion by my editor, Pascal Porcheron, who has been supportive and helpful from the beginning, as has his team at Polity Press, especially his assistants Ellen MacDonald-Kramer and Stephanie Homer. Thanks also to production editor Evie Deavall and copy-editor Fiona Sewell. Polity is a great press to write for.

Once the manuscript took shape, a number of people read it in various forms and offered helpful readings and reactions. These include two anonymous reviewers for Polity Press; my friend Jeremy Black; my "MilDude" colleagues at West Point, Major Kevin Malmquist, Major Ron Braasch, and Major Steve Beckmann; and a set of friends and relatives who gave me the critical "non-specialist" view that made sure I was being at least marginally comprehensible beyond the ivory tower, including Brigid Manning-Hamilton, Cynthia Sutton, and Shane Blackman. And my smart and lovely wife Lynne was, as usual, an invaluable critic both of ideas and of my prose and its tendency to devolve into paragraph-long complex/compound sentences featuring nested lists and other horrors of the "drafting ideas into usable English" process.

But above all, this book developed through a set of seminars I taught to undergraduates at both Wabash College and West Point, and discussions with them helped me wrestle a vague outline into the book's current form. I would like to thank those students: at Wabash, Simon Brumfield, Nick Carson (who deserves extra thanks for work as my intern one summer putting notes and references in order), Chris Dabrowski, Evan Frank, Chris Hartkemeier, Ben Klimczak, Davis Lamm, Ivan Martinez, Michael Ortiz, Wes Bedwell, Josh Blackburn, Cameron Graham, Gordon Harman-Sayre, Will Harvey,

Owen Ryan-Jensen, Evan Schiefelbein, Dylan Torbush, and Luke Wallace; and at West Point, Cadets Patrick Hachmeister, Hunter Harrison, Will Hogan, James Johnson, William Mitchell, Temuulen Sodgerel, Andrew Waldrep, and Parker Woodworth. It is to them and to all students of history that I dedicate this book.

Figures

Introduction

War and conflict in the Middle Ages is a vast topic spread over a long time period. Looking at armed violence over more than a thousand years from a global perspective means that the picture is also painted across a global canvas. How can such a vast topic be analyzed within the confines of a relatively short book?

The approach taken here is to break the analysis into two parts. Part I of this book examines the "Common Rules" of medieval warfare, the limits, mostly but not exclusively physical, that shaped how conflicts were fought. Part II then turns to a chronological survey that sees medieval warfare as a response to changing "Scenarios" and analyzes warfare as a form of discourse that was central in medieval people constituting their own world.

But before moving into the details of this analysis, the first two chapters of this book make up an introductory part. Chapter 1, "Three Battles," takes us into the topic by examining three fascinating battles from various times and places in the medieval world. The variety of combatants, locales, and fighting styles we can see in just these three battles raises a number of questions about our topic. Chapter 2, "Questions and Methods," explores those basic questions and outlines the philosophical and methodological assumptions this study makes in answering those questions.

1
Three Battles

This is a book about war and conflict in the Middle Ages from a global perspective. So let's make an initial exploration of this topic by recounting the stories of three battles (broadly defined, as we shall see), all of which took place in the era usually designated "the Middle Ages" (one each from the early, middle, and late thirds of that era), in places that were part of our globe. The combination of these stories should raise some questions about what we mean by "war and conflict" and "the Middle Ages," especially when viewed from a global, or world-historical, perspective. Then, after narrating the battles, we will explore some of those questions. Answering those questions and generalizing the lessons and features of our three battles will be the task of the rest of this book.

On to our three battles!

The Battle of al-Qādasiyyah

Kadiseyah — *638* *Muslims won*

In early January 638,[1] a small army of Bedouin Arabs, just recently converted to a new religion called Islam, stood at the edge of the Arabian Desert in southern Iraq, where the desert met the rich

---

[1] This book uses Christian (Gregorian) dating – also called "Common Era" (CE) dates – for convenience. The date of Qādasiyyah is disputed, ranging between 634 and 638 CE in the original Muslim sources. Armenian sources connected to forces that fought on the Persian side establish January 6, 638 as the correct (starting?) date: Kennedy, *Great Arab Conquests*, p. 18; Howard-Johnston, *Witnesses to a World Crisis*, p. 375, and on the chronological deformations of the Islamic historical record that affected the dating of Qādasiyyah, pp. 379–82, esp. p. 380.

alluvial soil of the Tigris-Euphrates valleys. Facing them was a larger
army of Persian soldiers from the Sassanid Empire, which ruled
Iraq and Iran. Sassanid influence had long extended well into areas
beyond the empire, including Arabia, the homeland of the Muslim
army. But this time, the Arabs were on the offensive, striking into
the realm of the sedentary, "civilized" world. In a remarkable set of
ways, the resulting battle pitted a potential new world order against
an established old world order. The stakes for both were existential.

Islam was the recent result of the preaching and organizing activities
of the Prophet Muhammad, who after much struggle had managed
to unite the mostly pagan tribes of the Arabian Peninsula under the
banner of Allah, the One True God. Muhammad had died in 632,
but the community had settled, after not inconsiderable conflict, on
the leadership of caliphs, or successors to the Prophet: Abu Bakr was
caliph for the first two years, but the next four caliphs either were
assassinated or abdicated. The first of these, Umar, directed campaigns of expansion against the Eastern Roman Empire (later known
as the Byzantine Empire) and the Sassanid Persian Empire starting
in 634. The Muslims immediately met with perhaps unexpected
success, conquering the rich Roman province of Syria by 636; Umar
then shifted Arab efforts against the Sassanids.[2]

Arab successes were in part the result of the fact that the Romans
and Sassanids had just been fighting each other for several decades.
This war saw initial Persian successes, including their conquest of
Roman Syria and Egypt, with a Persian army approaching the Roman
capital at Constantinople in 619. But the Roman emperor Heraclius
led a remarkable recovery that ended with the Persian ruler Chosroes
assassinated by his own followers in 628, followed by four years of
political infighting before Kavadh II reestablished order. Though the
extent of the damage to the two great empires can be exaggerated,
the war undoubtedly left both powers somewhat war-weary, their
subjects overtaxed, and morale on both sides needing to be rebuilt.
The Islamic invasions came before either side had fully recovered.

The war had had other effects on the political and economic setting
in which Muhammad had built up his new Muslim community. Both
Persians and Romans had invested resources in Arab tribal allies,
pumping unusual levels of wealth into Arabia, wealth that probably
served to enhance the possibilities for community and state building
in the peninsula, which was not normally rich enough to generate high

[2] For good narratives of the early Islamic campaigns of expansion, see Kennedy,
Great Arab Conquests, and Donner, *Early Islamic Conquests*.

levels of political organization on its own. Furthermore, the difficulty of the war had pushed both sides to intensify their cultural efforts to solidify internal support and gain allies. This meant that both sides turned to their religious traditions. Heraclius' Christianization of the war has led some historians to refer to his campaigns against the Sassanids as the first Christian Crusade; similar and parallel efforts on the part of Chosroes might be seen as the first (and last) Zoroastrian Crusade. (It should be noted, however, that the population of the Eastern Roman Empire was far more Christian than the population of the Persian Empire was Zoroastrian – the Iraqi portion of Persia may have been majority Christian when the Muslim invasion occurred.)[3] It is probably not a coincidence that Islam emerged in a time and region saturated with intense religious imagery and propaganda.[4]

Thus, the two armies that faced each other at Qādasiyyah represented on one side a new religion, Islam, one with a special relationship to a people, the Arabs; and on the other an old religion, Zoroastrianism, with a special relationship to a people, the Persians. Reflecting the social structures of the two peoples and their religious beliefs, the Arab Islamic army saw itself as representing an egalitarian society without hereditary rulers; the Persian army saw itself as representing a very hierarchical society ruled by the hereditary house of Sasan and its supporting aristocratic elite. The former fought to establish an identity for its newly created community. It had, naturally, almost no record of military achievement. The latter fought to preserve the long-established identity of its community, an identity (and empire) we can fairly call "classical." Although its confidence had been shaken by the sudden and disastrous end of the war with Rome, the Persian army could look back on a tradition of military success dating back a thousand years. If regional rivalries and divisions exacerbated by the Roman war meant that the Persian force was less culturally unified than the Muslim force, the presence of Armenian princes and their followers in the Persian army spoke to the obverse of that coin: the imperial reach of the

---

[3] Kennedy, *Great Arab Conquests*, p. 169.

[4] Islam clearly arose from and was framed by Muhammad as the final revelation of the Jewish and Christian family of beliefs. The large debt of Christian cosmology to Zoroastrianism is known but often underappreciated. It is reasonable, then, to see Islam as the last product of Zarathushtra's preaching of ethical monotheism (or dualism) centuries earlier. On this and the early Buddhist-Taoist-Pyrrhonist opposition that the monotheist idea spawned, see Beckwith, *Greek Buddha*.

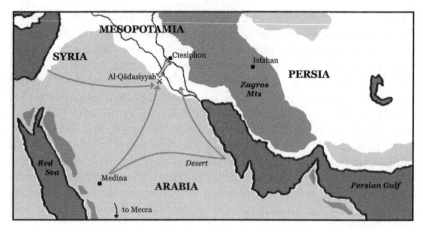

Figure 1 Map of campaign of Qādasiyyah.
Source: Author.

Sassanid Empire brought in subordinates and allies that reinforced its Persian core.

How large were the armies facing each other across an abrupt geographic divide and a chasm of cultural differences? Hard data is impossible to come by, but the best estimates are that the Muslim army was in fact rather small: perhaps 12,000 men. The original expeditionary force that had raided and then been driven back by a Persian counteroffensive had been reinforced by troops transferred from recently conquered Syria, and by a call for reinforcements that went out to most of Arabia in response to that counteroffensive (figure 1). Still, Arab resources were limited and some troops were already tied up in Syria.

On the other side, establishing numbers is even harder. The Arab sources claim that the Persians numbered as many as 210,000. This is clearly logistically impossible and, in the political circumstances, highly unlikely anyway. The Persian army, produced by an empire-wide effort, probably did outnumber the Arabs – but by how much? Guesses ("estimates" would overly glorify the "calculation" process) in the range of 20,000 to 30,000 seem reasonable, though lower is possible and much higher than 30,000 less likely, though the Armenian writer Sebeos claims there were 80,000 in the Persian army.

In terms of command, equipment, and accustomed fighting style, the differences between the two forces may have been visibly dramatic but in effect were probably less so. The Arabs fielded what we might call a ragtag force; commonalities of weaponry and armor resulted from a common background rather than central control.

Defensive armor was not heavy, and most of the Arab soldiers fought on foot in battle, even if some had horses or camels for long-distance mobility and raiding campaigns. They tended, however, to have good swords and good bows – Arab archery was known to be effective. The Persians fielded a mixed force: infantry whose main weapon was also the bow (spears and shields were not preferred); elite aristocratic cavalry formations wielding lances and reasonably well armored; and, at least at Qādasiyyah, a small number of elephants drawn from the empire's Indian frontier. While the Arab army included veterans of previous campaigns who would have been accustomed to taking the initiative in battle, the Persians seem to have preferred a careful, cautious approach to combat – centrally controlled and perhaps discouraging initiative. The Persians had probably established a semi-fortified encampment on arriving at Qādasiyyah. Each side's commanders – Sa'd ibn Abī Waqqās, an early Muslim convert from the important Quraysh tribe of Mecca who had fought alongside the Prophet, and the Persian aristocrat and chief minister Rustum – were respected, experienced, and had records of success. Rustum had in fact defeated a Muslim army months earlier at the Battle of the Bridge, one of the few major defeats early Muslim forces suffered and a key moment in the Persian counteroffensive that had driven Muslim raiders back into the desert.

And so the two armies faced off and came to blows. The Arab Muslim sources for the battle provide copious amounts of detail about the fighting, but most of it has a legendary character focused on specific actors who, because of the retrospective importance of the battle, were inserted into the stories that got attached to the legend of the battle. Overviews in the sources are few and unhelpful. [5] Indeed, the date of the battle is different in different sources (see note 1 above), in part reflecting specific deformations of the historical truths presented in the Islamic record where religious truths took precedence. And whether "the date of the battle" is the correct formulation is open to questions. Most of the sources that specify the length of the battle present it as lasting three days (and even into the morning of the fourth). On the face of it, this sounds implausible. Almost none of the open field battles we have reliable details about from the medieval world lasted more than a few hours, for reasons we will explore later in this book. Those that lasted longer were all associated with the permanent structures of fortifications and siege works: an attempt to

---

[5] Kennedy, *Great Arab Conquests*, p. 190.

relieve a siege might lead to a more extended conflict, as we will see, for instance, in the next section of this chapter. There was no siege at Qādasiyyah. Simple logistics – that is, the mechanics of keeping enough water and food within reach of the combatants over several days, for example – are difficult to imagine, especially with the field of conflict being at the edge of a desert. Is the commonly accepted length of the battle legendary?

Perhaps, but not necessarily. The desert was the natural operating environment for the Bedouin Arabs who had converged on the site; it is not at all impossible that they brought flocks and herd of animals with them that could have provided a mobile food supply, and the site may have been chosen (on both sides) for its access to wells and water. The Persian army had arrived gradually at the site, had chosen it deliberately, and was undoubtedly operating with a logistical tail – a supply train using carts and drawing on local resources from the irrigated, agricultural side of the geographic divide that shaped the campaign. Furthermore, the attested Persian habit of creating a hastily fortified camp (much as Roman armies on campaign had always done) when they reached the end of a march meant that while there was no permanent fortification (or dug-in siege works) for either side to use, the Persians did have a semi-secure base for their daily operations, while the Muslim commanders seem to have occupied a large building in/at the edge of the town as a headquarters, and the Muslim army as a whole, composed of nomads, would have had less need, at least psychologically, for a "structural" base of operations. The accustomed caution displayed by the Persians, especially in the face of Arab mobility, could have kept Persian offensive moves at a level that the smaller Arab force could manage, while the Persian camp would have made an all-out Arab offensive risky, at least until the enemy had been worn down physically and morally. So let us provisionally accept that the battle lasted an unusually long time, even up to three days and into a fourth.

It thus probably began with tentative attacks on both sides, with both generals probably preferring to remain in the position of maintaining a tactical defense, which for predominantly infantry forces was often the stronger stance.[6] The possible tiebreaker here, so to speak, was the Persian elephant corps, which seems to have been not large (under thirty elephants, certainly – elephant logistics were even harder than human and equine logistics). Still, there were enough

---

[6] See Rogers, "Offensive/Defensive in Medieval Strategy," which, however, overstates the generality and strength of its conclusion by focusing only on infantry battles.

to offer the Persians hope of breaking Arab resistance with an early attack, especially given that elephants were particularly difficult for horses unaccustomed to their presence, potentially neutralizing the Arab cavalry. This may have further pushed the battle into an infantry-heavy encounter in which archery played a central role, to the advantage of the Arabs, who as already noted had good bows – likely better than the Persians' – and apparently better protection against arrows. Archery probably also accounted for the ability of the Arab infantry to successfully resist the elephant-led Persian offensives.

A pattern of tentative attacks, successful defenses, periods of rest and reorganization, and breaks at night is certainly conceivable as lasting through two or three days. Gradually, however, the Arab army seems to have gained in confidence, worn down the Persians' superior numbers, and maintained a higher level of morale. Here, the more homogenous and socially unified composition of the Arab army certainly played a part, with the sense of divine mission provided by the new faith that held them together perhaps providing the ultimate advantage. By the third day, the Arabs seems to have been moving more consistently to the attack, and by either the end of the third day or the dawn of the fourth, after a night of harassing their foes, Arab attacks began to break through and the Persian army began to fall apart. Rustum and many of the other Persian leaders were killed. In the end, the battle turned into a rout. Arab forces pursued Persian fugitives throughout the last (fourth?) day. Persian Mesopotamia lay open to the invaders, right up to and including the imperial capital at Ctesiphon. Within four years, the entire empire had been swallowed by the caliphate and a new world replaced the old.

The Siege and Battle of Xiangyang

(Shangyang) Song Mongols & China US (South)

With the armed conflict that centered on the fortified city of Xiangyang (and its twin city of Fanchen, attached by a pontoon bridge to Xiangyang across the Han, the two forming an effective whole) in the years 1268–73, which encompassed a number of battles (skirmishes, perhaps) in the field and, certainly more centrally, a long siege, we are stretching the usual concept of "a battle" well beyond its usual limits. Histories of twentieth-century military conflict might more readily accept a "battle" that took months or years to resolve – at Stalingrad in 1942, for example. But many modern battles and campaigns have tended to merge and metastasize into vast and lengthy contests because of the industrially supported growth in army sizes and logistical support systems that made everything bigger and longer, at least in "Great Power" military conflicts. And yet, the conflict at Xiangyang is not necessarily so different from "modern" battles when it is carefully examined with the factors that sometimes make modern conflicts so large kept in mind.

This is because the forces that met at Xiangyang were, especially in thirteenth-century terms, stupendous. Attacking from the northwest toward the city were the forces of the Mongol Empire, the preindustrial world's offensive behemoth, creators of world history's largest contiguous land empire, conquerors whose destructive (and often, constructive) footprint was large enough to have temporarily cooled the global climate[7] and killed more people, as a percentage of the global population of the time, than World War II. Already masters of a huge piece of Eurasia, they aimed, starting in 1268, at their most formidable opponent, Song China, a defensive behemoth to match the Mongols' offensive prowess. True, the Mongols already ruled the northern half of what had been, in the eleventh century, Song territory, and aimed simply to complete their conquest of the world's largest, richest, most organized society. But the Southern Song were, in many ways, hardly diminished by the loss of the north. Probably over 80 percent of the population and perhaps as much as 90 percent of the economic production of Song China were in the south. Song China could deploy a military establishment of over a million men, supported by the world's richest, most advanced economy, one which easily led the world in iron production, had invented paper money to lubricate the vast scale of its internal economy, maintained maritime trade connections with the world through its port cities on the southeast coast, and was the inventor, not just of paper and paper money, but of gunpowder, whose military purposes were on full display at Xiangyang. It possessed the world's biggest, most technologically sophisticated naval forces, both oceanic and riverine: among its ships were paddle-wheel-driven river craft (albeit the paddles were human- not steam-powered) that could launch gunpowder bombs from shipboard catapults. The navy was crucial to defense of the south, divided as it was from the north by the Yangtze River and its tributaries. Xiangyang, in other words, witnessed the mother of all medieval Great Power, heavyweight battles. No wonder the battle (in the broad sense, primarily the siege) lasted five years, making it one of the longest sieges of the entire medieval period.

---

[7] Pongratz et al., "Coupled Climate–Carbon Simulations."

What is odd, however, is that, given the scale and consequences of this meeting of giants, the conflict at Xiangyang has received very little attention in military history writing, either in the Euro-American mainstream (though the Eurocentric focus of "western" military history makes this perhaps less surprising)[8] or even in Mongol and Chinese military history writing.[9] It appears that, despite the siege part of the conflict, in particular, displaying some significant technological developments, the conflict is seen as militarily uninteresting: its eventual outcome – victory for the Mongol forces and the subjugation of Song China – is somehow taken as inevitable, despite the length of the Song resistance, which, including the five years at Xiangyang, lasted over forty years, far longer than any other Mongol opponent managed to hold out.

This sense of inevitability probably reflects not just the widely held perception (then and now) that the Mongols were unstoppable, a perception the Mongols themselves did as much as they could to foster, but also the historiographical underrating of the Song dynasty. Viewed objectively, the Song was an era of remarkably good, effective governance of China in the face of some very tough challenges. Militarily, in particular, the Song suffer from bad historiographical framing. They succeeded the Tang, who carefully cultivated a reputation for military success and expansion from the time of the second Tang emperor (and effectively co-founder of the dynasty with his father), Li Shimin, who was and wished to be seen as a bold and successful general. The Tang dynasty as a whole are usually seen as an expansionist high point in Chinese dynastic history. The Song were, of course, followed by their conquerors, the Mongols, or in Chinese terms the Yuan dynasty, who were militarily, of course, *the Mongols*. The Song appear in this frame, especially militarily, as a trough between peaks.

The dynasty contributed to this reputation by emphasizing civilian virtues and civilian rule and control of the military, which is often interpreted as having reduced the effectiveness of the Song army. The dynasty is best known for economic advancements (for which the state probably receives less credit than it is due) and a

---

[8] Xiangyang receives *no* mention in the standard reference work, Dupuy and Dupuy, *Encyclopedia of Military History*, or in Curry and Graff, *Cambridge History of War. Vol. II*, etc.

[9] It receives one brief mention in May, *Mongol Art of War*, and none in Graff, *Medieval Chinese Warfare*. It is mentioned in Wright, "Northern Frontier," p. 73. The essential analysis is Lorge, *War, Politics, and Society in Early Modern China*, pp. 249–74. Another analysis of the conflict, based in large part on Lorge, is by Hanson, "Mongol Siege of Xiangyang."

"renaissance"-like flowering of Neo-Confucian philosophy and the arts. Yet the two "peaks," Tang and Yuan, had considerably shorter periods of effective rule than the Song (arguably, 630–750 for the Tang, or barely over 100 years, and 1270–1350 for the Yuan, less than a century, as opposed to roughly 1000–1270 for the Song, nearly three times as long – even granting that the loss of northern China occurred in there, again perhaps more a matter of military image than true loss of effectiveness). And the Tang and Yuan both fell to internal divisions and rebellions, whereas it took the world's mightiest war machine to bring down the Song after a long struggle.

In short, Xiangyang really was a meeting of giants that probably deserves more attention than it has received. It stands as our second "battle."

Our analysis must begin with geography, and why the Mongol–Song confrontation focused on Xiangyang. Northern China was a wheat-growing region, relatively dry, flat, and centered on the Yellow River valley. It had been the cradle of Chinese civilization, but by the Song period, as we have already noted, the economic and demographic center of gravity of China had shifted to the hotter, wetter, in places more mountainous rice-growing lands focused on the Yangtze valley. Still, the north, distinct from yet open to the steppes of central Asia, remained the center of Chinese military power, including horse breeding and equine trade with the nomads of the steppes. More open to steppe influences, northern China was also open to conquest by the peoples of the steppes: the Mongols in taking northern China displaced already extant northern kingdoms and dynasties of steppe origin more than they conquered the Song themselves.

When they turned their attention to the south in 1268, the Mongols faced unusual challenges. The climate was hotter and more humid than they were comfortable with; the many rivers, lakes, and marshy areas were far less suitable for their accustomed mass cavalry campaigns than the north had been. And the Song were as prepared for the coming Mongol assault as they could be. Unlike many of the polities the Mongols had already conquered across Eurasia, which had often been centered on a single large fortified city, or perhaps a number of scattered ones, the frontier region between north and south China was heavily urbanized, full of well-fortified cities connected into mutually supporting networks to create, effectively, a defense-in-depth system well suited to frustrating the independent mobile columns the Mongols favored for strategic operations. From Sichuan in the west down the Yangtze and including its major tributaries, especially the Han River running into the Yangtze from the north, and on which Xiangyang and Fanchen sat, the frontier between north and south China formed a deep and flexible defense region where riverine naval forces could support fortified positions and the infantry units that occupied them.

By 1268, the Mongol leadership was focused in the person of Chinggis Khan's grandson Kubilai Khan, who had solidified his position as Great Khan and thus as leader of the fractured Mongol Empire by defeating a revolt by his younger brother Arigh Böke. Böke represented the "purist," steppe-oriented side of Mongol cultural interests, who objected to Kubilai's Sinicizing moves, such as establishing a Chinese capital in the region of modern Beijing and emphasizing the Chinese bureaucracy, which were designed to solidify Chinese support for Mongol rule. This trend would culminate in Kubilai formally proclaiming a Chinese-style dynasty, the Yuan, during the campaign to subdue the Southern Song.

Kubilai and his key advisors had decided to focus Mongol efforts on one key target, responding to the difficulties presented by the fortified defensive zone they faced and taking a lesson from the slow progress Kubilai's brother and predecessor Möngke had made with a traditionally organized campaign into Sichuan in the late 1250s. The Xiangyang–Fanchen fortification complex guarding the Han River, and thus access to the Yangtze valley, was that target (figure 2). They made no attempt to hide this focus from the Song government and its military leaders, as strategic maneuverability and the surprise that enhanced its effectiveness in other Mongol conquests were abandoned as useless. Instead, the Mongol leadership seems to have decided to draw the Song into an extended battle of attrition at Xiangyang where the southern resistance could be broken once and for all. What ensued might reasonably be called a medieval version of the Western Front in World War I, with Xiangyang playing the role of Verdun: Great Powers fighting toe-to-toe to the death.

The Song army was overwhelmingly infantry-based, reflecting the failure of the Song to hold onto any of the northern territories where horses could be bred and raised; furthermore, the Mongols controlled the central Asian supply of equine power. (It has been estimated that the Mongols at their height controlled well over half of the world's supply of horses.) The infantry were usually armed with iron crossbows, and some carried spears or swords. They were centrally trained, and benefited from the experience that a long-term professional army could accumulate. But no one would claim that the Song infantry were, man for man, among the world's best soldiers. They were decent. What made the Song a military behemoth is that,

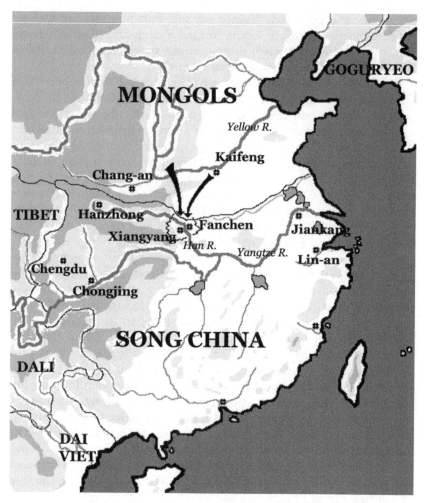

Figure 2   Map of campaign of Xiangyang.
Source: Author.

first, there were a lot of them. The entire Song military establishment was in the many hundreds of thousands (and had probably been over a million in the early decades of the dynasty). And they were well armed by the world's largest, most productive economy that produced technologically sophisticated arms and armor. This technological expertise was deployed to best effect in the Song navy that guarded the main rivers, the Yangtze and its tributaries, that anchored the Song defensive frontier.

The potential weakness in the Song system was its leadership. In reaction to the warlordism that had fragmented and destroyed the Tang dynasty, the warlord who founded the Song instituted a system that emphasized civilian control of the military and loyalty to the dynasty as its central features, perhaps, at times, to the detriment of military efficiency. Generals were rotated through regional commands to prevent their forming local bonds with their troops; attempts were made to institute a written exam system for military promotions like that in effect for the civil service, though this never proved successful. What really held the Song system together, however, was an informal substructure of military families who held commands hereditarily, giving the system continuity, expertise, and a set of social bonds among commander families that could tie larger regions together outside the formal chains of military command. But as an informal system, it was subject to political pressures and competing demands for loyalty and official rewards. Put another way, the Song court and its army were not strongly linked politically, a serious potential weakness.[10]

By contrast, the Mongol (or Yuan) military system was centrally led by the khan/emperor, Kubilai, who, once he had suppressed his brother's revolt, commanded the complete loyalty of the system politically and militarily, including not just subordinate Mongol leaders, but Chinese generals who threw their lot in with the rising power from the steppes. On the other hand, the Mongol army was more complicated than the term "Mongol" conveys. There was a core of Mongol soldiers who probably were, man for man, about the best soldiers in the world. They were mostly horse archers, with some proportion of them carrying heavier melee weapons and wearing more substantial armor. But the number of actual Mongols was limited, and those were split among the four major pieces of the empire by Kubilai's time. Additional steppe-style horse archers were provided by the many central Asian groups, including various Turkic and related peoples, who had been incorporated into the Mongol Empire and military system. But the Mongols also folded large numbers of Chinese infantry into their armed forces, infantry who provided the necessary military labor for siege work and attritional warfare. And in preparation for a campaign into the navally defended south, they had created their own naval forces, built and manned by further Chinese specialists recruited into

---

[10] Lorge, *War, Politics, and Society*, p. 255.

the new dynasty's system. Finally, recognizing the key role siege warfare would play in the assault on the south, they recruited (or conscripted) Chinese engineers and imported specialist engineers from Persia to construct siege engines and other equipment. The vast reach of the empire and all its resources, human and material, in other words, could be focused on the targeted Song, and targeted at one key location, mitigating the Song superiority in overall resources, as the Song had to defend everywhere along the frontier, given Mongol mobility, while Kubilai could choose his point of attack.

Starting in late 1267 and then throughout 1268, the Mongols began to bring pressure on Xiangyang–Fanchen. They built forts to constrict access to the area, and began to concentrate their naval resources to contest control of the Han River. The slow buildup gradually became clear to the Song, who attempted to counter the emerging siege. It was in this stage of the campaign that some small open field battles were fought as the Song tried to prevent the Mongol army from settling in around Xiangyang. But at this point, luck and the nature of the Song leadership system coincided to deal the defenders a serious blow. Lü Wende, the leader of the defense of the Xiangyang region and head of a family network that tied the whole defensive structure together (his brother Lü Wenhuan was in charge of Xiangyang proper), died in 1270 just before he could lead an attack on the Mongol army. His replacement, Li Tingzhi, alienated the Lü family from the court (the court, in fact, already did not trust the Lü family fully) and was unable to unify the command of the defenses of the region.[11] Li's attempts to dislodge the Mongols – or even, by 1271, to relieve the tightening siege of Xiangyang and Fanchen by getting fresh supplies through to the fortifications – failed. The Mongols increased the pressure. The blockade tactics were wearing down the defenders without causing the Mongols large casualties. By the end of 1272, after five years of pressure, Kubilai and his key advisors decided it was time to force the issue. They further decided that taking Fanchen was the easier half of their goal, and that doing so would make the defense of Xiangyang itself untenable.

In early 1273, the Mongols first attacked the bridge that connected the two cities across the Han. The Mongol river fleet defeated the Song fleet while the Mongol army directly attacked the bridge,

[11] See Lorge, "Northern Song Military Aristocracy," and Fang, "Military Families."

destroying the wooden piles that anchored it. With the bridge destroyed, the Mongol army attacked the city. The direct assault on strong city walls, though supported by siege engines including new "Muslim" trebuchets – counterweight trebuchets built by Persian engineers with experience of southwest Asian warfare where counterweight trebuchets, which were far more powerful than the traction trebuchets in use in east Asia at the time, had been developed – was costly in Mongol lives but ultimately successful against defenders isolated from any relief. Fanchen fell by February 2. The Mongols massacred its entire population, piling bodies up outside the walls in full view of the defenders of Xiangyang, and setting up their Muslim trebuchets to bombard Xiangyang from across the river.

At this point Kubilai paused, allowing Lü Wenhuan time to consider his position: he was in an indefensible city whose inhabitants would also be massacred if the city resisted further, and he and his family were mistrusted by the Song court. It is therefore not shocking that Lü not only surrendered the city on March 14, but went over to the Mongols.

With the defensive frontier decisively breached at Xiangyang, the following three years of campaigning by the Mongols into southern China, ending with the final surrender of the Song court to the invaders in 1276, took on the character of a mop-up campaign. When the last Song emperor died that year, all of China was under Mongol rule. This marked the high point of Mongol expansion, even if the aura of Mongol invincibility had been broken farther west by the Mamluk victory over a small Mongol army at Ayn Jalut, in Syria, in 1260. But unlike the results of the battle at Qādasiyyah, when the Arab conquest of Persia permanently and decisively altered the cultural trajectory of one of the world's oldest imperial cultures, the Mongol conquest of China was in many ways ephemeral. The Mongols under Kubilai's leadership, unable to impose Mongol identity on the vastly more numerous Chinese population, had already begun to adopt a Chinese imperial identity to reinforce their legitimacy. Nevertheless, by 1368, Mongol rule in China was over. Stressed by outbreaks of epidemic disease and facing growing peasant revolts, the Mongol Yuan dynasty fell to a peasant-born leader who established the Ming dynasty that year. The Ming would follow a path of conservative reaction against the period of Mongol rule, consciously looking to pre-Mongol models of Chinese identity and policy to reestablish the Middle Kingdom in its place of centrality in the medieval world.

The Battle of Morat

By 1476, when the Battle of Morat took place, western Europe was a century and a half into a period of crises that had started with the catastrophically cold, wet summers of 1316 and 1317, had been seriously compounded by the Black Death pandemic that reached Italy in 1348 and within three years had killed a third of Europe's population, and included the self-inflicted wounds of widespread warfare, especially the Hundred Years War, religious schism, and class conflict.

One result was that the dominance of the major kingdoms of the thirteenth century (including the papacy as a major political power even if it was not technically a kingdom) over the political space of western Europe had been loosened considerably. New polities emerged into newly opened spaces. Communities seeking to find a path through the crises and claim a collective identity in troubled times launched experiments in governance that, given the nature of European societies, had to defend their claims to existence on the battlefield.

Western Europe by the thirteenth century had evolved a heavily militarized socio-military system whose three major components existed in a tense but complementary balance. At the top of the system was a class of heavily armed warrior aristocrats and their servants: the knights in shining armor whose image is central to popular western conceptions of medieval warfare. The knights exploited their social dominance to extract the economic resources necessary to support themselves in the style befitting their claimed role as the defenders of society: ownership of large, specially bred warhorses capable of carrying the knight in his full armor, which by the 1400s had shifted from mostly mail to more and more plate armor. Their possession of landed estates, often as fiefs granted to them by a higher lord in exchange for their readiness to perform military duties at the lord's command, supported them not just in terms of buying equipment, but by letting them devote their lives to military activity as a lifestyle. The knights' resulting skills and resources made them the dominant force in medieval European warfare. They were vital in combat; because of their equine mobility they were necessary to the prosecution of campaigning activities such as scouting and pillaging; and they acted as the armored spear tip of siege warfare.[12]

---

[12] Rogers, "Role of Cavalry."

Siege warfare was critical and constant – sieges were far more frequent than pitched battles in Europe, the inverse of the move-ment-and-battle-seeking patterns of Mongol warfare on the steppes. This reflected the dynamics of the settled, sedentary worlds that surrounded the steppe world of horse warriors and was thus not unusual. But Europeans had taken this pattern to an extreme, as the knightly class that ruled the region had settled centuries earlier into a lineage-based kinship system whose family centers were small private castles very different from the vast urban fortifications of China. While urban fortifications and "public" castles – strongpoints built or at least owned by a central authority – existed all across Europe, it was the plethora of fortified positions created privately that domi-nated the military infrastructure of the society. And again, this was a socio-military system: castles served as military bases of operations, but thus also served as the points from which elite dominance over the countryside and its peasants emanated, a dominance exercised not just by arms but by the operations of the courts and other bureau-cratic mechanisms of rule located in the castles.

But if knights and castles represented the two rurally based, elite parts of the socio-military system, its third component filled out the social spectrum and rounded out the military capabilities of the system. Bodies of infantry, drawn from largely urban communal groups who gave the infantry their cohesion and were in turn pro-tected and defended by the infantry they nurtured, joined the knights and their castles. They filled out army numbers in a world where horses were rare and expensive, performed many of the vital tasks of siege warfare, and often supplied the missile component of arms combinations and the defensive formations in battle that the knightly horsemen could maneuver from.

This system was spawned and held together by a civilizational set of values that put notions of militarized law at the center of social organization. Such values necessitated in turn that any social group with a claim to some set of privileges or status had to be willing to defend those claims by force, and the operations of the system were characterized by many informal or ad hoc obligations and terms of service. But the operations of military activity by the fourteenth century, in the context of an expanding European economy, had become increasingly monetized. In other words, variations on paid soldiers, called by many names beyond just "mercenaries,"[13] had

---

[13] See Morillo, "Mercenaries, Mamluks and Militia."

become not just common but increasingly central to the organization of military forces by the 1400s.

Returning to the century and half of external shocks and stresses with which we started this section, however, those stresses caused the formerly complementary pieces of the socio-military system to come apart at the seams a bit, giving rise to increased levels of internal conflict and bloodshed. This conflict not only pitted unsettled or newly emergent political formations against each other, but also expressed regional and class rivalries and disagreements.

The Battle of Morat, fought on June 22, 1476, encapsulates this entire set of trends.[14]

The battle was brought about by the ambitions of Charles the Bold (alternatively, the Rash or the Cruel – to some contemporaries, he was "Charles the Terrible," whose reputation for cruelty and brutality was exceptional even for the time), the ruler of the duchy of Burgundy. Charles aimed to turn the duchy into an independent polity positioned between France and the Holy Roman Empire – a late medieval successor of Lotharingia, the middle portion of the tripartite division of Charlemagne's empire in the ninth century. Charles built his centralizing state around the army that would define and defend it, drawing first on some of the best knightly elites in Europe for a core of heavily armed and armored cavalry and a core of local rulers for his state. But as a thoroughly modern military thinker, Charles added to this offensive core of knights the best mercenary infantry units he could find, including English longbowmen and German arquebusiers, whose firepower complemented the offensive potential of the heavy cavalry. Even more, he gathered one of the largest artillery trains in Europe at the time, which he used not only as a very effective means of taking fortified towns, but on the battlefield as well, despite the cannon of the day still being relatively hard to maneuver and limited to a slow rate of fire. Charles drew on Roman models to organize his forces into permanent, numbered units, partly as a way of overcoming the difficulties of coordinating a polyglot, culturally diverse collection of units into a cohesive whole.

Standing in the way of Charles' ambitions was the Swiss Confederation, a coalition of small polities that were, essentially, city-

---

[14] A good detailed narrative of Morat and its setting, embellished by a touch of Swiss national pride, perhaps, is Winkler, "The Battle of Murten." Murten is the German form of the name Morat, a not uncommon doubling of nomenclature in the region, including much of Switzerland itself. I will admit to choosing "Morat" arbitrarily.

states. The Confederation, dominated by the eight oldest and largest cities of the region, headed by Bern, Zurich, and Lucerne, controlled much of modern-day Switzerland and both blocked and threatened the expansion of Burgundy that Charles planned. Strategically, Burgundy could be cut in half by a Swiss westward offensive.

Adding to the obvious strategic and territorial tension was an ideological component of the Burgundian–Swiss rivalry. Against Charles' very traditional, monarchical-aristocratic duchy, the Swiss Confederation was collectively and cooperatively run – each of the major units of the Confederation was an independent player, and each was collectively run internally. "Democratic" is undoubtedly a somewhat anachronistic description for their politics, but the Swiss were certainly at the opposite end of the medieval European ideological spectrum from Charles' Burgundy.

Like Burgundy, the Swiss Confederation's military forces arose from and thus reflected closely their social and political structure. But unlike the elite-dominated (and thus cavalry-led) Burgundian army, the Swiss communal associations produced what such associations had always produced, dating back to the Greek city-states of classical times: masses of heavy infantry who fought as they lived, side by side. For the Swiss, this meant large squares of infantry called *Haufen*, or "a mass," armed with pikes and halberds. The pikemen formed the outer four to six ranks of the formation on every side, and their 18-to-20-foot spears could repel any cavalry charge. The halberdiers filled the middle of the wide, deep blocks. The halberd, a polearm topped with a business end that combined a spearpoint, an axe-head, and a hook, was the perfect melee weapon for close combat with heavily armored knights. Though shorter than the pikes, the spear end let the halberdiers contribute to the defensive wall against cavalry attacks; the heavy axe-head, swung at the end of a 10–12-foot staff, could cleave into most armor; and the hook was designed to snag a horseman and pull him off his horse. Thus, though the Swiss *Haufen* bore some resemblance to Greek or Macedonian phalanxes, they were deeper and less linear, and the difference in weaponry between the two resulted from the threat to the Swiss posed by a sort of heavy cavalry the ancient infantry had never had to face.

The real similarity to their ancient forebears was that the Swiss drew on the political, social, and economic cohesion of their communities to create cohesive infantry formations just as the ancients had done, and deployed those units often enough that they gained further cohesion and skill from abundant practice. These were not infantry on the model of imperial Roman legions or the Chinese infantry of the Song, whose existence and effectiveness depended on a large, rich central state to both gather recruits together and train them. This was social infantry.

Crucially, they gained enough practice and experience, honed by the trick of (re?)learning to march in time to music, that Swiss *Haufen* could maneuver rapidly on the battlefield without losing their cohesion or opening gaps in their formation. They were therefore capable not just of standing on the defensive, which various infantries throughout the medieval period had managed with greater or lesser effectiveness, but of attacking, often with astonishing rapidity and terrifying effect. It was this army that faced off against Charles of Burgundy's model of combined arms modernity.

The Swiss–Burgundian war opened formally in 1474. The Swiss Confederation formed an alliance with the Hapsburg archduke of Austria; former enemies driven together against Charles by his perceived threat to both of them. Charles' side of the war opened with an unsuccessful siege of the city of Neuss in the summer of 1474. At the same time, under the pretext of avenging previous outrages by Charles, the Swiss invaded Burgundian territory and took a number of towns, cities, and castles, defeating a Burgundian relief army at Héricourt in November. The next year they invaded the Vaud region of Burgundy's ally Savoy and took the fortified town of Morat. Over the following year a series of offensives and reprisals intensified the war on both sides, and acts of cruelty and slaughter of non-combatants multiplied. Charles' first attack into Swiss territory ended in a chaotic defeat at the Battle of Grandson on March 2, 1476, where the Swiss ability to launch sudden, rapid infantry attacks caught Charles completely of guard. He lost many of his cannon, but re-gathered his army, pulling together perhaps 20,000 men, some of whom were less than fully trained militia and mercenaries, and rapidly gathered cannon from all over his realm. He invaded again, aiming to retake Morat as the first step toward attacking Bern directly. He arrived outside the town on June 9. The Swiss quickly raised a relief army and began force marching it toward Morat, some contingents covering over 80 miles in three days.

Morat was on the shore of a lake, and Charles deployed his army – unwisely, even rashly, one might say – partly facing the town to prosecute his siege, and partly facing the opposite way toward the direction the Swiss relief force would come from. He set up many of his artillery pieces to aim at a possible Swiss attack and had a defensive palisade constructed to defend his position. But this left the lake behind his forces, in their natural line of retreat.

The Swiss relief army, probably slightly larger than Charles' force, arrived in the vicinity of Morat on June 21. They closed to attack the next day, arriving around midday. A dense wood kept their approach hidden from Charles, who furthermore, probably from aristocratic arrogance and partly just sheer stupidity, underestimated his opponents' marching abilities. A serious thunderstorm that night made a Swiss attack seem even less likely. That some of his newer troops were, on the morning of the battle, negotiating with him to be paid before they would fight indicates the sad state of Charles' preparations. Thus, when the Swiss emerged from the woods in the early afternoon, the Burgundian defensive line was only partially manned (figure 3).

The Swiss advance force, the first of three large *Haufen* and numbering perhaps 5,000 infantrymen supported by 1,500 allied knights, advanced in the teeth of an artillery barrage, followed closely by the main block. Their rapid advance kept casualties from the slow-loading gunnery low, and they forced their way through gaps in the defensive hedge. A Burgundian counterattack with their cavalry failed to stem the advance, and the Burgundian position rapidly collapsed. The Burgundian troops around the city fled east along the lake, much of the main body fled west, and a significant portion of the Burgundian center was trapped against the shore, driven into the water, and drowned. Charles escaped leading a rearguard action and fled with his scattered troops.

The Swiss captured great riches from Charles' camp. Burgundian losses were probably in the range of 10,000, while the Swiss lost no more than a few hundred men. After days of flight, Charles reorganized his army, adding new recruits as he could, though the loss at Morat meant he was cut off from the southern parts of his realm. Even worse, between Grandson and Morat he had lost the great bulk of his artillery train, his key technological edge on his many opponents. Returning to the offensive, he besieged the city of Nancy in January 1477. He was attacked on January 5 by a coalition of his enemies including a substantial body of the Swiss. His army was crushed and Charles was killed in the retreat. He left no capable heir, and Burgundy effectively ceased to exist as an independent power. The Swiss Confederation, on the other hand, had guaranteed its independence and set about renting out its now-feared pikemen as mercenaries to the competing powers of Europe. Their lineal descendants still serve as the symbolic Swiss Guard of the papacy in the Vatican City.

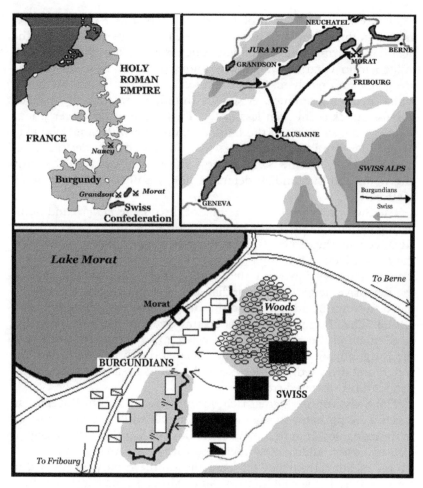

Figure 3 Map of campaign and Battle of Morat.
Source: Author.

Questions

Three battles, six different forces, many of which were actually coalitions of various armed groups, themselves the products of a variety of different societies and cultures, and three very different geographical settings, spread across eight centuries of time. What makes all these battles part of "War and Conflict in the Middle Ages"? What do they have in common, if anything, beneath the wide array of weaponry, tactics, political organization, and cultural motivations for fighting on display here? Answering these questions is the purpose of this book.

The variety of participants in just these three battles, from small groups of Arab desert nomads and Swiss mountain villagers to allegedly vast hordes of Mongol horsemen and provably vast numbers of Chinese state-raised soldiers, explicitly raises the question of what role the scale of forces plays in defining "war" as opposed to other forms of armed conflict, though we will avoid some of the issues of this problem by casting a broad analytical net over "war and conflict" generally.

More problematically, the chronological and geographic range of these battles will force us to consider what we mean by "the Middle Ages," or what constituted "the medieval world." The central problem here is that the concept of "the Middle Ages" arose in European history and certainly does not apply easily *in European terms* to the rest of the world. Just by way of example from our three battles, the Persian army at Qādasiyyah could arguably be called "late classical" rather than medieval; and the Song dynasty is often taken in Chinese historiography to constitute the beginning of the "early modern" period. The same "early modern" label might be applied to the Burgundian army at Morat. Even while admitting that periodization is always contested and somewhat arbitrary, we shall have to decide whether there are cross-cultural grounds for viewing the period covered by this book as in some definition "medieval," and if so where that term might apply. In terms of "where," we shall attempt as much as possible to take the global perspective advertised in the subtitle of this book and make our analyses apply as broadly as possible. How to do so raises its own issues, as we shall see.

Next, how might we approach the problem of answering questions such as "what constitutes a 'global' (or at least trans-regional) Middle Ages?," or even "what underlying commonalities unite battles as diverse, even just militarily, as the three sketched here?" Clearly, we cannot simply narrate every major and minor engagement that occurred over the course of the many centuries in our view. We shall have to engage in some comparisons and generalizations to arrive at a comprehensible picture of war and conflict in the Middle Ages from a global perspective.

Finally, why answer these sorts of questions at all? Your author will certainly not deny that military history holds plenty of intrinsic interest for many readers. He shares that interest! But it is still a fair question to ask about the patterns and details of medieval armed conflict, "so what?" Why is this topic important? It is in offering a particular answer to this question that this book attempts to see medieval armed conflict from a new angle: to understand armed conflict from the perspective of its cultural role in the construction of the medieval world. The general argument is that armed conflict played a central role in shaping medieval societies individually and indeed in shaping the cross-cultural interactions that united and divided the medieval world, dynamically and in constantly contested ways. Armed conflict was, ultimately, a central form of communication and negotiation through which medieval people defined themselves and their world and made it a meaningful place to live.

The book will adopt the following schema for presenting my answers to these questions. The next chapter, chapter 2, will answer our basic definitional and methodological questions, in effect extending the introductory section of this book. When and where were the Middle Ages? What constitutes the scope of "war and conflict"? What theoretical and methodological tools can we bring to bear in answering such questions?

Most of the rest of the book is divided into two parts, conceived of in terms of understanding medieval warfare through the metaphor of game rules. Part I, made up of chapters 3 and 4, presents "The Common Rules of Medieval Warfare," the underlying commonalities that characterized armed conflict across the medieval world throughout the period. Many of these commonalities were grounded in the constraints and realities of the physical worlds in which warfare took place. That is, part I presents a materialist perspective on the contexts and mechanics of armed conflict. Chapter 3, "Geography, Politics, and War," covers the constraints imposed on warfare by human societies' relationships with the natural environment, from means of subsistence to where, for example, horses (that supremely important weapon/weapons platform) could be kept and bred. The human geography of states, grounded (literally) in agrarian production, counts as part of this fundamentally materialist background. Another part of this analysis offers a first pass at the question "What was the function of armed conflict in the medieval world?" from the materialist perspective of the "Common Rules." The close relationship between armed forces and coercive political structures underlies most of this chapter. After these "strategic-level" aspects of the contexts of medieval war, chapter 4 "Technology and War, or The Common Rules of Combat," is mostly a close analysis of the implications of medieval weaponry for patterns of warfare. But it also includes thinking about the limitations imposed by transportation technology on those same patterns. Throughout part I, the emphasis is on the constraints and resulting patterns that were common to armed conflict wherever and whenever it happened in the medieval world.

Having established the Common Rules and the main elements of continuity underlying medieval military history, part II, "Three Scenarios: Medieval Warfare in Changing Conditions," then breaks up our medieval, "between the cold and plagues" world into three chronological chunks, which we can think of as scenarios that posed particular challenges to the societies of the time, to look at wars in somewhat more specific detail against the background we outlined above: first, wars of defense and rebuilding that encompassed a process of *medievalization*; second, wars of expansion, encounter, and engagement; and third, wars (again) of defense and rebuilding, or indeed of continued building, given the success medievalized societies had in meeting challenges that had brought down classical societies. Comparisons here must be more tentative and perhaps even speculative, including as they do a larger component of cultural reactions and constructions, which are inevitably more malleable and variable than physical constraints. The chapter titles indicate some of this variability: chapter 5, "The Early Middle Ages, 540–850: Wars of Medievalization," chapter 6, "The High Middle Ages, 850–1300: Wars of Encounter and Connection," and chapter 7, "The Late Middle Ages, 1300–1500? Or 1800? Wars for New Worlds." Yet, to emphasize one goal of this project again, we will aim at seeing war and conflict as a *process*, a form of discourse and transformation that contributed to the formation of a global Middle Ages.

Thus, chapters 5, 6, and 7 outline the major instances and patterns of warfare in the periods 540 to 850, 850 to 1300, and 1300 to 1500(?) or 1800(?), or what we might call the early, high, and late medieval eras, though the questions about the final date warn that the "end of the Middle Ages" will come under special scrutiny. Each period had its own character in terms of the challenges societies faced in the era, and the wars of each period therefore took on their own dynamics. These chapters will be as close as this book will come to a systematic chronological survey of medieval armed conflict. But much more importantly, these chapters constitute this book's full answer to the "So what?" question about medieval armed conflict. It answers that question in terms of the cultural function of war and conflict in the medieval world: what purpose it served and what significance it held.

Finally, chapter 8 presents the conclusions that flow from our examination of medieval armed conflict.

Most military historians (and indeed, in all likelihood, most readers) will probably think of "the function of warfare" as having to do with something like a political science problem (how did warfare serve the ends of the state or the individual rulers of a society, for example) or, in a more strictly military way, as being expressed in the grand strategies, or at least just the strategies, of warfare. Alternatively, some analysts might talk of "military tasking," again a conceptualization that places war in a political and strategic framework of analysis.

This book, by contrast, looks at warfare through a cultural historical lens, and conceives of war and conflict as performing functions aimed at (whether intentionally or not) the construction of a comprehensible and manageable world by those living in it. It sees warfare, in other words, as a tool of identity formation and the construction of meaning, processes that, carried on in a connected way across the variously connected pieces of the globe during this era, *created* the medieval world as a coherent whole. Our accounts of the three battles narrated above have already hinted at some of the sorts of outcomes this admittedly abstract description refers to: the existential struggle at Qādasiyyah between an ancient Persian imperial world and a newly emergent Arab-Muslim world; the titanic clash of nomadic and sedentary worlds at Xiangyang; the ideological and existential stakes of the clash between Burgundians and Swiss at Morat. Chapters 5 to 7 will delve more deeply and systematically into such questions.

That violence – or perhaps more precisely the violent assertion of power (and the often violent resistance such assertions usually engendered) – should have had such a central role in the processes that created the medieval world may be seen, probably rightly, as unfortunate and at times even tragic. But central it was, and understanding the patterns and dynamics of armed conflict in the medieval world therefore is (or should be) an important concern for historians of the Middle Ages.[15]

---

[15] Put another way, I am *not* saying that armed conflict in the medieval world was an *efficient* or *preferable* tool for accomplishing anything beyond killing many people and keeping a few people in power, any more than it is in today's world. But as one of the more common tools that societies turned to in the medieval world – far more commonly and pervasively employed across the whole range of armed conflict than it is in most societies in the twenty-first century – it is certainly worth historians' time to understand its dynamics better.

2

Questions and Methods

This is a book about war and conflict in the Middle Ages from a global perspective. As even our brief tour of three battles in chapter 1 has already shown, each element of this topic is potentially problematic. What counts as war? And when "conflict" is included, the topic might threaten to be endless: what kinds of conflict count? Only conflict in which armed men contest the issue? Clearly, our topic needs some careful definition.

And when were the Middle Ages? This question is more than a chronological query, because the very concept of a "Middle Ages" or "medieval" period derives from European history and is therefore questionable for an examination of a slice of global history. Investigating whether there are globally (or at least trans-regionally) grounded reasons to see the period from 540 (or "roughly 400" in conventional terms) to (perhaps) 1500 CE as more than just an odometer convenience will be one of the goals of our inquiry.

Finally, what makes for a global perspective? Since a view from outer space would be both impossible and of questionable productivity, "global" here will mean a view that takes in as many of the world's regions and societies as possible within the limitations of space and sources. But the result cannot be a mere patchwork quilt of regional views; we will need methodological tools that will allow us to compare, synthesize, and examine the larger patterns that underlay regional diversity and particularity.

Given that a simple statement of the topic of this book raises such serious questions about the definability of the project, one might be tempted to ask at this point whether the investigation is worth it. What can an analysis of war and conflict in the Middle Ages from a global perspective tell us? This book argues that the dynamics of war

and conflict make an excellent lens through which to view a critical
and often underappreciated period of world history, a lens that helps
us see what is central to the period and what distinguishes it from the
eras before and after it. Indeed, war and conflict make a revealing
lens because violent dispute resolution was central to how this world
emerged and developed. In other words, the role of war and conflict
in the making of the Middle Ages, globally, is the theme of this book.

The Making of the "Middle Ages"

Whether we call our period the "Middle Ages" or "medieval" (simply
a Latinate linguistic form of the same underlying idea), the implication is that this is a period that came between two other periods, with
a strong suggestion, if we move a scare quote one word to the left,
that "*the* Middle Ages" occupy the middle of a triad – one usually
expressed as "ancient, medieval, modern," with "ancient" transform-
able into "classical" when connections between the first and third
segments of time across our contested middle are stressed. Such
connections assign the middle age a position of stasis, at best, when
nothing much happened, or at worst a character of loss, decline, and
decadence between the foundational creativity of the classical and the
renewed stasis breaking and achievements of the modern.

 Such a picture is a grossly misleading caricature of the Middle Ages
(in any region), and one that no self-respecting medievalist accepts.
Yet the implications still lurk in the term itself, so part of our project
will be not just to avoid such implications, but to actively deconstruct
them. Why? In part, because the implications of "medieval"ism go
well beyond their European origins. As Kathleen Davis and Michael
Puett argued in introducing the journal *The Medieval Globe*,[1] part of
the danger of the term "medieval" lies in its historiographic origins:
colonial Europe identified itself as modern, having broken free of its
medieval past, and projected "medieval"ism (stasis, decadence, and
so forth) onto the rest of the world, justifying its colonial projects. But
as these authors also argue, recasting a "medieval" period as global
has the potential to replace the loaded chronological triad with a
period, defined globally, that invites comparisons and cross-cultural
analysis of what defined the period in its own terms as an era of world
history. "If anything defined it," we might add, as Davis and Puett

---

[1] Davis and Puett, "Periodization and 'The Medieval Globe'."

frame their conversation as an invitation, not an answer. This book will attempt to provide at least some answers.

Emergence?

It seems unproblematic to assert that the period we will call the Middle Ages was not the opening period of world history.[2] The logical implication is that the Middle Ages emerged from an earlier period of world history, though "emerged" hides the necessity for identifying changes that, in retrospect, marked the beginning of a new age. Standard world-historical accounts usually point to some combination of the decline of classical empires (Rome and Han China), the rise of the salvation religions, and (in more recent historiography) the growth of network connections between major societies that sparked growing cultural contact and conflict, often expressed through war, as the major markers of transition from ancient/early/classical to medieval. Not that such markers are wrong. The clash between the Persians and the Muslim Arabs at Qādasiyyah, as we have seen, is one event that plausibly marks (and indeed helped create) a break between classical and medieval worlds. It should be noted, however, that such markers are *descriptive*, and beg for a deeper, causal explanation of change.

The standard historiographical characteristics of the global Middle Ages emerged logically from the terms of the transition: this was a period both of the fragmentation of political authority (a "decline" from the mighty imperial states of the classical age) and of religious fervor, which contrasts neatly with a very modernist reading of classical paganism, in European history, at least, as less "zealous" and more tolerant and "enlightened" than medieval religion, and with the claimed secularism of the modern.

Again, it is not that the piety and political fragmentation of the medieval world are necessarily wrong, as much as it is that the implicit (and often explicit) contrasts with the periods before and after are almost always both illusory and polemical, and that the implicit character of these characteristics is "medieval": static, decadent, less

---

[2] Although what that opening period was is also problematic: was it the stage of the earliest state-level societies, the ones that generally invented literacy and record keeping, and thus "history"? Or, as I prefer, was it the long, deep "prehistory" of the modern human species and its immediate ancestors? Fortunately, we can set that question aside for now.

than. To be sure, recent medieval history, both European and global, has increasingly stressed the positives of the period. These include growing networks of exchange and connection, as for instance the creative connections fostered by the rise of the Islamic world after Qādasiyyah, or the role of the Mongols in fostering networks of exchange of goods and ideas. Network growth led to the diffusion of technological innovations and people who made them, like the Persian engineers who built counterweight trebuchets for the Mongols at Xiangyang. Another positive was the rising rootedness of states and hierarchies in their societies, even if the political units were often smaller than the classical empires they succeeded, a rootedness expressed through the growing sophistication of their cultural tools of coherence and rule (and indeed, this is where the religious and political usually meet) – the Swiss Confederation can stand as an example of this trend. Finally, as a result of all of this, the Middle Ages saw the emergence of cultural "worlds," characteristic combinations of religions with political systems or hierarchy patterns, that continued to have relevance into succeeding periods, even up to today. Yet we may observe again that much of this is descriptive (albeit productively), more than analytic.

The End of the Middle Ages?

Similarly, the end of the Middle Ages is, in standard world-historical views, often presented in terms that are both descriptive and often value-laden in that they implicitly define the characteristics of a succeeding "modern" era. The continued growth of network activity culminates in 1492 with the creation of a Global System that progressively (double entendre intended) breaks down the parochialism of the multiple medieval worlds. "Modern states," or at least states with increasingly "modern" characteristics,[3] begin to appear all over the globe (sometimes abortively, as in Charles the Bold's Burgundy), connected by the network into a seemingly vast League of Leading Empires. Finally, [insert your favorite characteristic of modernity here; choices might include philosophical humanism or the idea of individualism] appears, though perhaps only in nascent form, across the world, maybe in comparable "renaissances" of learning. The uni-

---

[3] Such as greater professionalism, bureaucratization, and the employment of more "scientific" knowledge via map-making and anthropological descriptions of non-state peoples as part of states' projects of sovereignty assertion.

versal historiographic result, building an earlier term of convenience
into a paradigm, is the invention of an "early modern" world as a
successor to the Middle Ages.[4]

This book's position is that the "early modern" is a chimera, a
historiographical monster jury-rigged together from an assortment
of ill-fitting parts, that serves to connect "medieval" to "modern"
across an impassable terrain of continuities, a connection that must
be constantly rebuilt as the "modern" target continues to move. (The
"modernity" of Charles' Burgundy looks decidedly odd when the
armored knights of the Burgundian state and army are placed at its
leading edge.) One solution is to agree with Davis and Pruett that the
term "modern," as anything more than a sloppy synonym for "where
we are today," is a counterproductive and dangerous analytical category that must be jettisoned from historiography. But while this is
undeniably true, the problem with this position is that it is essentially
negative, leaving a gap into which "early modernism" will simply
reflow unless we fill the hole with something positive.

So how should we periodize? And can we do so, especially in geographically non-restrictive terms, in a way that makes a non-arbitrary
period out of what has traditionally been called "the medieval world"
or "the Middle Ages"? I think we can. In large terms, this book follows
the fundamentally materialist and demographic-ecological chronological scheme developed in my world history textbook, *Frameworks
of World History*. Human history has, in this view, fallen into three
major periods defined by the dominant mode of production in each
age: the hunter-gatherer era, the agrarian era, and the industrial era.
We must recognize that the transitions between each era were never
clean, sudden, or universal. That is, the transitions between eras were
(and continue to be) slow, non-linear, and – to agree with James C.
Scott's argument – not stages in a story of the March of Progress.[5]
Drawing detailed boundaries between hunter-gatherer, agrarian, and
industrial eras simply affirms that periodization has an irreducible
element of arbitrariness to it. But the underlying truth of this division
is best illustrated by a graph of total human population in the world

[4] The "early modern" formulation became necessary as soon as the "modernism"
of the time of the inventors of the Middle Ages began to look decidedly less modern.
In political terms, the monarchical character of "modern" European states seemed
problematically less modern at least by the time of the French Revolution. The
paradox of "early modernism" is that the "early modern state" was simultaneously the
ancien régime. "Ancient modernism" brings the ridiculousness of the "early modern"
formula to the fore.

[5] Scott, *Against the Grain*.

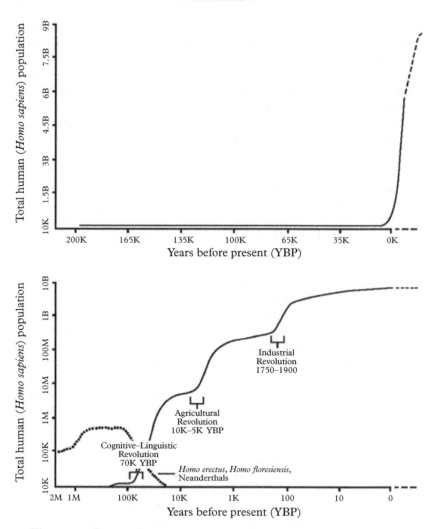

Figure 4 Graph of total human population. (Top) Arithmetic scale.
(Bottom) Logarithmic scale for time and population.
Source: Author.

(figure 4). Set on a log scale both chronologically and in terms of
population in order to equalize rates of change, such a graph makes
visible a large-scale periodization for world-historical analysis.

In terms of the question we are approaching here – what defines or
distinguishes the medieval period from what came before and after?
– this graph apparently doesn't provide us much except some larger

context. This is because the entire period we want to get at (again, from roughly 400 to 1500 in conventional dates, or 540 to 1500 or as late as 1800 in this book's terms) falls along the virtually flat-line part of the curve between the Agricultural Revolution and the Industrial Revolution. Let us *not* take this placement as evidence for the supposed "stasis" claimed for the medieval world in the traditional view, unless we wish to attribute the same stasis to our own time, which also falls (increasingly) along a relatively flat part of the curve. "Flat" shows simply that overall population was not changing rapidly, not that change of any sort was absent.[6]

We can, however, take the relative stability of population during the Middle Ages as evidence for the possible coherence of the era on its own terms, and for the comparability within that era of the various societies and cultures into which the world was divided. It also demonstrates the fallacy of the traditional triad of eras, since the medieval world falls into the same part of the curve as the "classical" version of the early world and as the entire period commonly designated as "early modern," from roughly 1500 to 1800. That is, the "medieval" is part of a larger era between the Agricultural and Industrial Revolutions – in other words, is part of the agrarian era – and shares multiple fundamental features of that world with the "classical" and "early modern" periods. The best we might do constructively with this is to see classical worlds as part of the early agrarian, when rising population enabled – indeed required – the experiments that created the foundational states and civilizations that came to be seen as "classical"; to see the medieval period as the high agrarian (which any medievalist should like!), when relative population stability enabled the working out of the lasting cultural patterns noted above; and to see the period 1500–1800 as the late agrarian, when medieval patterns and trends reached maturity. We shall explore later in this book what this means for dating "the end of the Middle Ages."

Thus, the largest transformations, the ones brought about by agriculture and its associated developments at one end and by industrialization at the other, long preceded the beginning and (perhaps) long postdated the end of the standard medieval period. So again,

---

[6] Again, population is graphed on a log scale; thus, changes significant in local terms (the death of one third of western European people during the Black Death, or the addition of perhaps three billion people between today and roughly 2060, when demographers expect global zero population growth (ZPG) to arrive) do not show up as globally significant.

aside from simply kind of being in the middle of the agrarian era, is there a way to delineate our period that respects its fundamental continuity with the eras immediately before and after, maintains a global perspective, and does so without falling into arbitrary invention and its potential for polemics?

A Climatic-Demographic Middle Ages

One potential answer lies in the climate variations that have occurred naturally (at least until the drastic and probably catastrophic industrial warming of our own day) during the relatively warm period since the last of the Ice Ages about 20,000 years ago. Indeed, we can mark off the last 200 years of fossil-fuel-powered industrial development as constituting, to borrow again from James Scott, a "thick Anthropocene" of drastic human impact on the earth. What follows logically is that the global age since the glaciers retreated saw the worldwide diaspora of the African species *Homo sapiens*, our domestication of fire, then plants and animals, and all of the achievements of historical "civilizations" before the Industrial Revolution. This long era constituted a "thin" Anthropocene.

This era periodically witnessed times of serious cooling that, to some degree or another, (often seriously) disrupted the patterns of settlement and food gathering or production established during the warmer norms – "cold snaps" that have irregularly threatened to return the world to a new Ice Age. The first and longest of these was the so-called "Younger Dryas," which lasted from about 10,800 to 9,600 BCE. This cooling has been implicated in explanations of the subsequent appearance of domesticated animals and plants: they formed part of the adaptive subsistence strategies adopted by various human communities, particularly in southwest Asia, in response to the Younger Dryas. A much briefer but more intense cold snap, from 6,200 to 6,100 BCE, was followed (over the next 3,000 years, again primarily in Mesopotamia) by the appearance of permanent towns, by heavier dependence on domesticated crops and livestock, and eventually by the first small states, the invention of writing, and thus of "history" and the development of agrarian societies, states, and "civilizations."[7]

We may note that the great empires of the classical era flourished in a climate age known as "the Roman Warm Period." (The tem-

---

[7] Scott, *Against the Grain*, p. 4.

perature variations referenced here are drawn, however, not just from European data but also from central Asia, and can be seen as representing at least the northern hemisphere generally.) Then, in the mid–500s, the good times suddenly came to an end, as a series of major volcanic eruptions triggered what is usually referred to as "the Late Antique Little Ice Age" (LALIA), which lasted *c*.540–660.[8] By this time, we have enough historical records that we can correlate (though not necessarily assign causation without dispute) climate change with other evidence, probably most significantly with the widespread outbreak of epidemic diseases – in the Roman Mediterranean, the outbreaks known as the Plague of Justinian (541–3 and periodically thereafter), caused by the *Yersinia pestis* bacterium. Thus, it is reasonable to look for the transition from the "classical" or foundational period of the agrarian era to the "medieval" period in the climate and disease shock of the LALIA.

A period of warmer climate eventually ensued. Between *c*.800 and 1300, the "Medieval Climate Anomaly" saw warmer temperatures, longer growing seasons, rising populations, and the expansion of many of the major societies of the Afro-Eurasian world and their associated cultural traditions. This was the period, for example, of the Viking expeditions that reached North America and of the remarkable economic expansion within Song China, among others.

The climate then again turned cooler, less dramatically but for a longer time than in the LALIA. This is perhaps first visible in western Europe with the cold, wet summers of 1315–16 that led to widespread famine, but the cool period extended for several centuries into the early nineteenth century, encompassing a period commonly known as the Little Ice Age (during which, famously, the River Thames regularly froze over in winter). This too was accompanied by and probably contributed to another round of epidemic disease, this time the pan-Eurasian spread of the Black Death, or the bubonic (and associated) plagues again caused by the *Yersinia pestis* microbe. The combined effects of climate change and pandemic disease suggest an end to the "medieval" period by roughly 1500, though note (again as an argument for continuity and against setting off any "early modern" period between 1500 and 1800) that the Little Ice Age lasted to the dawn of industrialization, and that events such as the fall of the Ming dynasty in the mid-seventeenth century

---

[8] This section draws on Büntgen et al., "Cooling and Societal Change."

have been explained, at least in part, by the effects of "Little Ice Age" climate and weather patterns.[9]

Given this continuity, the argument here for the traditional date for the end of the medieval period rests less with the emergence of something new than with the more notable disruption and transformation of the patterns and stabilities that had emerged during the warm period of the Middle Ages. While this inevitably entailed the emergence of "the new," the medieval-centric emphasis should be on the period itself, its birth in a time of troubles and its extended demise in a time of troubles, with construction centered in between. (The same emphasis on continuity could be highlighted for the beginning of the period, when the Middle Ages emerged gradually from the breakdown of the classical world.) Bruce Campbell has put forward a far-reaching and persuasive climate-and-disease analysis of the end of the medieval world.[10]

In a generally favorable review of Campbell's work, Monica Green notes:[11]

> It seems a strange coincidence that the Middle Ages are bookended by two plague pandemics: the Justinianic plague, from ca. 541 to ca. 750, and the Black Death, which we usually date from 1347 to 1353 but which should now be seen as the beginning of the much longer Second Plague Pandemic. Historical periods are conventions we create, and the transition from antiquity to the Middle Ages, on the one hand, and then the Middle Ages to the early modern period, on the other, were fixed in historiography long before questions about the environment or history of disease loomed large. Yet both pandemics share more similarities than could have been imagined even a decade ago, which suggests why they should have been implicated in two of the greatest turning points in Afro-Eurasian history. Not simply were both caused by the same organism, *Yersinia pestis*, but climate science confirms that both emerged in periods of pronounced, and quite sudden, global cooling.

This environmental formulation of the Middle Ages as a time "surrounded by cold and plague," or more actively as a time birthed and killed off by outbreaks of cold and plague, points to more than just a strange coincidence. It raises some of the questions, about war and conflict and their connections to the broader patterns of this world,

[9] See Brook, *Troubled Empire*.
[10] Campbell, *Great Transition*.
[11] Green, "Black as Death." I thank Ron Braasch of the US Military Academy for bringing this review to my attention.

that we will explore in this book. What effects did the LALIA and Little Ice Age have, and do those effects mark off a period that we can characterize distinctly from the periods that preceded and followed it? (That is, do these climate events do more than provide chronological markers; how did they contribute to the ways in which the historical road actually turned?) And was the period after the LALIA perceptibly shaped by the conditions of its birth?

Let us be slightly more precise about this question. Climate change and disease were not sentient agents attempting to change societies. They were natural conditions that made established patterns of human existence at least temporarily difficult or impossible to sustain. Human communities reacted to these conditions, in attempts to resist change and defend what already existed, or failing that to rebuild something new (likely with the memory of what had existed previously preserved in collective memory as a target, a model, or at least an ideal for rebuilding); depending on the success of those efforts, they kept building and expanding, perhaps in what now looks, in retrospect, like a new pattern; they then encountered and interacted with other communities engaged in the same process; and at the end of the period faced again the problem of resistance, defense, and rebuilding as natural conditions again turned against them. How did this set of processes work?

It is the argument of this book that war and conflict were central to these efforts at defending, rebuilding, expanding, engaging, and again defending. Our opening three battles have already given us a glimpse of these processes: old versus new at Qādasiyyah, the clash of worlds at Xiangyang, the cultural conflicts behind Morat. In other words, war and conflict were part (indeed, a crucial part) of a *process* of cultural construction and reconstruction across the medieval world. Furthermore, war and conflict, when it came to engagement within societies or between them, formed a process analyzable as a dialogue or discourse between antagonistic parties, with the result that the larger worlds into which the medieval globe can be divided (we'll examine the geography of the medieval world further as part of our survey) shared this process and influenced each other. In other words, war and conflict were a central means by which medieval societies defined themselves and thus the entire medieval world.

Indeed, the more detailed claim I will defend is that the global Middle Ages, militarily, fell into three stages shaped by the climatic-demographic structure of the period: wars of defense and rebuilding; wars of expansion, encounter, and engagement (or, to unify this category, wars involving the meeting of communities rebuilt in the first period); and wars (again) of defense and continued building. Furthermore, the success of the initial period of defense and rebuilding *created* richer, more complex and deeply rooted medieval societies – our first period constituted, to coin an ugly word, a process of *medievalization*. The resulting strength of medieval societies made the second round of defense and rebuilding far more successful than the first. Medieval societies were, in other words, success stories compared to their classical forebears, and thus carried on their building projects far more coherently than the classical world had. This has important implications for how we see the end of the medieval world. Again, our opening three battles encapsulate these stages. The character of such types of war and conflict will constitute part of our investigation.

Clearly, this is more than a "purely military" claim, if there is such a thing. We will therefore examine war and conflict across a range of topics, some of which are not usually associated with military history. To take only one representative example, one of the historical "rules" about agrarian-era societies is that labor shortage leads to lower labor freedom.[12] The Climatic-Demographic Middle Ages were born in a period of relative labor shortage resulting from weather- and pandemic-induced demographic contraction and consequent economic recession. These shortages were alleviated only by population growth during the warm middle of the period. We should therefore expect a world of bound, dependent labor forces – an expectation certainly met, at the peasant level, by various forms of serfdom, to use the European terms for such labor, around the world. No surprise there, nor, in the largest terms, much of a change from antiquity. But, at the risk of falling back on the overly broad characterizations of the classical Marxist schema, if the ancient era was characterized by dependence on slave labor (certainly true of Hellenic and Hellenistic Greece and of Rome) and of wars that therefore often focused on obtaining slave labor through making captives, were the Middle Ages any different? That is, using the Marxist terms, what is the effective difference between classical slavery and "feudal" (manorial) serfdom?

More specifically for our investigation from the perspective of war and conflict, what was the role in medieval warfare in, for example, slave raiding and slave taking? Did it decline with medieval population growth? And what about soldiering as a form of labor? Where do

---

[12] As opposed to the market-based expectation common to industrial societies today, that labor shortage should lead to higher wages. For an explanation of this, see Morillo, *Frameworks of World History*, *passim*, but especially pp. 67–71, with exploration of the most significant (apparent) counterexample in pp. 427–31.

soldiers (fighters lacking elite social status) and even warriors (fighters who have elite social status as a function of their military role) fit into this equation? How did armed conflict mediate social conflicts over labor and freedom in different societies? Is there a characteristic "medieval" pattern to the answers to these questions?

We shall explore such issues in subsequent chapters of this book. For now, we can simply note that the environmental and demographic background indicated by our definition of the Middle Ages will help us ask appropriate questions of a large number of data, and it will contribute influences on our answers. My hope, in other words, is to fit military history into the scientific and philosophy-of-history advances going on in climate and disease history, and in so doing to place military history at the center of historical analysis of the medieval world.

The Scope of this Book

Defining the medieval period climatically (within a larger "subsistence-demographic" vision of world history periodization), with the result that we can limit our inquiries to the period, roughly, 540–1500 (or 1800), with two periods of climate change and reaction (540–850 and 1350–1500 or 1800) around a warm middle period, is only the beginning of defining the scope of this book. Within the chronological parameters we have chosen, there remains a vast and varied pile of historical data to sift through and analyze. The vastness of our topic is generated in two directions, geographically and by the topic of war and conflict.

Geographic Scope

Taking a global perspective on war and conflict in the Middle Ages entails trying to include (or at least notice) the patterns and practices of war in as many societal regions of the globe as we can. I say "societal regions" because, as we shall see when we explore geography and war in more detail in chapter 3, our survey can effectively ignore many geographic regions because they did not host armed conflict for various reasons. Given the naval technology available in most of our time period, much of the world's open seas was simply inaccessible to armed forces, for example.

But even focusing just on areas where armed conflict could happen leaves a great variety of geographies to analyze. These supported an even greater variety of social structures and organizations that engaged in conflict. One goal of this study will be to attempt some fairness in our survey of these regions of conflict – fairness defined not just in terms of geographic inclusivity, but also in terms of complexities of social organization. Here I recognize (and plead guilty to contributing to, in my earlier publications) the charge laid by James C. Scott in *Against the Grain*, that the largest, most complex state-level polities and empires have dominated historical coverage of warfare. As he then says, "a more even-handed history would chronicle the relationship of hundreds of smaller states with thousands of nearby nonstate peoples, not to mention the relation of predation and alliance between those nonstate peoples."[13] This very charge, however, makes clear the daunting (impossible?) labor that would be involved in creating such a chronicle, involving hundreds or thousands of conflicts.

Which is *not* to dismiss the charge or the task. Especially in the medieval period, when even the strong states of the world were far less strong and organized than states in our day, when much of the world was not under the control of states, and when many areas that were claimed by states were only tenuously governed, a fair analysis of war and conflict must give due weight to non- (and sub-)state events and perspectives.

War and Conflict

Which brings us to the variety and vastness of the topic advertised as "war *and conflict.*"

What counts? Again, given the weakness of even strong medieval states in modern terms (such as monopolizing, or at least claiming to monopolize, the legal use of violence), restricting the topic to the official, organized military forces of sovereign states will not do. But where to stop, in a world where the equivalent of a "Hatfield–McCoy" family feud might, when fought between major elite families, have political stakes at the royal or imperial level?

The approach here will be to attempt an analysis that is as comprehensive as possible about conflict between armed groups. This will include not just fights between foes "foreign" to each other, but struggles between political factions, social groupings within a society, and so forth. Obviously, when such a broad definition of the topic is spread across an entire global collection of societies of every level

---

[13] Scott, *Against the Grain*, p. 252.

of complexity ... well, "vast and varied" barely does justice to our potential pile of data.

Presented with this much material to analyze, the historian has several options, some more theoretical than others. One, utilizing the capacity that computers have unleashed for crunching "Big Data" in meaningful ways, is unavailable. Most medieval data are not amenable to "datafying" – categorizing, coding, quantifying, and so forth – in ways that computers could make sense of, especially across a data set so vast and varied.[14] Furthermore, the vastness of the data set disguises the fact that the more we focus in on particular questions, the fewer real data we actually have. This is typical for medieval history: time alone has caused much of our potential evidence to disappear. Moreover, the data are distributed in a very "lumpy" way: some regions and complexity levels (for instance, those areas where big state/imperial administrations governed regions whose climate and information-recording systems have generated large numbers of documents in conditions propitious for archival survival) are overrepresented, while others (non-state, non-literate societies in tropical areas, whose major building projects were in wood, for example) are seriously underrepresented. Crunching numbers generated by such a flawed data set might well produce, following the "garbage in, garbage out" principle of computer science, flawed conclusions.

A second possibility for dealing with a vast topic is to write a vast analysis (this seems to be the approach implied by Scott's critique). This is not the approach taken here.[15] Nor is an exhaustive detailing of wars and conflicts necessarily the most productive way to present our topic. No one could remember thousands of pages of details; the important takeaway would be an understanding of the patterns that emerged from such a survey. This book attempts to get at those patterns without exhaustively compiling the data first. Such an approach is of course inherently flawed: how can you, the reader, trust that the patterns I point out are really there? At some level, you can't. Yet there are enough data to be suggestive of large patterns, so as long as we maintain an appropriate level of generalization, we can hope

[14] Some medieval topics can be "datafied" in this way: my colleague Cliff Rogers ran a History Research Lab at West Point on "Quantifying Siege Warfare in the Hundred Years War" that was based on "datafying" the relevant medieval chronicles. The restricted focus of the project makes his approach possible and productive. See also Braasch, "Skirmish."

[15] For a superb example of what a vast (if not exhaustive) survey of medieval military history looks like, see Curry and Graff, *Cambridge History of War. Vol. II*, outlined in the next section.

that the patterns we see are *generally* true. And you should, further, take this book as an initial exploration of a vast and mostly uncharted territory. Which is, in other words, an invitation to further research, exploration, and correction of the initial maps I will sketch.

With Big Data analysis unavailable and an exhaustive survey beyond reach, the approach here will follow a third path: a set of thematic analyses of the data.

Doing thematic analyses, of course, requires that we first establish ways to divide up the data pile productively. What this means is that we must establish some theoretical tools of analysis that will act as data-pile slicers and processors. It is to this methodological problem that we now turn.

Theoretical Tools

Sources and Historiography

Before we dive into the more theoretical side of this study's methods, we need to acknowledge some even more basic questions of method. To start, as we noted briefly just above, there is the uneven distribution of the sources available for a global study of war and conflict in the Middle Ages. Some of this has to do with climate and the materials from which the primary documents we'd like to have were originally produced. More survives in dry and temperate places than in subtropical and tropical locales. Since temperate areas, as long as they are not too dry, also tend to correspond with the agricultural conditions that produce state-level social organizations, which are in turn the great producers of writing and thus of historical documents, some regions of the globe have been vastly overrepresented in histories of medieval warfare because of the availability of written and archaeological evidence. Western Europe, China, and Japan lead this list, and at times drag other regions with which they were in contact somewhat into the light (though Japan was isolated enough that Japanese historical evidence applies largely to Japan).

The gaps in our knowledge produced by the differential survival of primary source material is compounded by two further factors, one unavoidable but relatively benign, the other more potentially insidious. First, the primary sources that survive come to us in a wide range of scripts and languages, wider than any one historian could hope to master. While this problem does potentially privilege the sources and associated cultures of the most widespread languages (headed by the Chinese and Indo-European language families), what this issue really shows us is that history, especially world history, is of necessity a collective enterprise, at least in the sense that any one historian will depend on the prior work of many others; the collective will cast a far wider net of language comprehension than any individual could.

The second, however, affects that dependence on earlier work: research into medieval military history has long been shaped not just by the availability of sources, but by the profession-wide assumptions by historians about *what is important*. Such assumptions go back into the birth period of history as a modern, "scientific" academic field in the mid-nineteenth century in western Europe. That context endowed academic history with a racist, gendered view of the world, and a nationalist view of history that put the nation-state (a cultural construction) center stage. Indeed, medieval history was born as part of the project of finding the historical "roots" of nineteenth-century nation-states, historical roots that helped legitimize the state-building projects of a revolutionary time. When those states became colonial powers, the European "medieval" was imposed on the rest of the world.

Thus, the danger in the collective enterprise of world history (and the reliance of individual historians on the prior work of others) is the perpetuation of bad assumptions that have colored history as a field since its birth. But a further danger arises: because Europe has been a center of investigative attention supported by a relatively rich documentary base, even attention to the rest of the world that escapes the worst of old assumptions runs the danger of falling into the kind of Eurocentrism in which European patterns of development and the theoretical models that help explain those patterns are exported to other regions, whether or not they fit well (and if they don't, the evidence from elsewhere might be "shoehorned" into the European model in order to make the strange new evidence more comprehensible).[16]

This kind of Eurocentrism has certainly affected the military history of "medieval" regions beyond Europe. But the (ironic?) advantage that the medieval military historian who wishes to escape this Eurocentrism has is that there is so little history writing that can claim to be about medieval military history from a global perspective that it can exert only minimal influence (I hope) on how a book like this is written.

There are only a few military histories that examine premodern warfare in some detail with some breadth of coverage. Four of the most prominent are:

[16] For a more detailed discussion of this problem in the context of the analysis of a specific history, see Morillo, "Guns and Government."

- *The Cambridge History of War*, especially *Volume II: War and the Medieval World*. A truly excellent collection encompassing the work of many experts on medieval warfare around the world. It can be criticized (albeit mildly) for some of the issues I have already outlined in this chapter – its view is largely state-centric, and as the editors admit in the introduction, the approach of the volume as a whole is not comparative: "Although a few chapters, such as the one by Stephen Morillo dealing with 'Justifications, Theories, and Customs of War,' adopt a universal and comprehensive approach, the great majority of them are regionally specific." [17] Pages 1–5 of the introduction and the footnotes therein provide a thorough and fair overview of the historiography of medieval warfare. While the volume is much more a quilt of regional coverage than a synthetic global overview, it is the new gold standard for exploration of the details of medieval war (though not necessarily of conflict more broadly conceived).
- *War in World History: Society, Technology, and War from Ancient Times to the Present* is a world military history textbook written by myself, Jeremy Black, and Paul Lococo. It is fairly comprehensive in its geographic coverage, though with the emphasis on the major state-level societies that I noted earlier with respect to my own previous work, and it is not as rigorously comparative as it could be. Still very solid as a survey, but could use some updating.
- *Waging War: Conflict, Culture, and Innovation in World History*, by Wayne E. Lee, is an excellent thematic history of warfare in human history, focusing on key episodes or instances of innovation that had far-reaching military consequences even if they were not military in the first instance. It does not attempt to be comprehensive in coverage either of places or of wars, but rather explores its themes through select case studies. An excellent book, but not focused on the Middle Ages: aside from the invention and spread of gunpowder, Lee's instances either predate the medieval world (e.g. the rise of the state) or postdate it (e.g. industrialization).
- *The Cambridge History of Warfare*, edited by Geoffrey Parker, is

[17] Curry and Graff, *Cambridge History of War. Vol II*, p. 5. The editors call for new interpretations: "Bringing all these stories together in one volume covering most of the medieval world … facilitates the identification of universal processes, local differences and variations, hitherto unsuspected connections between developments in far-flung geographic regions, and perhaps even helps to inspire the creation of new master narratives for understanding war in the global 'Middle Ages'" (p. 5). The present book may be seen as a companion exploring the themes and comparisons underlying the rich regional detail that volume presents.

glossy, slick, excellently produced, and fatally flawed by a deep Eurocentrism in both its coverage and its intellectual take on the topic. A multi-author work, it also suffers from being somewhat incoherent from chapter to chapter. Finally, its medieval sections are the work's weakest. To be carefully distinguished from the *Cambridge History of War* that led this list.

The historiography of medieval European warfare is, by contrast, substantial and thriving. Among the best more general works, perhaps two to start with, because they point fully to the historiography of the field, are *Soldiers' Lives through the Ages: The Middle Ages* by Clifford Rogers, an essential introduction; and *Medieval Warfare: A Reader* by Kelly DeVries and Michael Livingston, a collection of primary sources that also manages to give a good overview and introduction to the topic.

Broader thematic analyses of war in global history (as well as many older surveys of global military history, which were usually very Europe-focused), while often valuable, have tended to pay comparatively little attention to the Middle Ages. It is, admittedly, a difficult period at least in terms of sources. But more importantly, the military history of the Middle Ages, as this book will try to show, does not fit easily into conceptual schemes built on the state-centered histories of the post–1800 world, whose paradigms, furthermore, can be applied fairly easily (though deceptively, I believe) to the major states of the classical world. The period therefore tends to get overlooked in military history in much the same way as in more general histories mentioned above, as the "dark regression" between classical foundations and modern developments. Let us escape this problem. Again, this book examines war and conflict in the Middle Ages as much as possible on its own terms, globally and comprehensively.

Approaches and Models

So, to the question of how to do this.[18] The goal will be to look at our vast collection of data and see significant patterns that show up across large portions of it. The breadth of our geographical and chronological investigation is necessary partly to make sure that patterns

[18] This section draws on my essay "Ibn Khaldun Views Olitski," which considers the challenge for world historians of making sense of the vastness of the global past in the context of seeing world history's relationship to the humanities.

we claim to see really do apply to more than just a local and perhaps idiosyncratic area. In other words, the more of the medieval world we can see, the more likely that the patterns we discern are true of that whole world, not just a small part of it.

Seeing the patterns of the medieval world requires making comparisons. But comparative history applied across multiple cultures raises various methodological issues, especially related to making sure the comparisons are of functionally equivalent items, not just apparently similar ones based on possibly misleading terminology. For example, the role of the office of "emperor," even if we accept that English word as an adequate translation of the respective words in medieval Latin (and then German) and medieval Japanese, is a functionally very different thing in the tenth-century Holy Roman Empire and eleventh-century Heian Japan; comparing these two "emperors" may therefore not reveal much of significance.[19] But some comparisons, those grounded in physical realities, for instance, are somewhat easier to make productively than others.

This fact determines the organization of the rest of this book, as we noted in chapter 1. The metaphor is that these parts present medieval military history as the rules of an historical simulation game. Part I, "The Common Rules of Medieval Warfare," presents the common rules that apply to all instances of the game. Part II, "Three Scenarios: Medieval Warfare in Changing Conditions," presents the various scenarios, with any special rules necessary to creating a more accurate simulation of the game instances happening within the divisions of the medieval time period as a whole. The basics apply everywhere; but as historians, we know that things change over time, and our rules should try to convey that.

Now that you know the plan, let's explore the military Middle Ages.

---

[19] On comparative methodology questions, see Morillo, "Guns and Government"; and on problems of terminology, see Morillo, "Milites, Knights and Samurai."

PART I

The Common Rules of Medieval Warfare

Historians are usually concerned with change over time: explaining why something changed, when it changed, and what the consequences of that change were. The very notion of periodization – the thing that allows us to partition off war and conflict *in the Middle Ages* as a separate topic – presumes changes that marked off "the Middle Ages" from what came before and what came after.

But periodization is also frequently disputed among historians, partly because what counts as significant enough change to mark a chronological break can be disputed, but also (perhaps more fundamentally) because continuity always exists alongside change. Outside of the truly catastrophic moments in the earth's history, such as the meteor strike that wiped out the dinosaurs 65 million years ago, change tends to come only to some portion of the range of human (or prehuman!) experience, while other aspects of existence carry on in familiar ways.

This part of this book examines continuities: those aspects of war and conflict that remained relatively consistent, that were played according to the same "rules" throughout the medieval period and across the medieval world. Such rules, as we shall see, tend to be grounded in physical realities, or the social and political structural realities that existed within those physical realities, and so tend to produce an historical perspective that can be termed "materialist." To put this metaphorically, what we will examine in part I is the stage on which medieval warfare was played out, and the props with which the action took place.

3

Geography, Politics, and War

Introduction: The Common Rules of Medieval War

One would expect that, if there are "universal" truths about medieval war and conflict, they should be at the level of the physical
world where cultural beliefs and perceptions can't change realities
that impose limits on "the possible." (This does not deny the fact
that every culture sees the physical world and its *meaning* through
its own cultural frame, and that the world therefore looks different to different groups. But the presence or absence of food for a
marching army, for example, though it may mean different things
to different people, will still influence what an army can do in that
area, whatever they believe about it.) The necessity of reading
narrative stories in our sources critically against physical reality is
what Hans Delbrück, the influential nineteenth-century German
military historian, called *Sachkritik*. Reading against physical reality
was one of Delbrück's central insights when he argued that the
numbers attributed to ancient armies by classical historians were
often seriously inflated. Logistics (available food and water) and
sheer considerations of space made many numbers in the sources
implausible or literally impossible. Yet the limits imposed by physical reality are fairly broad and can be exaggerated; we will stick here
to the broadest, most general patterns, where the direct influence of
physical reality on the conduct of warfare is clearest.[1] We also need,
however, to examine the *indirect* influence of physical reality on the

[1] On *Sachkritik* and its limits, see Morillo, "Contrary Winds."

patterns of medieval warfare – influences that operated through the common political patterns and structures that physical reality imposed on the preindustrial world. Thus, the physical and political constraints that imposed common, virtually universal patterns on the conduct of war and conflict in the Middle Ages are the topic of this chapter.

Physical Realities: Where War Could Happen

Conflict, if we include interpersonal disputes at the one-on-one level, could happen anywhere humans lived in numbers greater than one. (We will exclude intrapersonal psychological conflicts from this survey!) During the Middle Ages, this means conflict could happen just about anywhere outside of Antarctica. We will come back to the topic of conflict and the varieties of forms it could take at the end of this chapter, though we can point out here that our categories are not hard and fixed: non-war conflict could be ramped up to something that could qualify as war. Furthermore, in the medieval world, the lines between varieties of conflict were fuzzier and more malleable than we are used to today, and in general the medieval world knew a much less clear distinction than most societies today do between war and peace, because medieval daily life was, on average, significantly more violent than modern industrial societies are accustomed to. We shall explain this more when we come to the role of the state in shaping medieval warfare.

War, on the other hand, was more limited in terms of where it could happen. But seeing how requires that we define what we mean by war as opposed to the broader category of conflict.

Defining War

To distinguish war from interpersonal conflict or even the violence of large-scale riots, let us start with a fairly standard definition of war as "organized armed conflict." Having just put an examination of conflict off until later in the chapter, we need therefore to think about what "organized" and "armed" mean in our definition.

"Organized" for armed conflict has generally meant, historiographically if not historically, that the conflict was conducted by a hierarchically arranged society with a command structure, whether permanent or improvised on the spot, that gave to masses of armed men at least a modicum of direction that they would not otherwise have had. The most common form for this organization is "the state." Let us take "state" for the moment to mean the kind of political organization characteristic of complex hierarchical socie- ties. That is (to avoid complete circularity), a "state" is a political organization featuring something that can be seen as an institu- tional existence that transcends the personal influence of individual leaders, usually with a form of record keeping more permanent than memories and oral transmission (that is, with writing), and an internal hierarchical organization reflective of the complexity of the society it rules. Often (always?), this level of institutional develop- ment is accompanied by self-conscious conceptualization of "the state" (in our period, usually closely tied to a ruling family) as a thing separate from and standing above society – a "res publica," to use the Roman term that continues to inform our world today. The key implication of socio-politically based organization for the conduct of warfare is that the influence of states tends very strongly toward warfare becoming an activity conducted by humans massed together in large numbers.

States did not have a monopoly on war making, however, espe- cially in our period. Warrior chiefdoms (the commonly recognized next step down the organizational ladder of political hierarchies) were common, and warfare even at lower levels ("tribes" and "bands," to use the usual anthropological categories for the political organizations of less complex societies) was not uncommon, though the role of states in propagating warfare among less complex societies is another topic we will return to later in the chapter. Indeed, what most his- torians would recognize as warfare could be conducted by sub-state social groupings – in our period, for example, by guilds, or by that smallest and least organized but nevertheless still war-making social group, the Viking shipload.[2] (Note that especially for social organiza- tions such as guilds, which were truly sub-*state*, that is, which existed within a state structure, the militarized tendencies of the state level of organization, as we shall see, tended to permeate downward through its subgroupings, so that they shared a military culture engendered higher up. Viking shiploads, on the other hand, are representative of groups whose militarization had happened within the political

---

[2] Attempts to draw a cut-off line below which armed conflict is not "warfare," what H. H. Turney-High in *Primitive War* called "the military horizon," have not been ter- ribly successful; by analyzing "war and conflict," this book will effectively ignore the problem, while recognizing the prominent role of states in historical warfare.

confines of an emergent state, and who fled to retain a freedom of action the nascent state threatened. In both cases, the state played a central, if indirect, role in such groupings as the model of the "organization" aspect of war making.) And the tendency toward mass, of gathering all available human resources together for a collective effort, existed at all levels of social organization of violence, though usually with less effectiveness than that displayed by organizations "purpose built" to create soldiers.

"Armed" might seem to be more straightforward than "organized" as part of our definition. We can specify, however, that the "arming" process that marks warfare was as intentional as the organizations that emerged to prosecute warfare. That is, groups organized for war almost always carried implements designed and specifically created for the purpose of killing human beings, especially humans armed with similarly intended implements.[3] Specifying this has one significant implication: it works against the assumption that warfare as organized killing evolved "naturally" from hunting, an activity practiced just about universally, as far as we can tell, across all early groups of *Homo sapiens*. Yes, hunting was also organized killing. And it is true that some hunting weapons, above all the bow and arrow, proved useful in war. But stopping there is to confuse technology with technique. Even weapons such as the bow that could be used for either activity were used differently in each case – en masse, in a way shaped by the organization using the implement, in the case of war; individually, in a way shaped by the prey and preferences of the individual hunter, in the case of hunting. (Even today, rifles designed for military use *can* be used for hunting, but for optimal use in hunting are often modified in various ways.) Even with the bow and arrow, the shape of arrowheads varied according to the target. The simple spear, when adopted for masses of foot soldiers, tended to become more standardized, to get longer and heavier than a spear a hunter would use, as it was less likely to be used javelin-like for throwing and more likely to be used for stabbing at an armed and armored opponent. It is no coincidence that when armies accustomed to fighting "real war" (that is, organized in masses with implements adapted for that kind of use) met "primitives" (people from less socially hierarchical societies, producing armed men in smaller masses and armed with weapons much more like the hunting implements they lived by – native North Americans when Europeans encountered them, for

---

[3] We examine military technology in ch. 4.

example, or armed forces in Ireland when Normans, English, or even early Viking shiploads encountered them in our period) they met foes who, outnumbered and "outgunned," resorted to forms of guerilla warfare that much more closely resembled hunting: ambushes, skirmishing, and so forth.

Like the militarization of sub-state social groups to create "organizations" producing armed forces, the militarization of weaponry by association with state-level tools and practices meant that when implements designed for other purposes, most likely hunting or farming, were taken up for warfare, they tended to be modified for military use using models provided by "real" weapons. And like the lesser effectiveness of non-military organizations at producing soldiers, ad hoc tools of war were almost always far less effective than the purpose-built kind.

This discussion of the terms embedded in our definition of warfare, despite caveats about sub-state social organizations and the role that could be played by improvised, "sub-state" weaponry, clearly establishes state-based warfare as the center of gravity in our definition. This gravitational centering is reinforced by the tendency of the historiography of warfare to emphasize state-level military conflict, and by a long (several millennia) political ("polemical" is probably the more accurate word) emphasis by state-centered cultures on warfare as legitimate only when conducted by proper state authorities; the most formal version of this emerged in Christian Just War theory, which drew on Roman legal traditions, and was echoed closely by Islamic Just War theories. The monopolistic motivation for states attempting to limit legitimate warfare to their own military efforts, either coercively or at the least rhetorically, is obvious; whether state propaganda makes good history is a different question. Yet historians through the ages have tended to adopt the state-centric perspective on war, either intentionally or by default, as well. Is such a perspective justified?

As long as we take a state-centered view of warfare as the dominant image produced by a "weighted average" of historical cases, and bear in mind that especially in the Middle Ages there were many significant exceptions, as we have already noted in building our definition of war, the image is not unreasonable. Indeed, as we shall explore in the next section, states and warfare have gone hand in hand, for reasons that are not merely coincidental, since the earliest states emerged in southern Mesopotamia about 5,000 years ago. States make war, and in the process draw non- and sub-state peoples into the war-making dynamic throughout history. The next section explores why.

War and States: Geographic Limits

The origins of state-level societies have long been subject to a semi-heroic, "progress"-oriented narrative that in fact does not capture very well the impact of the emergence of states on human lives.[4] States, though they generated most of what we think of in terms of the "achievements" of "civilized human history," undoubtedly made life worse – nutritionally, cognitively, and in terms of what today we call "quality of life" – for the vast majority of the individuals who lived under them. War was one of the mechanisms that contributed to the deleterious impact of state rule.

The short version of the reason for this negative impact is that states emerged as macro-parasites on the most densely settled, sedentary sources of assessable and confiscatable wealth available: grain-growing human communities. Cereal crops have always formed the agricultural foundation of states because of their legibility (or readability to surveyors during production and as product), assessability (including ease of measurement), and storability by potential state authorities (i.e. tax collectors). States latched on to such communities, extracting the surplus wealth they created and erecting mechanisms (such as walls) to protect and *control* the sources of that wealth: not just the grains, but the populations who grew them.

The hierarchical, coercive character built, of necessity, into state-level organization of human society spawned some of the preconditions for the use, if not the invention, of warfare as a tool of state policy: control of masses of manpower under central direction, and the need, in the eyes of those running the state, to defend and if possible extend their gold mine.

Put in these terms, we also have a path to explaining the universally patriarchal, male-dominated character of all preindustrial societies. The wealth of the state lay, as we have said, in the human and agricultural resources it controlled. Grain growing was one of the ways this resource self-perpetuated; but human reproduction was the other. Thus, the types of people who found themselves with highly restricted freedoms in agrarian societies were farmers (who became at best peasants, at worst slaves), and women of all social classes and occupations

---

[4] See Scott, *Against the Grain*, especially ch .7, "The Golden Age of the Barbarians," for a nuanced and theoretically comprehensive account of the relationship of states to non-state societies. For Scott, states and "barbarians" competed to exploit grain-and-population core regions.

(who were subordinated politically, socially, and economically). Well into the Middle Ages globally, reproductive-age women were the most valuable people captured in the slave-making function of war, which was far more central than most accounts allow for.

Thus, it is not a coincidence that war in the Middle Ages was largely a male activity (as war continues to be, even when recent gender integration of armed forces is taken into account). In the Middle Ages, of course, females had close connections to warfare as victims of rape, abduction, slaving, and killing; as producers in the economies that supported war; as camp followers, wives, and a key part of "home fronts"; as cementers of alliances through marriage; and as pretexts for going to war, even if there never was a Helen who saw a Troy. But females participated in war only occasionally as leaders and even more rarely as fighters.

Returning to the "grain-and-people" core around which all ancient and medieval states were ultimately built, and given the centrality of states to the patterns and methods of war making (as revealed by our exploration of a standard definition of war), even without anything like a state monopoly over the legitimate use of armed force, "Rule 1" about where war happened was that it was restricted to geographic areas within striking distance of grain-growing economies. "Within striking distance" means that this is not as tightly restrictive a rule as it might at first appear: indeed, pastoral and semi-pastoral economies (as prevailed in the central Asian steppes or in early medieval Ireland, respectively) appeared to support war-making societies without having much if any grain growing (figure 5).

But pastoral and semi-pastoral economies were never truly independent of interactions with grain-growing cores, and so neither was their warfare. War in the Middle Ages centered on control of grain cores by states, generating a fair amount of warfare internal to states, and then generating war between states, between states and the "barbarian" penumbra of non-state societies that surrounded them, and among those many barbarian societies.[5] The clash between Song China and the Mongols at Xiangyang exemplifies this "state–barbarian" conflict at the highest level (high enough, in fact, that both sides are claiming to be, and have the trappings of, states – indeed, states as empires, the most expansive form of medi-

---

[5] See Scott, *Against the Grain*, especially ch .7, "The Golden Age of the Barbarians," for a nuanced and theoretically comprehensive account of the relationship of states to non-state societies. For Scott, states and "barbarians" competed to exploit grain-and-population core regions.

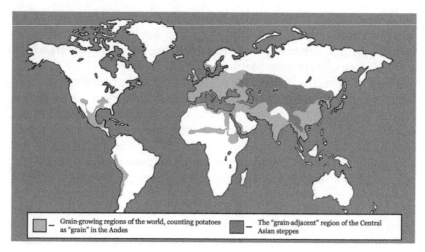

	Grain-growing regions of the world, counting potatoes as "grain" in the Andes	The "grain-adjacent" region of the Central Asian steppes

Figure 5   Map of the major grain-growing/agricultural regions of the world.

Source: Author.

eval state). The Persian–Arab clash at Qādasiyyah similarly pitted a grain-state core area (Persia) against a "barbarian" penumbral area (Arabia), with the latter having risen to state-level war making largely through the influence of Persian (and Roman) goals, organizations, and resources via subsidies designed to secure alliances with the Arab tribes.

The dynamics of state formation and war making that determine this rule explain why war was not an activity, during the Middle Ages, that happened in mountains, swamps, jungles, deserts (except, as at Qādasiyyah, on the edges where deserts met grain land), tundra, and so forth: terrain where grain growing was either impossible or possible only in tiny, isolated oases. And not just war: these were the sorts of terrain that were inhospitable to state formation, and thus where state authority rarely ran, even if a state were adjacent to such lands. Even relatively accessible hills and uplands were difficult for states and armies, and were notorious as the places where bandits hid out, rebels retreated under pressure, and populations more generally might retreat in times of trouble – beyond the reach of both raiders and states desperately seeking extra resources with which to deal with troubles. One reason states were less stable and lasting formations in major parts of India than in other centers of "civilization" was that its geography more closely intertwined grain- and state-friendly terrain with "internal frontiers" of state-unfriendly terrain.[6] The ability of the Swiss to create an independent polity in the face of opposition by major powers such as Burgundy rested not just on Swiss military prowess, but on their unattractively mountainous homeland (which nevertheless was productive enough to support the Swiss themselves, though rarely an invader and certainly not the cost of conquest and governance).

The restriction imposed by Rule 1 was most obvious at the level of the largest wars involving that most characteristic form of grain-state armed force, the massed infantry army. Such armies on campaign, numbering 20,000 and above (though rarely if ever over about 100,000 in one place for any length of time), were larger than most cities in the medieval world, and thus absolutely depended, whether via forage, market options, or transport, on the same resource that sustained cities: cores of concentrated populations and grains. Even when they operated within grain-growing areas, all the mechanisms of forage, markets, and transport of grain were themselves subject to pretty serious limitations, setting bounds to the range of military campaigns and shaping patterns of strategy in ways we shall explore further later in this chapter (see "Geography, Politics, and Warfare," below). The centrality of the Yangtze valley and its tributaries to the Xiangyang campaign and its mass armies, with the rivers as routes for the movement of troops and supplies as much as they were defended barriers, exemplifies this perfectly.

The limits of foraging, markets, and transporting grain from depots were aspects of the more general technological-social limits of the preindustrial world on large-scale organized human activity, whether armed or not. Thus, the combination of geography and technology produced contexts for the use of armed force that help explain both where and why warfare occurred in the medieval world.

War and States: Techno-Political Contexts

The fundamental limits on human activity in the medieval world, as they had been since the emergence of complex agrarian societies and would be until the Industrial Revolution, were low productivity and slow communications. The preindustrial world operated with sources of power that were limited to wind, water, and above all muscle, whether the muscle was human or animal. Thus manufacturing, as

[6] Wink, *Al Hind*, ch. IV.

the Latin roots of the word demonstrate, was mostly a matter of hand crafting; techniques of mass production were limited in the extreme; hence low productivity. Travel happened mostly at a walking pace and had limited carrying capacity – the central importance of water transport in the moving of goods (especially bulk goods like food) to cities and armies resulted from the vast decrease in friction and increase in load capacity that water transport allowed over land transport; yet even water transport was limited to wind, water (tide and current), and muscle as sources of power; hence slow communications. With most relevance here, the "low and slow" combination shaped the possibilities and dynamics of the political structures of human societies in ways directly relevant to the history of war.

We can offer a thumbnail portrait of agrarian-era hierarchies, a short list of their common (indeed, practically universal) characteristics, all of which flow from the "low and slow" limits of agrarian-based production and technology.[7]

First, the limits of slow communications meant that it was difficult or impossible to get large numbers of people together quickly to make critical decisions. Even getting a smaller, select group together if they came from a wide geographic area was unfeasible. In other words, mass democracy was, except at very small scales (i.e. one city-state with very limited definitions of citizenship, as for example in classical Athens or medieval Bern), impossible, and even restricted collectives – oligarchy, aristocracy – were usually impractical, with poor communications also contributing to a strong tendency for such groupings to be torn by factionalism and infighting. No wonder that virtually every preindustrial society considered monarchy the "natural" form of government. It was "natural" (or at least highly determined by the universal "low and slow" context of state building), whether the state was headed by a "king" so called or a unitary political leader by another name, while those societies that resisted monarchy, such as the Roman Republic, allowed for king-like officers (e.g. dictators) in emergency situations that simply heightened the usual conditions that led every agrarian society toward monarchy. And given that the main organizational job any polity had to undertake was warfare, which required rapid, centralized decision-making, kings were war leaders, and even limited collectives tended in times of war to move toward unitary leadership, as we have just noted about early Rome.

---

[7] See Morillo, *Frameworks*, for a more extended explication and model of agrarian-era hierarchies; see also Crone, *Preindustrial Societies*.

The same "low and slow" dynamics shaped social structures. Low productivity and the inability to distribute production efficiently via slow communications made for poor societies whose meager surpluses were concentrated upward by those with the coercive means to do so. Result: effectively "two-class" societies. At the top, a small group of (usually hereditary) elites; under them, the mass of the population ("commoners"), made up mostly of farmers whose production was sucked upward through taxes, rents, or the fact that their labor was to some extent unfree, whether via true slavery or limited unfreedom (serfdom and the like). The "political community" headed by the king consisted only of the elites, and usually only of a small segment of those. Neither elites nor commons were an undifferentiated mass: differences of birth, status, rights, prestige, and wealth meant that every medieval society was intensely hierarchical from top to bottom. But the fundamental divide between elites and commoners, marked by language, beliefs, outlook, mobility, and resources, formed a Great Cultural Divide separating all medieval societies into two.

The unfairness of such pyramidal social structures, so visible in a more egalitarian age, was not invisible at the time. This accounts for the fragility of medieval polities. The organic connections between any society's elites and its commoners were inevitably weak, and the state, the "top of the pyramid," could be, so to speak, "knocked off" and replaced by outside invaders with surprising ease. This was true of preindustrial societies generally, and particularly of "classical" or "ancient" versions of such societies. One of the patterns of the medieval world was the creation of stronger ties between the tops and bottoms of societies through cultural "technologies of social control" that attempted to bridge the Great Cultural Divide, chief among these being the spread of the "salvation religions" (Christianity, Mahayana Buddhism, Devotional Hinduism, and Islam). These ameliorated the evident unfairness of such societies by promising the downtrodden a better afterlife, while justifying hierarchy through creation myths and religious sanctions.[8]

A further set of common characteristics of agrarian societies had to do with their socio-economic structure. The dominant role of coercive political organization in the construction and maintenance of complex hierarchical societies reinforced and arose from the fact that market-based economic forces and activity were, especially by the standards of our contemporary global society, weak. This is not to say that trade

---

[8] Nationalism, with its "historical" creation myths and tales of common language, history, and culture, is in this perspective the modern religion of state building.

networks and economic exchange did not exist: they were pervasive, and had often been in existence far longer than political hierarchies. Furthermore, the scope and carrying power of networks (which
included networks not just of economic exchange but of cultural connection and human movement) tended gradually to increase across
the period of the Middle Ages, with some important consequences
that we will explore later in this book. But in big-picture terms, this was
a world of hierarchies first, connected by networks second, in which
political arrangements (i.e. questions of coercive power, distributed
unequally) tended to predominate over economic arrangements (i.e.
questions of cooperative exchange mediated by market mechanisms).
This was true from basic production – the pervasiveness of unfree
labor is indicative here – through the organization of trade, often controlled or at least regulated by guilds that were departments of a state,
up to strategic levels of gift exchange between polities that constituted
long-distance trade or at least colored and framed the trade that did
occur. A visible result of the weakness of networks of exchange is the
small size of medieval cities worldwide; a handful of megalopolises
such as Constantinople, Baghdad, and a disproportionate number
of major Chinese cities existed as urban islands in a rural (or at least
micro-urban) world, supported by vast regional and trans-regional
systems of trade (supported in turn by major state investment in supplying the megalopolises through infrastructure development such as
canals and direct provisioning arrangements reminiscent of the dole in
imperial Rome). Most cites were far smaller – 20,000 was the population of a very large city, and many were in the 2,000–10,000 range
– because that was all that low productivity and slow communications
could support in the absence of vast state investments in a political
and economic center, and even those were only rarely possible.

In sum, medieval polities, like ancient states before them and the
states of the period 1500–1800 after them, were built on a foundation of coercive inequality and political domination, if not outright
control, of grain-growing economic processes for the benefit of the
state and the elites who ran it and profited from it.

Medieval polities therefore existed under a constant shadow of
latent internal conflict. This leads us to "Rule 2" about medieval
warfare: the first and primary role of the armed forces of any state, Job
1, was defense of the hierarchy itself, *primarily* against the threat of
internal unrest (figure 6). Defense against external enemies, including
"barbarian" forces and the armies of other states, was simply a secondary aspect of Job 1. Indeed, even major public works apparently
designed for defense against external foes can be seen as having a

Figure 6 Peasant revolt. This image of the Jacquerie, a widespread and violent peasant revolt in France in 1358, illustrates the dangerous tensions at the heart of medieval polities, tensions that made defense of elites and their state structure Job 1 for medieval armed forces.

Source: Christophel Fine Art / Universal Images Group / Getty Images.

dual function: the Great Wall of China, perhaps the premier example of this phenomenon, was there not just to keep Mongols out, but to keep the Chinese subjects of the state *in* and under control.

This is a truth that must be borne in mind when evaluating the composition and effectiveness of various medieval armies: their fitness for doing Job 1 might render them suboptimal for warfare against external foes, but unless the results of foreign wars proved exceptionally catastrophic, Job 1 remained the dominant part of the military environment in terms of evolutionary pressure, accounting for the deep conservatism of *elite* armed forces in particular across the medieval world.

Put another way, agrarian hierarchical societies were ruled by three sorts of elites: priests, or those who wielded religiously sanctioned authority; scribes, or those who wielded the authority sanctioned by "tradition," written rules, and their role in the bureaucratic mechanisms that made up the state; and warriors, or those who wielded the authority given them by their ability to coerce. Warriors were thus the ultimate backstop of elite and state authority. Yet it should be noted that warrior authority, while perhaps the most basic and ultimately necessary, was the least efficient, because "might makes right" engenders little in the way of voluntary cooperation. Philosophically based scribal authority and religiously based priestly authority, on the other hand, while perhaps lacking ultimate coercive power, were built to engender cooperation, or at least to legitimize and thus make more bearable the coercion implicit in the system, and thereby reduce the need for naked coercion. The spread of the salvation religions, noted above, is a sign of their success at framing the inevitable coercion in ways that made it seem less coercive.

The hierarchical coercion at the heart of medieval states shows up in two other fundamental ways. The first is that, given the technological and social limitations of the medieval world, often the only way for a ruler to expand his resources (which was often the best way to maintain internal peace, as the additional revenue could then be doled out to the elites to build their unity and support for the central-royal government, which was crucial to its effectiveness) was for him to grab control of more grain-growing regions and people. In other words, because "economic development" (to put it in modern policy terms) that was aimed at raising the productivity of land and people, while possible, was rarely so in ways subject to centrally directed state action (the construction of vast irrigation projects being the very occasional exception), expansionism was a consistent feature of medieval state policy. Expansion, of course, did not always happen:

each state's desire to expand was subject to being checked by its neighbor's defenses and similar desires, as well as by limits imposed by geography and effective communications – an overly large state was subject to regionalism and breakup from within.

The second is that the medieval world's states, when not surrounded by other states, faced frontiers occupied by "barbarians" – that is, by non-state peoples.[9] This highlights the fact that the medieval world, unlike our world today, was not universally divided into states – the majority of the world's land area lay outside the control of states, though the density of settlement in state-controlled regions meant that a slowly growing majority of the world's population lived under state control. The relationship between state and non-state peoples was complex and deserves some explanation.

To begin with, the fact that non-state peoples are often referred to as "barbarians," or by other pejoratives such as "savages," "primitives," and so forth, is a result of state-centered perspectives dominating history. Non-state people were a threat to states, certainly. But not just because their people often made their livings in ways that proved useful for learning military or paramilitary skills – the lifestyle of the pastoralist nomads of the central Asian steppes is the best example, and one we will explore further below. Instead, non-state areas existed in a sort of hostile symbiosis with states.

Economically, states – based, again, on intensive grain growing and the subject populations necessary for that economic system – were not fully self-sufficient economically. They produced food and that specialization allowed sedentism and thus manufacturing, especially in terms of metallurgy and cloth. But almost all states found it necessary to supplement their own production with goods that had to come from non-agricultural regions. These included fish and game; forest products such as furs, honey, and amber; and in some cases political-economic necessities such as horses (a topic we will return to shortly). Thus, state and non-state regions were always connected by trade networks whereby states obtained what they could not produce in exchange, usually, for manufactured goods. Trade networks inevitably existed side by side with "barbarian" raiding of states, and trade-or-raid relations could easily morph into tribute relationships where states bought peace with (and/or influence among) the "barbarians" in exchange for tribute payments that were often dressed up as "gifts."

---

[9] See Scott, *Against the Grain*, ch. 7, "The Golden Age of the Barbarians."

Depending on the sort of land occupied by non-state peoples – especially whether it had potential for supporting grain-based agriculture, a category that gradually expanded as farming techniques and technologies (including new breeds of standard crops) opened new regions to grain farming – the dynamic of raiding and warfare could move toward offensive campaigns by state forces under the basic expansionist dynamic of states. Here we may consider the political-military challenges facing both sides of this pervasive tension between states and their non-state neighbors.

In immediate military terms, the advantage often lay with the "barbarians" because their lives as herders, hunters, or simply independent survivors gave them individual military skills that the vast majority of sedentary people did not have, as well as better basic health and nutrition. Farmers, in particular, made weak material for creating fighters. Thus, man for man, non-state military forces could often outperform their "civilized" opponents. The quality of the average Mongol soldier was the extreme case of this, and "barbarians" such as the Mongols from pastoralist regions such as the central Asian steppes could also deploy the vast advantage of mass horse riding, a fundamental division of the medieval military world which we will explore more in a moment.

But the contest was rarely if ever man for man, and states deployed several significant advantages that tended to develop and weigh more heavily over time, meaning over the course of isolated confrontations between specific states and non-state neighbors, and across the entire era of the Middle Ages. The key state advantages were manpower and organization. Grain-based agriculture could support a much greater density of population than any other preindustrial subsistence system, so farming states simply had far more people than their non-state rivals. That this demographic advantage could be made to count on the battlefield was not guaranteed; sometimes it simply meant more victims for the less populous but more warlike side to slaughter, as the Mongol piling up of corpses outside the walls of Fanchen reminds us. But this is where organization came in. Political organization meant that states could turn a part of their vast population into, if not warriors, then at least soldiers (taking the basic difference as "warriors were a product of lifestyle, soldiers were manufactured by systems"). Thus, sedentary armies often outnumbered their "barbarian" foes.

The political organization of states conferred another advantage, if not completely consistently: institutional continuity. As much as dynastic succession allowed, the state became its own person, and could usually therefore outlast any individual non-state leader, no matter how talented, applying consistent pressure over several generations in the same way that a corporation (a legal person, albeit a potentially immortal one) can outcompete an individually owned business over the long haul.[10]

Furthermore, the oppressive, hierarchical social organization of states allowed them to create their own warriors in the form of social elites whose dominance of the social order gave at least some of them the ability to adopt a lifestyle grounded in martial ability. These *warrior elites*, though not always existing in completely comfortable alliance with the "state," often formed the core, if not the entirety, of a state's military forces, and could be warriors the equal of non-state warriors. On the other hand, the social pyramid necessary to support warrior elites could only, because of low productivity and slow communications, sustain a tiny number of them. Thus, the non-state model could actually produce, usually, more warriors than the state model, unless the state were unusually large and militarized, which carried its own risks to political stability.

To social-political organization we may add the oppressive economic organization of states, which was designed to gather the surplus wealth of the state, however meager the surplus might be at the individual level, and concentrate it in the hands of the state's rulers. Thus, the leaders of states could deploy economic resources in their political-military contests that non-state areas simply could not match. This sometimes showed up as the ability of states to buy off barbarian threats through the payment of tribute, as noted above. But it also gave states the ability to hire away pieces of their opponents' military forces as mercenaries or subsidized allies, reducing the individual military advantages of the barbarians substantially. The Swiss ability to sell their (semi-)barbarian infantry skills exemplifies this; though the Swiss themselves did not suffer thereby, the main beneficiaries were the larger kingdoms who hired them. Thus, non-state peoples participated regularly and crucially in the subordination of non-state regions to state control – apparently paradoxically, since the reason there were non-state regions is that the oppressive state model was not automatically attractive (contrary to the narrative of "progress" that often colors histories of state warfare against non-state peoples).

---

[10] Indeed, a post-medieval example of this phenomenon was the British conquest of India in the eighteenth and nineteenth centuries, accomplished primarily by an actual corporation, the British East India Company, whose main advantage over often talented local Indian princes was that it kept outliving them.

Another aspect of state organization that assisted in states' conflicts with non-state regions was that same hierarchical oppressiveness that made states look (and be) unattractive to many non-state people. The social and political leaders of non-state regions could see the advantages their state counterparts reaped from controlling state mechanisms, and sometimes opted (to put it polemically) to sell out their own people for a piece of that pie. This could mean going over to the state and taking what followers they could, a path sometimes initiated by mercenary service. But it also meant that non-state leaders often initiated state-building programs within their own territories, in order not just to match the collective organizational advantages of states, but, at the individual level, to secure to themselves the "blessings" of being a social elite in a state. The fourteenth-century conversion of the pagan Grand Duchy of Lithuania to Christianity, after several centuries of successful resistance to Baltic Crusades that aimed at forcing their conversion, is a classic case. Lithuanian conversion was ultimately voluntary and led by Lithuanian elites who saw not just the advantages their Christian counterparts had, but the critical role of Christianity in justifying that more oppressive role.[11] Thus, state organization, though limited (along with most of the warfare it generated) to regions within reach, at least, of grain-based agriculture, was over the long haul "viral," tending to spread as new fields were opened up to its economic foundation.

A final note about political and military complexity and geography: the complexity and (to put it more judgmentally) sophistication of political and military systems around the world were higher in areas that supported multiple states and competing non-state forms of organization, because competition, while at times bad for stability, forced societies to come up with systems (governmental, military, and cultural) whose greater sophistication and flexibility allowed states that developed such systems to survive in more competitive environments. We can see the effects of connectedness, or by contrast the results of isolation, across the medieval world. A good part of this derives from a basic view of world history through the lenses of diseases, demography, and communications:[12] radically isolated Australia developed no state-level societies; the major societies of

---

[11] Hogan, "The Great Staring Contest"; see also, for the military side, Urban, *Teutonic Knights*.

[12] The classic and best-known example now being Diamond, *Guns, Germs, and Steel*.

the Americas and sub-Saharan Africa were somewhat less culturally complex than the leading powers of Eurasia.

More germane to this book's view of the medieval world, isolation and complexity as a theme gives us another lens on the Middle Ages as a coherent global period. At least in popular historiography, the medieval period often gets short shrift, in part (I suspect) because the polities of the medieval world are somehow less impressive than the great empires of the classical period – "the glory that was Greece, the grandeur that was Rome," the Han, the Mauryas. But a good deal of this is an effect of the differing competitive environments. The classical empires thrived in an emptier, less competitive world than their medieval successors survived in. In the wake of the breakup of the classical world in the climatic and disease catastrophes of the fifth century, multiple successor states emerged in all areas, and the spread of state-level organization outlined above created new competitors for the "grain space" available, even as that space itself expanded. In such a world, domination of vast areas on the classical model was much harder and in many cases impossible. China alone of the great classical empires saw a "revival" of its unified classical patterns, though close examination reveals the Tang dynasty as less impressive than its self-image proclaims, as we noted in chapter 1, and subject to more serious competition from polities such as Korea, Tibet, and the Uighurs than the Han had ever faced. Medieval polities thus appear more numerous and less imposing than their classical ancestors, but collectively marshalled more in the way of resources both material and moral.[13] The medievalization process traced in chapter 5 was in large part about leaders organizing and harnessing human and moral resources more intensively in smaller realms. Seen this way, even the apparent greater lasting power of classical polities is less impressive – as, in turn, the classical empires seemed less lasting than truly ancient states such as Old Kingdom Egypt. It is, simply, easier to survive when there's no competition.

Likewise, when a new period of climate- and disease-initiated disruption challenged the medieval world, its successors, though still

---

[13] A rough analogy might be the dominance of the Beatles in the early ("classical"?) phase of rock-and-roll history. There was never "another Beatles" because the landscape had changed: post-Beatles (the "medieval" phase?) there were more bands, more genres, and a more niche-based recording industry, precluding any Beatles-like dominance, even when there was continuity of a once-dominant name. Leading me to propose the Later Roman (Byzantine) Empire as the "late-career Elvis" of medieval polities.

operating in an agrarian world of predominantly grain-state polities, faced even more global and pervasive competition as the expansion of the global network of trade and communications, especially after 1492, raised the competitive stakes yet again. That the political continuity from medieval states to the modern world is much more direct than from classical to medieval, despite the increasingly competitive environment, speaks to the success of medievalization in creating polities that were more durable and capable than their classical ancestors had been. (And ironically, that same continuity allowed the invention of a "medieval" period of history.)

To sum up, the geographical center of gravity for the waging of war (as the narrower category than conflict generally) during the global Middle Ages was regions of grain-based states. Grain-growing economies created the demographic, logistical, and (via state building and structures) organizational conditions in which war could be waged, in addition to creating many of the social and political tensions that sparked war. This is not, however, to say that war occurred only in such regions. The direct and indirect influence of states on the areas immediately adjacent to them and even beyond meant that both economic activity and political organization in non-state, non-grain-growing areas were subject to becoming more grain-state-like. Even in regions where the discipline of grain growing long proved impossible to introduce, such as the central Asian steppes, the recourse to war proved capable of extension to some other economic foundations.[14] But the general rule, that war happened within "striking distance" of grain-growing economies, nevertheless captures the essential truth, or at least covers the vast majority of cases of warfare that historians have been interested in. Extended regions of mountain, swamp, jungle, desert, tundra, and (save for limited stretches close to grain-growing land) ocean could not, in the Middle Ages, support armed forces and warfare, even if small-scale conflict could (and did) happen in such settings.

[14] The tendency of state-based political and economic dynamics to "infect" neighboring regions with armed violence as a chief means of settling social conflict continued for centuries after 1500. For the impact of colonial states on the use of armed violence among Amazonian tribes, an impact which has muddied the debate about when war arose in human history, see Ferguson, "Archaeology, Cultural Anthropology, and the Origins and Intensifications of War.," See also his "Violence and War in Prehistory" on the influence of human activity in creating unnatural (state-like?) subsistence conditions on alleged occurrences of "warfare" among chimpanzees.

The Equine Geography of Warfare

Probably the second most important geographic influence on medieval warfare after the human geography of grain growing and state formation was the equine geography of the world – that is, where, and in what numbers, horses lived in the world. For although warfare is a human activity, horses were the most important domesticated animal to be drafted by humans into military participation. Admittedly, the range of animal participants is not large: aside from horses, elephants (of the smaller Indian and North African variety – sub-Saharan African elephants were untamable) were sometimes used in combat, as the Persians did at Qādasiyyah; camels occasionally played a horse-like role in carrying human warriors, as they probably had for the Arabs facing the Persians; mules, a horse hybrid, were useful not so much in combat but mostly as a pack animal or for pulling equipment; and that's about it. Dogs, despite the Shakespearean "let slip the dogs of war," were more humans' hunting companions than useful in actual warfare. And rhinoceroses, armored or not, are a pure comic-book/movie fantasy participant in combat, no matter how cool they look in *300*.

Horses were first domesticated on the steppes north of the Black Sea by the speakers of Proto-Indo-European (PIE), the language that is the fount of what is today the world's most widespread language family, indicating something about the competitive advantage horses conveyed to those who used them.[15] Horses were undoubtedly domesticated first for food, as were most other domesticates. Horses made good domesticates in their steppe context because of the snowy winters there: unlike cattle, horses will dig through snow for the underlying grass and thus survived winters more easily. But their domesticators soon discovered the capacity of horses to pull wheeled vehicles, which created two foundations of full steppe pastoralism.

First, horses could pull four-wheeled wagons, giving to entire communities the mobility to colonize and live from the full vastness of the central Asian grasslands. Second, they could pull lighter two-wheeled vehicles, chariots, at much higher speeds than heavy wagons. Manned by a driver and a warrior armed with a powerful bow, chariots became the first non-infantry component of ancient

[15] See Anthony, *Horse, the Wheel, and Language*.

armies, and indeed the weapon system of choice for warrior elites in the earliest combined arms forces. But soon horse-breeding people, starting with the same PIE speakers, learned to dispense with the vehicle and get directly on the backs of horses. The key technological advance here was the bit, which allowed the rider to control the horse in terms of direction as well as "braking." Riding horses was thenceforward until nearly the twentieth century a vital military skill (their use as pack animals and drawers of wagons lasted even longer). Even more than chariots (which had manufactured, often metal components that sedentary societies could specialize in more than steppe pastoralist nomads could), horse riding became the foundation of the vast military impact of central Asian steppe societies, reaching a peak under the Mongols.

This was because horses provided their warrior riders with several very useful advantages in combat and warfare more generally. The first, obviously, was mobility. Horses are faster than people, and speed was advantageous at both the tactical and strategic levels. Forces could arrive first to preferred objectives, outmaneuver their opponents face to face, and force the action on their slower foes. Sometimes overlooked, but also central at the individual level, mobility allowed a mounted warrior to escape a lost battle far more easily than a foot soldier could. When combined with effective bows, mobility made horse archery a devastating combination of fire and movement.

The second advantage conveyed by riding was elevation. Horse riders could attack down at the heads of foes on foot, who in turn had to attack up at the horsemen. Often, superior height was as much a psychological as a physical advantage: the horse–man combination was large and imposing, as not just the height but the weight of the horse added to the impression cavalry projected in combat. (The impact and effectiveness of the classic cavalry charge was largely psychological, a topic we shall return to in the next chapter.) The combination looked, to those unaccustomed to it, as for example the Aztecs when the Spanish arrived in Mexico, like a single intimidating organism.

Further advantages flowed from the intersection of social and military characteristics of the horse as a military technology. Horses could be, depending on the geography we will explore in a minute, expensive to maintain, and so possession of a horse became a good indicator of social status. Social status often coincided with the resources to focus on military training as a lifestyle, so warrior elites were often mounted warriors, especially in the Middle Ages, for reasons we will

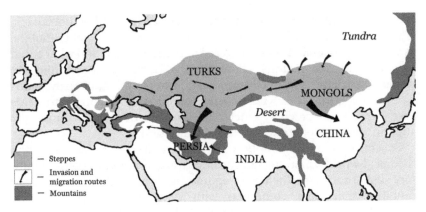

Figure 7 Map of the Eurasian steppes.
Source: Author.

explore further below. The Burgundian knights at Morat stood at an apex of this sort of development.

Given the many advantages horses could bring in warfare to both individuals and groups, the importance of equine geography to medieval warfare is not surprising. At its simplest, three sorts of worlds emerged depending on the availability of horses, at all or in numbers.

Horsed Societies

The successors of the PIE speakers who first domesticated horses, as well as the peoples they influenced or who adopted their "invention," came to dominate the largest and most important "horsed world," the central Asian steppes. This was a vast area of grasslands stretching from northwest of China westward to the region north of the Black Sea where the PIE speakers originally lived, with a small extension into the plain surrounded by the Carpathian mountains that would become Hungary when the Magyars, horse-riding nomads from the greater steppes, occupied it in the ninth century (figure 7). Lacking enough rainfall to support grain-growing agriculture, the steppes could nonetheless support vast herds of grazing animals, including horses, so that the peoples who exploited this environment became fully "horsed societies."

That is, everyone, men, women, and children, rode horses, and possessed horses enough that everyone had multiple mounts. Cities were non-existent, as steppe peoples followed their herds from summer grazing grounds in the cooler highlands to winter grounds in the valleys: steppe people lived in tents, in wagons, and on horseback. Thus, steppe-nomadic societies were highly and thoroughly mobile, as were the possessions that mattered to them: animals and what could be packed in their wagons. "Possession" of land was not a "thing" to nomadic societies. If forced from favored or traditional grazing lands by another group, the whole society could simply migrate to fields that were, if not greener, at least less contested, though joining the superior force's coalition was always an option.

Several consequences follow that had military significance in the medieval world. First, horsed societies were, if united, potential military juggernauts, as their vast equine herds gave them unmatched mobility that they combined with devastating firepower. The Mongols, again, stood at the apex of this line of development. As herders, they saw masses of sedentary infantry as just another herd to be split, maneuvered, harassed, and ultimately mastered. But living in smaller, mobile groups meant that they were not "naturally" united: political fragmentation and rivalry was the base condition of the steppes as a whole; building larger steppe-based political coalitions required the expenditure of some sort of energy (political-military and/or economic) to counteract the tendency to political entropy created by mobility. Steppe political culture was equally fluid: "tribal" or ethnic identities on the steppes often shifted with political shifts. Finally, the political-military reach of horsed societies was as geographically limited, over the long term, as that of the grain-based state-level societies we examined in the previous section. That is, steppe armies could not campaign for long outside the steppes, as no other place had enough fodder to support the numerous herds on which their military might depended. A nomadic coalition might conquer a significant sedentary society, but at least some of the conquerors could not remain steppe nomads if they wished to settle in a capital city and rule their conquest. Thus, nomadic rule of sedentary areas tended to be short-lived (while sedentary conquest and rule of nomadic areas was normally impossible, as grain-based armies could not penetrate the steppes logistically). We shall see these patterns play out repeatedly across those parts of the medieval world within range of the steppes throughout the medieval period; the experience of the Mongols in China was typical.

Partially Horsed Societies and Horsed Elites

Horses could, of course, be raised and maintained outside the steppes, though in far lower numbers than the steppes could support.

Their military utility meant that horses were raised wherever possible. But outside the steppes they were more expensive and rare, and thus, as we noted above, their ownership was dominated (as rare, expensive things that displayed their owners' superior status always were) by socially powerful elites. Ownership of horses and mastery of the skills of mounted combat then simply reinforced the political and social superiority of what became (or continued to be) warrior elites. European knights, Japanese samurai, the warrior elites of Tang China who were often closely related to actual steppe families, and the best units of the Byzantine army all conformed to this pattern and constituted the military elite of their respective societies (figure 8).

The cavalry of partially horsed worlds thus differed from steppe cavalry in being more socially exclusive and militarily differentiated. Although there were certainly status distinctions within steppe society that corresponded for the most part to differences in equipment and perhaps combat role, these were distinctions that held within a "cavalry" type. That is, lower-status steppe warriors might have fewer horses and less armor than higher-status ones, but they still had horses. Elite horse warriors were often the exclusive possessors of horses in their societies, which synergized with the elites' ability to afford better armor to distinguish them not just socially but in terms of military function from non-cavalry members of armies – that is, infantry and engineers. This had important implications for the role of armed force in the dynamics of internal social and political conflict.

The other common difference that emerged between horsed world cavalry and horsed elite cavalry was that, with horse breeding confined to specialized stud farms and with elite warriors usually acquiring the best (heaviest) armor and equipment they could, the horses of warrior elite cavalry tended to be bred for greater size and strength than steppe horses, which remained closer to the smaller size of wild horses. (The common name "steppe ponies" exaggerates this somewhat, but not hugely.) This was not universally true – Japanese horses were smaller and weaker than many sedentary breeds, for example. But it was certainly the common trend.

Larger horses sacrificed some endurance for their greater strength. This difference then corresponded with and reinforced the tendency for sedentary cavalry to be used more in a "shock combat" (hand-to-hand, melee-based) role, as literally "heavy cavalry," than in the mobility-and-firepower role that most steppe cavalry filled.

Nor were all partially horsed worlds created equal. Some warm dry regions bred excellent horses in limited numbers – Arabia and Spain were home to good breeds, both of which influenced the varied

Figure 8 Tang ceramic horse. The horses, often steppe-bred, of the elite warrior families who dominated the Tang dynasty were prized status symbols both in reality and in art. Tang ceramic horses expressed the cultural importance of the connection between the fully horsed world of the steppes and the partially horsed worlds of which China was a key part.

Source: niuniu / iStock.

breeds of wetter and cooler western Europe. Subtropical India had real problems maintaining good horses, which accounted for the vulnerability of India to conquest by places with more and better horses (especially the steppes) through the northwestern entrance to the subcontinent via the Islamic world.

Horseless Worlds

Finally, there were regions of the world where there were no horses. Given the military importance of cavalry, this might have made these areas highly vulnerable to conquest and domination by societies with horses. But in fact they were so isolated from the worlds with horses that this didn't matter, at least during most of the Middle Ages.

The Americas were where horses evolved, but they became extinct there about 12,000 to 10,000 years ago, along with many other species of American megafauna, possibly as a result of hunting by recently arrived humans who had come over the Alaskan land bridge during the last Ice Age. But horses apparently made it to Asia using the same land bridge, and begin to appear in the Asian fossil record just as they died out in the Americas. They were reintroduced to the Americas by the Spanish conquistadors, who indeed counted horses as one of their military advantages over American peoples such as the Aztecs. But horse populations rapidly spread beyond Spanish control to again influence American warfare at least into the nineteenth century, with parts of the Great Plains becoming a second "fully horsed world" for a brief time.

Australia, New Zealand, and Oceania, unsurprisingly, never supported native horses. There are today a few wild horses, descended as in the Americas from European imports, in Australia, but horses are militarily irrelevant in the history of these regions.

Finally, Africa south of the Sahara desert was a mostly horseless world that periodically in the Middle Ages was forced into the partially horsed category by trade across the Sahara from the Mediterranean coast. While kingdoms such as Mali and Songhai, in the Sahel, the grassland region south of the Sahara, briefly developed effective cavalry forces, these proved difficult to sustain. This is because African sleeping sickness and African horse sickness, both carried by insects, are widespread south of the Sahara and are fatal to horses. Thus, sub-Saharan Africa remained for the most part a horseless world.

Weak States and the Medieval Importance of Cavalry

We may make one final observation about the military patterns of the medieval world with respect to horses and cavalry use. We noted above the fact that the climate-and-pandemic-created fragmentation of the classical world that created the Middle Ages meant that political power was more varied and broken up than it had been under the great classical empires. Put another way, this was a world, especially at first but for much of its existence, of relatively weak and weakly centralized states. How does this relate to horses and cavalry?

The answer has more to do with infantry and the bases of its combat effectiveness than directly with cavalry. Infantry effectiveness is very closely tied to the cohesion that a body of infantry can maintain (especially in the face of a psychologically intimidating cavalry charge). There are basically two sources of infantry cohesion. First, the body of infantry drawn from an already cohesive social-cultural setting imports its social-cultural cohesion into its military role. The classic example is Greek phalanxes composed of the neighbors and citizens of a *polis*, and urban settings continued to be the breeding ground of potentially effective infantry in the Middle Ages – with Flemish and Italian city-states leading this trend in medieval Europe, for example, as well as the Swiss, as we have seen. Second, a state can bring together a group of men, even if randomly selected, and train (drill) them as a group until they achieve cohesion. This, however, requires the state to have fairly substantial economic and administrative resources. The classical model here is Rome and its legions; the same model accounts for the vast infantry forces of Song China. In the fragmented between-the-plagues medieval world, both sources of good infantry became much scarcer than they had been in the classical world – social cohesion mostly because the decline of networked economic activity created by climate and disease crises affected urban settings most severely; drill-based cohesion because few medieval states outside of China could muster the resources necessary to maintain drilled standing armies.

Cavalry, by contrast, depends less on cohesion for its effectiveness than infantry, and benefited in the medieval setting either from a lifestyle foundation of its effectiveness (as in the steppe-nomadic peoples) or from a foundation built from socio-economic exclusivity and advantage (warrior elites). Thus, the global Middle Ages saw an age in which cavalry forces assumed greater importance vis-à-vis infantry forces than they had had in the classical era or would have again in a post-medieval world of greater economic activity and revived state power. Military historians have sometimes called the European Middle Ages an "Age of Cavalry." It was, but because it was, fundamentally, an "Age of Bad Infantry."[16]

Varieties of Conflict

The relative weakness of medieval states affected more than just patterns of infantry and cavalry usage, and this topic allows us to circle back to reconsider our definition of war and how it relates to armed conflict more broadly. The "paradigmatic case" for warfare, as we noted above, is state-to-state conflict. Yet in a world of weak states, this paradigm applied far less broadly than at other (especially more recent) periods of history. Put another way, because of the weakness of medieval states, the shadow of armed conflict fell more broadly in the medieval world than did the shadow of "war" strictly defined.

To start at the most basic level, the medieval world lived with far higher levels of interpersonal violence than people today are used to or can readily imagine. Murder, rape, theft, and other forms of violent conflict occurred frequently and regularly. No medieval state had anything like a "civilian" police force designed to prevent or investigate crime; while most had some form of judicial system for trying crimes brought before it, the efficacy of such systems from a modern perspective was risible, consisting mostly of variations on the theme of attempting to "keep the peace" through state-sanctioned self-help procedures – as if community watch programs backed by judges whose courts employed a few state-hired thugs formed the front line of most policing. A state's armed forces, whether a regularly maintained army created through conscription or voluntary recruitment or drawn from the specialists in armed force constituting a particular social class (that is, a warrior elite), played the role of ultimate backstop to such local policing efforts, useful really only in cases of widespread peasant revolt or when banditry had become so pervasive as to spawn large armed gangs who threatened state control of local resources. These armed forces existed not to ensure the good of "the people" but to safeguard state control of the population and the goods they produced. Armed forces were, in short and as we have already noted, part of the machinery of compulsion and oppression that gave to states

---

[16] For a more detailed examination of this question focused on Europe, see Morillo, " 'Age of Cavalry' Revisited."

their character as macro-parasites on concentrations of the producers of wealth: farmers and women.

One important consequence of this for our understanding of the experience of war for the wider populations of medieval states is that the contrast between the conditions of war and peace was much less than it is for most populations today. The "horrors of war" certainly afflicted medieval people, but more as an intensification, in frequency, scope, and unpredictability, of the difficulties of life in peacetime than as a jarring change in fundamental expectations.

Another consequence for our understanding of medieval war and conflict is that much of the conflict happened well below the state level. It occurred as varieties of social conflict and, at higher levels of organization, as intra-hierarchy conflict that, if played out with less violence, would count as "politics," rising at the highest levels to regional, sectional, or "interest" conflicts that could easily become civil war. Much of this conflict, from the perspectives and expectations of a world of far stronger states, looks like (and indeed was) feuds, vendettas, and other versions of clan fighting that, again, states struggled to keep within bounds that minimized the chance of undermining state authority. This can be seen in the sorts of mechanisms that often characterized medieval (and indeed ancient) systems of justice. "Eye for an eye" laws, going back to the Code of Hammurabi and Biblical injunctions and on through the legal systems of medieval states, were designed to *limit* the scope of self-help. In other words, the rule is that if someone takes your eye, you are not sanctioned by the official state system of justice to take *more than* an eye in return. In parts of early medieval Europe, the limitation the state imposed (or attempted to impose) on the patterns of self-help that shaped sub-state conflict was to substitute *wergild*, monetary payment (not exactly a fine but compensation, as it was paid to the wronged party, not the state), for violent vengeance in cases from murder down through less serious crimes.[17] The differences between *wergild* assessed for different sorts of people – adult men as opposed to women, children, and so on – make explicit to us the hierarchical structure of these societies. This was the common social context for the raising and deploying of armed forces by states in the medieval world. Violence was expected and barely managed, or was deployed by the state; at the receiving end, the difference often didn't matter much. And the armed forces that states raised often arose from this

---

[17] Halsall, "Reflections on Early Medieval Violence."

context as groups already organized for armed conflict, with their own agendas and rivalries built in; creating a state army was often a matter of state officials or commanders redirecting the aggressions of such groups, molding them to state control, rather than making soldiers out of "civilians." Of the six armies introduced in chapter 1, only the Song does not really fit this pattern, and even the Song drew on networks of hereditary military families, as we saw, to organize the leadership level of their armed forces.

Geography, Politics, and Warfare

Thus far we have been talking about influences of geography and political structures on warfare that are "under the surface," deep currents of influence, beneath the waves of individual events and outside the usual decision loops of commanders. (If they influenced those decisions, it was by shaping the world and the assumptions individual commanders made about the world, not by throwing up a sudden unexpected obstacle.) In this section we move close enough to the surface that we do see direct geographic influences on patterns of campaigning and on battlefield decisions. Not that cultural perceptions are absent at this level: what some feature of the natural world "means" is always partly a product of the cultural frame through which a commander or soldier views it, as we shall see. In many ways, the influences we can see at this level, whether on strategy, operations, or tactics, are simply the constraints on military activity that the intersection of the natural world and human modes of subsistence created writ small. That is, the question "where can warfare occur?" that we explored above becomes "where can a campaign or battle happen?" or even "where on the battlefield can an attack happen?"

Thus, at the strategic level, we have already established that warfare had to happen mostly within striking distance of grain-growing (or pastoralist herding) areas. The sorts of terrain this excluded, including mountains, swamps, deserts, and so forth, created barriers to the movement of armies that channeled campaigns through some regions fairly predictably. The impassability of the Himalayas meant that invasions of India had to come through he northwest of the subcontinent, via Afghanistan and the Indus valley. The narrow channel from the Mediterranean to the Black Sea made it a favorable "choke point" of both land and maritime communication routes, while the pattern of valleys that led from there into the Balkan Peninsula was restrictive enough that Adrianople, the city that grew up in that choke point, was the scene of battles over and over again. The role of the Low Countries as "the cockpit of Europe" resulted from their location as the easiest non-mountainous route between the German plains and the main French grain regions.

Rivers, in this view, could play conflicting roles. River valleys often formed major invasion routes into the grain-growing regions that surrounded the river, and the river itself could act as a transport highway. But at a more tactical scale, a river could form a major barrier to the movement of ground forces, forming a defensive barrier even if the river were fordable. Thus, a key bridge could become the focus of a battle, as at Stamford Bridge in northern England in 1066, where an Anglo-Saxon army defeated an invading Norwegian force, or at the bridge that connected Xiangyang and Fanchen, which themselves sat as the defensive keys to a transport–barrier river system. The impact of terrain also depended, of course, on modes of transport and, at times, on cultural expectations. In the Mongol invasion of Russia in the 1230s, the Mongols confounded Russian expectations and defensive positions by invading in winter, when the rivers were frozen over and thus posed no barrier to the Mongol horse armies. And in a final example of the intersection of tactics and culture, the Roman military writer Vegetius advised that an army never deploy with its back to a river, as this cut off their path of retreat should that prove necessary. Vegetius expected Roman soldiers to fight bravely for their own glory and the empire, and figured that the general should give them room to make the best decision they could on the spot. But the Chinese military theorist Sunzi advised that an army before a critical battle be deployed with its back to a river. Why? Because soldiers of Sunzi's Warring States era were expected, in a different political environment than applied in Roman warfare, to be automata without initiative or motivation except for following the orders of their educated commander. Placing their backs to a river indeed cut off their chance of retreat, and so was designed to make them fight harder. Perhaps Charles the Bold, backing his army against a lake at Morat, had read Sunzi instead of Vegetius? (Or more likely he was too arrogant and self-confident to have listened to either, of course.)

Basically, terrain at the strategic, operational, and tactical levels either facilitated or inhibited movement, and thus channeled attacks or at least aided defenders, with the effects varying again with the modes of transport available – men on foot could often cross terrain that was more difficult for men on horseback (heavily forested areas, for example, as the Swiss traversed in approaching Morat) and impossible for wagons carrying supplies or heavy siege equipment.

We may outline, however, a more specific set of strategic patterns that tended to emerge when sedentary, grain-growing states fought each other, a set of patterns sometimes known among medieval European military historians as "Vegetian" because it conforms to the advice Vegetius – and indeed Sunzi – gives. The similarity between Roman and Chinese advice demonstrates its grounding in the economics and human geography of such states. The principal points may be outlined as follows.[18]

The major strategic principles embodied in Vegetian strategy are logistical and reflect the foundation of states in control of grain-growing lands and populations, as well as the equine geography, that we have outlined in this chapter. The limited productivity of traditional agriculture and the seasonal patterns of both that agriculture and the availability of wild fodder for horses led commanders to live, as far as possible, by foraging. Offensive campaigns sought to support themselves by foraging and pillaging in enemy territory, activities which not only supplied the attacker's forces but denied the opponent's own resources to him. If carried out widely and often enough, the devastation could directly undermine the defender's forces' economic capacity for continued resistance, and threaten the political coherence of enemy territory by exposing the inability of its leaders to protect its constituent parts.

What was the defense to do in reply? One indirect response was to launch a counterattack into the territory of the raiders, hoping to draw them back into defense of their own land. More direct responses included shadowing the invading army closely enough to prevent their foraging. Short of supplies and frustrated by a lack of booty from plundering, the invaders, it was hoped, would go home. But ultimately, Vegetian strategy assumed the centrality of fortifications in the defense of the territory on which the state depended. Even if raiders pillaged their way through some of the defenders' lands, if the defense kept their forts they kept their hold on the land and people the forts dominated, and thereby lived to fight again another day. Thus, the second major activity attackers engaged in was besieging fortifications, as at Morat and Xiangyang. This again often resolved into a logistical battle. Could the besieging army keep itself supplied longer than the besieged strongpoint could? If the defenders could keep an army in the field in addition to a garrison in the fort, that army might again stay close enough to the besiegers to hamper their

---

[18] This section summarizes Morillo, "Battle Seeking"; see also Rogers, "Vegetian 'Science of Warfare'."

foraging and so drive them off, as the Song attempted unsuccessfully to do to the Mongols.

Given a vital fortification, a determined and well-supplied besieger, and a determined relief army, a battle might result, as at Morat. But a final feature of Vegetian strategy, and the one that has earned it the opprobrium of armchair generals weaned on Clausewitz, is its somewhat limited use of battle as a tool in warfare. Battle, in the contexts Vegetian strategy assumes, was often an indirect path to goals more directly reached by pillaging and sieges. Furthermore, it was a risky option: the vagaries of chance could steal from a superior force in one day what it had worked weeks or months to obtain. Though an attacking force, especially, might seek battle for strategic reasons, such battle seeking was closely constrained by considerations of topography, tactical systems, relative force, and so on; on the defensive, only dire necessity constituted a good reason for actively seeking battle without overwhelming advantages of terrain (including fortifications) or force.

To summarize and then expand a bit, the "Vegetian" strategic patterns that describe much warfare in the medieval world prevailed when two conditions held. First, that the entities involved in warfare were settled agrarian societies. Second, that the entities involved in warfare lacked an agreed-on context for dispute resolution. Such a context could either consist of universally accepted cultural norms that governed conflict, or could reside in a superior power capable of enforcing cultural norms and/or legal rules. "Superior power" here can mean an entity which acted as the ultimate practical broker of military might, or an entity that constituted the exclusive source of legitimacy (of possession of landed wealth, above all) within a system. The practical result of any sort of agreed-on context for dispute resolution was to render warfare in important ways non-territorial and so non-Vegetian; if such contexts did not exist, territoriality tended to become central and led to Vegetian patterns.

In times and areas where these conditions did not hold, medieval warfare was characterized by a lack of fortifications (as a strategic choice) and by battle-seeking strategies, where both sides sought to end the conflict with a decisive engagement with the opposing army as soon as possible. The first and most significant exception to the Vegetian, territorial-based patterns of medieval warfare was when the pastoralist nomads of the central Asian steppes were involved. The mobile societies were not "territorial" in the way that states built on grain growing were; they therefore did not build fortifications, engage in sieges, or pillage each other's territories, and in conflicts among themselves and often with sedentary societies sought out battles. Only when they aimed at conquest by taking the sedentary society's fortifications did they fall into the territorial patterns of Vegetian strategy, as the Mongols did at Xiangyang.

The second set of exceptions, not exactly rare but far less systematic than the steppe exception, consisted of sedentary territorial societies and states in which warfare took place within a closed cultural or political world that in one way or another established rules that governed the meaning and practice of conflict (especially concerning the legitimate possession of landed wealth). These tended to appear in one of three ways: as agreed norms in a cultural world; as agreed norms in a political system; or as legal rules within a political system. The existence of such norms or rules obviated Vegetian strategies by rendering warfare non-territorial, either directly or indirectly. Directly, such norms or rules could dictate that warfare was not, in fact, about territory, but was about prestige, hierarchy, or elimination of rivals. Indirectly, such norms and rules could make possession of territory contingent not upon occupation protected by fortifications but upon legal or moral title conferred by some central authority.

A few examples will have to serve to illustrate these conditions for now. "Agreed norms in a cultural world" describes, before the medieval period, the warfare between classical Greek *poleis*, as well as much warfare in the Aztec part of the medieval world. "Agreed norms in a political system" describes warfare in Kamakura Japan, where battle seeking and slaughtering of enemies was the response to a world where legitimate control of landed income depended on the approval of the central government headed by the combination of emperor and shogun. The world of Anglo-Saxon warfare, except when the first wave of Viking invasions introduced an external element, can be analyzed according to either of these conditions, demonstrating that a "political system" is a culturally constructed artefact. And since both conditions resulted from "norms" unenforced by a strong central actor, both tended to be policed by notions of honor, face, and prestige – common cultural currencies for warrior elites, in particular, across the medieval world.

On the other hand, the last condition, "legal rules within a political system," pretty much assumes a strong state whose legal rules are binding on participants in warfare. Wars such as the Wars of the Roses for control of the central government of medieval England, the legitimacy and authority of which all contenders accepted, are the best example of this condition, and again produced battle-seeking strategies and killing of rivals. While one might say that civil war tends to be non-Vegetian, it would be more generally true to say that civil war tends to be non-Vegetian because civil war tends to happen within a political system with agreed norms or agreed legal rules.

Finally, in addition to patterns of strategy, geography and modes of subsistence also shaped patterns of conquest, or how conquering polities extracted resources from – and perhaps even governed – the territories they gained in warfare.[19] Not surprisingly, consolidating victory meant, for sedentary grain-based states, control of the land itself (often with a secondary need to gather in new sources of man-power through war as slave-making expeditions). Steppe peoples and their non-territorially based forms of warfare aimed at "gather-ing in the people" of conquered populations; against other steppe groups, this usually consisted of simply absorbing the newly subject population into the ruling coalition; against sedentary populations, the conquered would often be gathered in for sale into slavery (to sedentary states) or at least for removal from the land as part of a move to convert farmland into pasture. In even more "barbarian" or less developed societies where hunting and gathering still featured prominently in the subsistence package, the goal was to empty the land of its previous occupants to open it for a form of exploitation by the conquerors that required no new additional manpower, as sed-entary agrarian exploitation did. The indigenous societies of North America, in the medieval period (down through 1800), are the key example here.

Conclusions

What this chapter has attempted to examine are the "subsurface conditions," the tides and currents in the ocean of medieval warfare (to borrow an image from the *Annalistes*), that pervasively shaped the patterns of medieval armed conflict, but in ways that were not always obvious in the moment. We have laid them out in this way because they were always there; when we examine the courses of specific wars in part II of this book, we will be able to refer to these conditioning contexts in brief, rather than having to point them out repeatedly. Or, to return to the scheme behind the organization of this book,

[19] For a good theoretical analysis of these patterns, see Lee, "Conquer, Extract, and Perhaps Govern," on which this section is based. The "early modern" world of this study continued to operate according to the "medieval" (or agrarian-era) rules laid out here.

this chapter has outlined many of the "Common Rules" of medieval warfare. Armies followed these rules because they had to – the rules reflect the physical and organizational realities of the medieval world. As we shall see in the next chapter, they also followed "Common Rules," conditions based in physical reality, when it came to weapons systems.

4
Technology and War, or The Common Rules of Combat

Introduction: The "Common Rules" of Medieval War 2

In the last chapter, we laid out the "Common Rules" of medieval warfare in terms of geography: the physical constraints that determined where warfare could happen, mostly having to do with the economic bases of both warfare and state formation in grain growing; the global distribution of horses; and the ways in which the intersection of geography with political structures and cultures shaped strategic options and preferences. The same factors shaped who the participants in warfare tended to be.

In this chapter, we focus in more on the operational and tactical levels of medieval warfare, though again in terms of physical realities and constraints. In particular, the technological patterns and possibilities of medieval weaponry were more constrained than is often acknowledged, producing similarities across the medieval world that can be disguised by the mesmerizing minutiae of weapons variation. Thus, this chapter is the second part of the "Common Rules" of medieval warfare: the "how" rules to go with the "where" and "who" rules of chapter 3. (The "why" of medieval warfare is the topic of part II of this book.[1])

We will start by framing questions of military technology in philosophy-of-history terms, as the great risk in examining this topic is falling into "technological determinism." An examination of military

---

[1] Though approached from a somewhat unusual angle: "why" as a question of the underlying cultural function and outcome of war and conflict as opposed to the usual questions about social or state policy.

technology in the context of the sort of deep historical background that we deployed in the last chapter to frame state formation and its impact on warfare provides the context for understanding why technologically determinist views are inappropriate for understanding medieval warfare. The deep historical perspective again shows how the medieval world is a part of the longer agrarian era of world history, even though it does have an internal coherence.

The bulk of the chapter will survey the intersection of technology (mainly weaponry) and warfare at the tactical level. This survey in turn divides into three sections: the technology of combat in land warfare; the technology of siege warfare; and lastly the technology of naval warfare. In each case, we must analyze not just technology and its impacts, but how technology combined with, shaped, and was shaped by the organizational systems that deployed the technology. This, as we shall see, perhaps mattered most in naval warfare, itself the most organizationally and technologically complex arena of medieval warfare.

Finally, we will examine the technological constraints that shaped warfare above the tactical level: the various technologies of communication and knowledge transmission, including mapping, that influenced operational and strategic patterns of medieval warfare. These same constraints force us to consider the question of how medieval grand strategy was conceived and implemented.

Technology and War: Theoretical Considerations

Assessing the role of technology in medieval warfare requires that we frame the inquiry carefully, because the medieval world worked very differently from our own in terms of technological development or lack thereof. The modern pace of technological change, often with admittedly significant consequences, has showed up in military history's tendency to slip into technological determinism as an interpretive framework – one that simply does not work for the Middle Ages (if, indeed, it ever really works).

Technological Determinism in Military History

The history of warfare – or of human society generally – over the last 150–200 years has conditioned people to look for technological innovation as a (or the) driving force of change. From steamships and railroads to tanks, submarines, and aircraft, it looks as if technological advancement regularly transforms how war is fought. Whether this view even over the last two centuries is as true as it appears on the surface is a topic beyond the scope of this book.[2] But the expectations that recent history, largely of the industrializing world, creates are, this book will argue, inappropriate for understanding the medieval world. Those expectations, at their most extreme, constitute what historians refer to as "technological determinism": the idea that technological change exists virtually as an independent variable with major, if not primary, effects on the causal chains of world (or at least military) history. But not only is it clear that the use of technology, military or otherwise, is heavily dependent on the cultural context into which it is introduced, meaning that technology is far from an independent variable in causal equations, but the fundamental limits of technology in the medieval world were serious – a position captured neatly in the title of Kelly DeVries' article "Catapults are not Atomic Bombs."[3] What do we mean by these fundamental limits?

Preindustrial Technologies of Warfare

Global Similarity

The argument here is that weapons technology across the medieval world displayed a global similarity that meant that no power or set of powers had a decisive technological advantage over its foes. This was an inevitable result of the global foundations of technology and its use in the Middle Ages. The most basic of these was that almost all medieval weapons technology (like all preindustrial technology) rested on a limited set of sources of power, namely wind power (the main motive force for sailing ships and for some mills), water power (again, mainly for mills, though the currents of rivers were useful

[2] For a good general introduction to this issue at the philosophy-of-history level, see Black, *Rethinking Military History*, ch. 4. See also Black, *War and Technology*. Note, however, that Black's latter survey starts with European warships of the post–1600 era, and though it also examines the evolution of gunpowder weaponry, it does so for the period 1490–1800, and thus lies predominantly outside the medieval world as it is usually conceived. See "The Normality of Stasis" below, and chs. 7 and 8 for discussion of when the "end of the Middle Ages" might be seen as occurring.

[3] DeVries presents a clear anti-technological determinist argument linked to criticism of the "Military Revolution" paradigm that often accompanies technological determinist arguments, as well as the technological determinist narrative behind common depictions of modern technological breakthroughs. More generally on this point, see Lynn, *Tools of War*.

for navigation in one direction, at least), and muscle power, human and animal. While simple machines (levers, pulleys, and so forth) could multiply and at times store power for a carefully timed release, these still constituted a very limited set of motive forces for doing damage to military targets – humans, animals, buildings, and other machines. Probably the most consistent "technological" advantage visible in the medieval world came from the use of horses. As we saw in the last chapter, horses as "technology" were important enough that we divided the world based on their availability, and the central Asian steppe nomads who dominated equine technology were, when united, the medieval world's military superpower.

In terms of destructive force being limited to wind, water, and muscle, the application of fire in the destruction of dwellings and ships is the one consistent exception, and was restricted by the constrained degree of control users had over it. (We shall deal with fire in the sections on siege warfare and naval combat below.) The one other exception, gunpowder, brought the potential for chemically generated power to warfare, as we will discuss further below, but this resource remained in its infancy at the end of the medieval period (as it is usually defined), impressive as Charles the Bold's artillery train at Morat was at the time. Thus, the damage inflicted by medieval weaponry came almost totally from human (or equine) muscle imparting force through an instrument designed to cut or bludgeon its target, either directly or at a (limited) distance.

This limit remained dominant through the entire medieval period (again with the emerging exception of gunpowder) because of another limit: no medieval society had developed what could be called a "scientific culture" for the development of weapons (or indeed any technology). Accurate measurements of relevant data, controlled experiments, applicable understandings of the natural world more generally – no culture had yet developed essential elements of the science that lay behind industrial-era weapons advances. Innovation and experiment were not unknown, but could not be harnessed systematically, and still operated within the limits of the sources of power noted above.

The basic political structures of the medieval world militated against the development of technologically oriented scientific cultures or their application to military technological development. Machines, including of the military variety, are almost always what economists would call "labor-saving devices": mechanisms for multiplying the efforts of individual humans in the production of "work," whether that work is destructive or constructive. But the medieval world, globally, was one in which the basic foundations of political power consisted of the domination of labor, as we saw in chapter 2. With political power measured fundamentally by the number of laborers a powerful person could command, labor-saving devices were inherently subversive of established power. There was, therefore, virtually no demand for such innovations – new machines had to prove their worth to the powerful first, constraining the possibilities for their development.

Furthermore, particular styles of warfare grounded in the deployment of already extant weapons were often at the base of the cultural identities of various warrior elites. Any new weapons technology that threatened the dominance of established warrior elites would meet resistance on these grounds, no matter its military effectiveness. Both the crossbow and hand-held gunpowder weapons met such resistance in various regions (including western Europe) on exactly these grounds. Whether the technology spread and affected warfare then depended only partly on the purely military effectiveness of the weapon: if warrior elites could exert monopoly control over the warfare in a cultural region (which might depend on the political unity or lack thereof of the culture), the new weapon could be suppressed despite its apparent usefulness.[4]

The limits on weapons technology stemming from the limits of sources of power, scientific cultures, and political structures, however, did not lead to unvarying similarity across the medieval world. The varying styles of weapons and warfare that produced the cultural identities of various warrior elites meant that there were many nuances – regional and cultural specializations in the use of military technology – within the fundamental limits and similarities of the medieval world. These could create local asymmetries between combatants (the apparent superiority of Arab archery over the Persians at Qādasiyyah is a possible example of this), but advantages for either side tended to be relatively short-lived and not overwhelmingly decisive, given the limits within which all medieval military cultures operated.

---

[4] The most famous example is the suppression of gunpowder technology by the Tokugawa shogunate in Japan after 1605, which was grounded far more in the shogunate's political fear of the subversive and disruptive social and political effects of guns than in a romantic cultural devotion to the sword as the samurai weapon. The cult of the sword was invented in the Tokugawa era as part of the suppression of gunpowder for socio-political reasons. See Morillo, "Guns and Government." And see Turnbull, "Biting the Bullet"; Turnbull argues against a "revolutionary" spread of gunpowder weapons into Japan.

The one significant exception to this generalization, which like gunpowder came into play only at the very end of the "standard" medieval period globally, was that those societies that were more heavily networked together, and so shared the incremental advances in military technology that various of them might develop, had some advantage over more isolated societies who had to depend much more exclusively on their own innovations within their own limits. The world-historical encounter between the late medieval military technology of Eurasia, the most populous and heavily networked part of the medieval globe, and the military technologies of the most complex and hierarchical societies of the American continents, the Aztecs and the Incas, illustrates the extreme case of a networked technological advantage. But even in this case, the weight of technology in the equation that saw the Spanish conquer both American empires can easily be exaggerated.[5]

The Normality of Stasis

One consequence of an essentially stable technological and social-political set of foundations for warfare is that the Middle Ages witnessed nothing that can convincingly be called a "Military Revolution."[6] This is simply another way of saying that throughout the medieval period, everyone was playing by the same "Common Rules," as we are calling them here. This claim, however, requires first that we deal briefly with the possible exception of the introduction and spread of gunpowder technology during our period.

Gunpowder was indeed the first military technology (and indeed, technology of any sort outside the steam engines invented by Hero of Alexandria, which as far as is known had no real practical application) to perform "work" using a motive force other than wind, water,

---

[5] On the Incas, for example, see Guilmartin, "The Cutting Edge," and cf. Hemming, *Conquest of the Incas*. On the Aztecs, see Hassig, *Aztec Warfare*, whose analysis shows why political and cultural factors were at least as important as technological ones in Spanish success. Finally, the Aztec and Inca cases are paradigmatic in Diamond, *Guns, Germs, and Steel*; but of those three titular factors, germs were undoubtedly the most important (and communications technology in the form of writing should probably have made Diamond's title, based on his own analysis).

[6] Military Revolutions and the related but more limited concept of "Revolutions in Military Affairs" (RMA) have generated a vast and contentious historiography, originating with the arguments over the ("early modern," European) Military Revolution: see Rogers, *Military Revolution Debate*; Parker, *Military Revolution*. See the following paragraphs for more.

or muscle. Though to be clear, it is not gunpowder alone, which is simply an explosive, that accomplishes the destructive ends it came to be used for so effectively. To be useful for more than making fireworks or impressive but undirected "bangs,"[7] the explosiveness of gunpowder must be contained and used to force a projectile through a tube. In other words, you need guns as well as gunpowder. It took several centuries for this step to reach even minimal levels of military usefulness, and for the remainder of the medieval period after guns first appeared in both China and then Europe, even minimally effective guns remained heavy, somewhat dangerously unreliable, and slow to use. This meant that they played only a very small role in medieval field combat, and that only in a few restricted circumstances in western Europe, as at Morat (on the losing side!); and played little significant role in naval combat until after the mid–1500s.

Where medieval guns and gunpowder did make a difference was in siege warfare, where lack of mobility and slow rate of fire were less critical limitations. But here again, it made this difference only (in the "standard" medieval period) in western Europe, where a variety of factors allowed the production of the earliest effective cannon, and then only after the early 1400s. A technologically influenced military change, in other words, may have roots dating to the Middle Ages, but only blossomed later.[8]

We may go a bit farther. What do the medieval roots of gunpowder technology and its deep contexts as outlined here tell us about the "early modern Military Revolution"? We have already argued in chapter 2 for the sort of deep continuity in social, economic, and political conditions that unified the agrarian era of which the Middle Ages were only a "middle" part. From this perspective, claims for a truly revolutionary set of changes in military practice before the end of the agrarian era with the Industrial Revolution should be viewed with some skepticism. And indeed the historiography of the "Military Revolution" includes many works that critique the supposedly revolutionary character of the military developments of the period 1500–1800, as well as questioning the focus on Europe that

---

[7] Or to be ingested as an elixir of longevity, which may well have been the goal its first inventors were aiming at. On the history of the invention and spread of gunpowder technology, see Chase, *Firearms*.

[8] It is telling that even a "Military Revolution"-friendly work such as Knox and Murray's *Dynamics of Military Revolution* includes only one "standard" medieval case (ch. 2 by Rogers), and that is described as an "RMA," the far more limited category of military change.

characterized the earliest conceptions of a "Military Revolution."[9] Combining context and subject, the view here is that there was no real "late agrarian Military Revolution."[10]

The Frame for Stasis

This view may be amplified by comparing the military changes that characterized the periods before and after the period of technological stasis in which the Middle Ages fell.

In the earliest stages of the agrarian era, when the potential of grain-and-population-based societies for complex organization was only emerging, the clearly revolutionary invention of socio-political forms such as the state had military corollaries. Nothing in the Middle Ages came anywhere close to matching the invention, for example, of massed infantry, the domestication of horses (first for drawing chariots and then for true cavalry, in military terms), combined arms armies, fortifications and siege engines, and navies – the fundamental pieces of medieval military organization and technology, in other words, which were not added to for millennia. These organizational (and indeed sometimes *conceptual*) breakthroughs were connected to basic technological developments including the use first of bronze and then of iron as the materials for armor and weapons. Ancient societies, in short, created, in a series of revolutions, the military environment of the medieval world.

At the other end, the industrial nineteenth century saw again a vast set of revolutionary changes in economic, political, and social organization that brought military corollaries along. Capitalism, nationalism, and science called into being steam power (for ships and trains as well as mass manufacturing of weaponry) and the continuous process of innovation and arms-racing that by sometime in the twentieth century was threatening the existence of the very technological societies engaged in these processes, whether through the potentially nearly instantaneous destruction of nuclear holocaust or through the slow suicide of climate change. Set in the frame of ancient invention

---

[9] Among many others, see, e.g., Black, *European Warfare, 1660–1815* and *European Warfare, 1494–1660*; Lorge, *Asian Military Revolution*; Andrade, *Gunpowder Age*; Morillo, "Guns and Government"; and the further reading in the bibliographies of those works.

[10] This is not to say that there was not significant change, especially in siege warfare and – perhaps most significantly – in naval warfare after 1500, but that it did not add up before the nineteenth century to a "revolution."

and industrial acceleration, the long agrarian era, especially its medieval middle, takes on even more the character of a period of technological stability during which variations in socio-military organization and culture played far larger roles in the shape of war and conflict than military technology did.

Technology and War: The Tactical Level

The Limits of Medieval Weaponry

The main limit on the effectiveness all medieval technology including weaponry was that the sources of power available to get work done (work here including the destructive work of killing people and eliminating obstacles to the killing of people such as fortifications, other buildings, and even ships) were, as we noted above, wind, water, and muscle. Wind could drive ships and water power could be used to grind grain and perform other fixed-place tasks, but neither could really be applied to military tasks. They could provide sustained, low-level power, but not the sort of concentrated and movable applications of force that military problems usually required. Thus, human and animal muscle provided the motive force for destructive work.

These sources could be mechanically multiplied (as for example by bows, or at a larger scale by the lever mechanism of traction and counterweight trebuchets); and they could be supplemented in limited ways by the destructive potential of fire and, as we have noted for the end of our period, by the harnessing of gunpowder. But in the vast majority of cases, power for destructive work was weak, and when stronger was often hard to focus.

Medieval offensive weaponry could do damage to its targets in two main ways. First, by the blunt-force trauma that the impact of a heavy weight could have on flesh or on structures. Second, by the penetrating ability of the sharp points and edges of weapons. (The two could of course be combined, as a penetrating point or edge could increase the damage inflicted by sheer blunt force.) Medieval power limits meant that medieval offensive weapons were correspondingly limited in their weight and penetrating power, and limited in the range over which they could be projected. Thus, medieval weaponry produced combat that occurred face to face, or across a line-of-sight range of, at most, a couple of hundred yards. "Line-of-sight" means that, while limited techniques of indirect fire – projectiles sent over intervening obstacles toward their target, as in rocks cast over castle walls onto the structures and people within – were possible, most missile fire happened over short ranges where the target could be seen (and thus aimed at) by the person projecting the missile. We shall return to the consequences of this sort of weaponry after a brief survey of the actual variety weapons and armor assumed in different combat environments.

The Technology of Land Combat: Weapons, Combat, and Battles

Melee Weapons

In land combat, the weight of weapons that could be wielded effectively, via muscle power alone, to inflict blunt-force trauma was limited enough that pointed or edged weapons predominated. Clubs could still be useful, especially if given a penetrating facing, as with many maces, but were found mostly in one of two circumstances. First, where the limits of metallurgy made edged weapons impossible. Incan warfare in the Andes was conducted almost exclusively with wooden clubs for this reason, as the only Incan metalworking was in gold and silver, precious metals too soft to make effective edged weapons. Second, where some cultural imperative made blunt-force trauma the preferred method for inflicting damage. The major case of this was in medieval Europe, where, if clerics participated in combat (which they did, though not regularly), the religious injunction against their shedding blood was interpreted to mean that clubbing was acceptable whereas slicing was not.

Thus, bladed weapons dominated, including knives, swords, and axes. Blades could be designed to emphasize their ability either to slash or to stab. Stabbing blades tended to be shorter and come to a strong point; slashing blades could have one or two longer edges, and furthermore tended to vary between straight-blade and curved-blade designs. The latter proved easier to wield from horseback, and the "sabre," probably originally of central Asian origin, came to predominate among cavalry swords. Blades designed for use by hand included a grip and a hand guard of some sort – sometimes no more than a metal crosspiece – such that if blade met blade and slid along each other, the wielders' fingers would be protected from being sheared off.

Hand blades varied in length, of course, producing varieties variously called knives or daggers (usually under 18 inches), short swords (usually around 20–4 inches), and long swords ranging from two feet long up to massive blades many feet long that had to be wielded two-handed (figure 9). A set of trade-offs governed blade design. First, larger, heavier weapons carried more inertial force, but were harder to

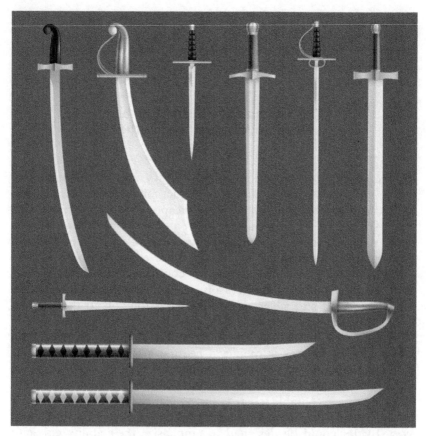

Figure 9 The variety of medieval swords. The shape of swords varied with their intended use. Curved, single-bladed sabers and scimitars (top left and middle) were slashing weapons primarily used by cavalry. Straight swords (top right and middle left) were generally double edged; broader blades were slashing weapons, while narrower blades or shorter ones that came to a sharp point were stabbing weapons. Japanese swords (bottom) were relatively straight, single-bladed, two-handed slashing blades made from some of the finest steel on the planet.

Source: Macrovector / Shutterstock.

swing rapidly. Central grooves served both as channels for blood and to lighten a blade for ease of use. Second, longer blades gave an advantage in reach to their users, but the usefulness of reach was dependent on tactical goals. Longer swords, requiring room to swing for effective use, entailed looser, less dense formations, whereas shorter blades could be used en masse, tending toward stabbing attacks.

Blades could also be mounted on wooden handles. These could be so short as to create something like the Frankish francisca, a small axe that was more often used as a throwing weapon than for slashing, or could be longer, as in the two-handed battle axes the Anglo-Saxons used to great effect at Hastings: a Norman source says that such weapons could easily cleave through the mailed leg of a rider and well into the side of the horse in one blow. Even longer handles produced polearms: when a stabbing blade extended out from the pole, resulting in spears (of 8–12 feet in length, often called a lance when used from horseback) and pikes (heavier, longer spears of around 18 feet in length, usually with a counterweighted back end for balance); or, if the blade end got more complicated on a spear-sized pole, weapons like what medieval Europeans (the Swiss at Morat, for example) called a halberd. The business end of a halberd usually included a stabbing point, an axe-head that gained great force from the mechanical leverage of the pole, and a hook designed to snag a horseman off his mount. The infantrymen of Flemish towns used a short polearm that combined a stabby point with a club; it was called a *goedendag*, or "good day," the origin of which name is disputed but may reflect a grim sense of humor on someone's part.

The other key variation, especially from a global perspective, in bladed weapons was the choice of material. Pointed stabby "blades" could be made from simple wooden spears. But the effective materials were almost all metal: initially bronze; then iron, which was harder; in some areas of the medieval world, including most famously Japan and Iberia, blade makers learned to temper iron blades into steel, which was both harder than iron and could thus hold a razor's edge longer, and less brittle and thus less liable to break. The Aztec world was like the Incan world in lacking weapons-grade metallurgy, but substituted obsidian, a volcanic glass that could produce shards as sharp as any metal blade, for their slashing weapons. The brittleness of obsidian, however, meant that "swords" had to be constructed from a wooden shaft in which the shards were embedded. Compared to the steel swords of the Spanish, Aztec swords were heavier and less handy to swing, and lost their cutting edge more rapidly, though they still proved fearsome enough.

And again, the use of any weapon in mass formations mattered: though a wall of pikes proved a formidable obstacle to cavalry, men carrying long polearms were sometimes vulnerable to close-in attacks by enemies with short stabby swords, though infantry with shorter weapons were more vulnerable in turn to cavalry attacks.

Missile Weapons

Moving beyond the range of hand-to-hand combat meant missile weapons, which again could do either bludgeoning or penetrating/ slicing damage, and which, like hand-to-hand weapons, were dominated by the latter. There were three major methods of delivering missile fire before the invention and spread of guns and gunpowder.

First, of course, objects could be thrown or cast at the enemy. We've already noted the Frankish throwing axe; javelins (or thrown spears) were common. Less common in organized warfare were spears thrown with the assistance of a spear-thrower, whose mechanical multiplication of the thrower's arm action could significantly increase the range and power of a cast spear. The atlatl of indigenous North American peoples is perhaps the best known example, but may have been more useful as a hunting weapon than in warfare. Slingstones had been more common in ancient warfare but decreased in use in medieval times as defensive armor got better, with slings probably giving way to improved bows.

Bows, which shot arrows using the stored energy of the bow, constituted by far the most common and widespread type of medieval missile weapon, and came in a wide variety of designs and effectiveness. Simple self bows, or sticks that rebounded when bent, were the baseline for bow-and-arrow design. Self bows varied mostly according to their length, with longer bows providing greater power but requiring greater strength and room to use than short bows. This usually put them outside the realm of use from horseback, with the interesting exception of medieval Japanese bows, which were up to six feet long but could be fired from horseback because they were strung and drawn asymmetrically: the draw point was about one third of the way up from the bottom, rather than in the middle as with most bows. Even with this added length, however, Japanese bows were not especially powerful – making an oddly fitting match with the undersized and underdeveloped horses used by medieval samurai.

Greater power within a length still usable from horseback was achieved by the construction of compound or composite bows, or bows made from a combination of materials (figure 10). This characteristically central Asian sort of bow was made from an inner layer of bone, which springs back powerfully when compressed, bonded with fish glue to an outer layer of sinew, which snaps back powerfully when stretched. These bows gained added power from being built with a natural curve the opposite of the bow when strung. These short but tremendously powerful bows required strength and

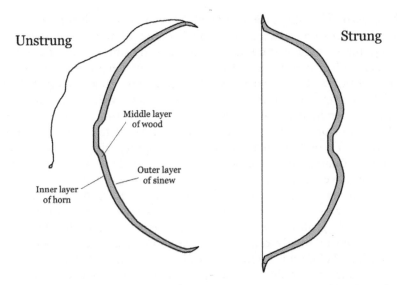

Figure 10   Steppe bow. Recurved and made from a combination of materials, such bows offered great strength in a bow short enough to be used from horseback.

Source: Author.

practiced technique to draw, but the resulting combination of horsed mobility and firepower, as we noted in chapter 3, formed the foundation of dominant steppe-nomadic military power.

There was a self bow that was more powerful and had greater range than the central Asian compound bow: the famous English longbow. Longbows gained some power from their roughly six-foot length, but a peculiarity of the yew wood from which they were made mimicked the construction of compound bows. The staves for longbows were cut such that the outside of the bow was sapwood, which springs back under tension like sinew, while the inner part of the bow was heartwood, which resists compression as bone does. As with Asian compound bows, effective use of the longbow required years of practice both to build the archer's strength and to master the technique of drawing such a powerful bow. One could not simply "take up" the longbow; archers had to be "brought up" to its use.

The specialized lifetime of training that both Asian compound bows and English longbows required limited their spread. By contrast, the last major type of bow, one characteristic of the medieval era across a large range, provided power with minimal training: the crossbow. Made from a variety of materials up to and including iron, the crossbow could store significant mechanical tension in a locked position whose release required no more than aiming the loaded bow and pulling a trigger. It could be readied using simple muscular effort (albeit applied using the archer's whole body weight and core musculature) or with the assistance of mechanical cranks that put draw weights comparable to Asian and English bows within the reach of a minimally trained archer. This came at the cost of a relatively slow reload rate: professional archers could deliver a far greater volume of fire than crossbowmen. But minimal training with iron bows that shot iron quarrels gave crossbows an easy-to-achieve range and penetrating power, a major advantage in the raising of masses of missile troops, as was demonstrated from China to Iberia in our period.

This very ease of use, however, made crossbows socially suspect, as it seemed to professional warriors, who were often socially elite, that the lack of skill involved in using a crossbow made their lethality dishonorable. While this seems to have had little effect in China, where warrior elites were only sporadically present (as in the early years of the Tang dynasty) and thus state-determined interest in achieving mass military efficiency won out, the crossbow never caught on in the more elite-dominated fields of Japanese warfare, and though crossbows became a common part of western European warfare, they faced elite opprobrium and were even (unsuccessfully) banned by the papacy as an inhumane weapon. In this characteristic, crossbows presaged many elite responses to the introduction of gunpowder weapons, particularly handguns. Cannon, as big, expensive investments with utility as display devices as much as militarily, especially early on in their development, faced much less opposition: the gunpowder siege train rapidly became both an enforcer and a symbol of elite and above all royal or state power, as only the richest of the rich could afford a significant number of them. Charles the Bold's extensive artillery train demonstrated his state-building ambitions, for example.

Artillery takes us into the final category of battlefield missile weapons. The easy generalization here is that the Middle Ages saw little use of battlefield "artillery" of any description. The Romans had deployed "super-sized" crossbows, or ballistae, but mostly for use in sieges or assaults on towns and villages. Until the extensive development of cannon after 1500, artillery was effectively not a battlefield arm. This was because the deployment of masses of cannon was expensive and limited by their complexity of design, consequent difficulty of maintenance, and very limited mobility. Large, heavy weapons simply were unsuited to the fluidity of the battlefield, as the fate of Charles the Bold's artillery emplacements at Morat also demonstrates, bringing his state-building ambitions to an end. It was not until incremental technological improvements after 1500, mostly in European warfare, made cannon lighter and mountable on wheeled carriages that the big gun battery became a part of the standard battlefield array.

Defensive Armor and Shields

The extreme vulnerability of bare flesh to injury by weapons of tougher materials meant that defensive protection had emerged as early as the use of weapons to attack humans. Defenses consisted either of shields carried as an extra device in battle, or as "enhanced clothing."

A full range of materials was employed for defensive purposes. Shields often had wooden components (at least frames), and defensive clothing ranged from various types of cloth through leather (usually treated to toughen it) up to various uses of metal. Simple padded cloth jerkins could add significantly to a body's ability to withstand either bludgeoning or slicing attacks. Central Asian warriors, in an archery-rich environment, often wore a layer of tough raw silk cloth as part of their protective gear: it had the ability to resist being punctured by arrow heads, and so even if an arrow penetrated the flesh underneath, it could sometimes be extracted again simply by pulling up on the cloth. Leather toughened by boiling and drying formed a common part of body armor throughout the world, and could be hardened and shaped to protect specific body parts.

Metal, including bronze, iron, and steel, had the greatest resistance to damage, but was also the most expensive to create and obtain as armor. Three main forms predominated: metal scales, sewn in an overlapping pattern to a backing (usually of leather); mail, or rings of metal interlocked into a flexible "fabric" from which hauberks (long shirts), leg coverings, gloves, and hoods could be fashioned; and plates of metal that could cover whole body parts, most often as a helmet for the head, and then as protection for the main torso (breastplate and backplate), as connecting and articulating plate armor for the limbs was difficult and only became common in some areas (mostly western Europe) late in our period, and then only for the most elite, richest warriors. Almost all mail and plate armor was worn over a padded undergarment, both for comfort and to protect the flesh from armor driven inward or pierced into an inner sharp edge by an attack. King Henry I of England, in battle at Brémule in 1119, took a sword stroke to the head that his helmet turned aside, though the blow drew some blood, likely from the edge of the helmet being driven into his forehead.

The choice to wear protection of some sort always involved trade-offs. The protection it provided came at the cost of increased weight carried by the warrior, affecting both his endurance and his mobility, and at the cost of comfort. Metal, as a conductive material, made cold weather feel colder and hot weather dangerously hotter. Finally, helmets mostly protected the skull but not the face, except in some cases for a nosepiece or perhaps an extended brim over the brows, because greater protection came at the high cost of limited visibility – both seeing and being seen. It is easy to imagine the hell of trying to fight with one's only view of the world coming through the holes and slits of a full faceplate. But recognition of friends and foes in battle, especially recognition of leaders, could depend on exposure. At Hastings in 1066, William the Conqueror, attempting to rally his Normans from an early panic, rode along his lines with his helmet lifted away from his face so he could be recognized – and this was a simple Norman conical helm with no more than a noseguard extending over his features.

The Intersection of Technology and Battle

Given weapons and armor with the characteristics we have just outlined, what were the consequences for how battles were fought? Understanding this intersection is in fact vital to understanding the dynamics of medieval combat (dynamics that are shared with much ancient and post-medieval combat before the vast technological changes of the nineteenth century – that is, across the agrarian era of world history).

First, combat happened in close contact with the enemy: face-to-face in melee combat, and even with missiles with the enemy no more than a couple of hundred yards away and usually much closer. Psychologically, this meant that fighting men confronted their foes personally, and especially in hand-to-hand combat killed them as individuals. This probably accounts, in large part, for the emphasis among medieval warriors, above all among elite warriors for whom armed conflict was a lifestyle more than a job, on honor: killing other men whom one confronted so personally probably had to be constructed as honorable so that it wasn't unbearable. But this emphasis on honor had serious limits, tending to operate most strongly between members who shared a military culture. This meant that opponents who faced each other across cultural divides were more likely to avoid the moral weight of combat by dehumanizing or even demonizing their foes. The most significant of such divides in the medieval world was that between sedentary and nomadic worlds, as illustrated by the Armenian Grigor of Akanc, who described the Mongols as "terrible to look at and indescribable, with large heads like a buffalo's, narrow eyes like a fledgling's, a snub nose like a cat's, projecting snouts like a dog's, narrow loins like an ant's, short legs like a hog's, and by nature with no beards at all."[11] But it is important to recognize that notions of warrior honor could cross apparent divides, as illustrated by the Christian construction of Saladin as a chivalrous opponent during the Crusades, demonstrating that the conditions of combat were intense enough to unite as well as divide combatants.

Those conditions, beyond the personal emotional intensity of close-quarters fighting, included that the battlefield was a place of potentially overwhelming sensory input. Battles for those in them were terrifyingly loud with the clashing of arms and armor and the shouts and cries of participants (including animals), the air often choked with dust and the smells of sweat, blood, and excrement, and experienced through a tunnel of vision focused on the foe just in front of you and confined by the press of humanity all around. Even commanders on horseback in the midst of masses of men on foot could experience little beyond their immediate reach; if entire units were mounted, no one had a superior view. The confusion of battle accounts both for the unreliability even of eyewitness accounts, which might convey only a limited portion of a large conflict, and the importance of the common techniques of command, designed to be visible or audible above the fray: commanders on horseback (limited as they might be), banners, drums and trumpets. Battlefield chaos and the concealing effects of armor noted above account for the common use of various symbols of identification, especially among commanders; the developed systems of European heraldry were exceptional only in their detailed rules and conventions (some of which, ironically, probably acted to reduce the instant identifiability of the warriors bearing them). And certainly not least, medieval battlefields must have been, at times, incredibly bloody affairs, with literal gallons of blood spilled.

---

[11] Grigor of Akanc in Rossabi, *Mongols and Global History*, p. 25. For a more detailed explanation of the impact of cultural divisions on warfare, see ch. 6 below, where I outline distinctions between *intracultural* warfare, or war within a culture, and *intercultural* and *subcultural* conflicts, or war that crossed different types of cultural divides.

Relatively recent battlefield archaeology has reinforced the grue-some picture of what medieval combat must have been like at "the face of battle." The record of fatal wounds inflicted at the Battle of Visby, in Gotland, in 1361, which produced a mass grave that has been excavated, shows the massive damage that polearms and other such weapons could cause to heads, limbs, or any part of a human body. Even the anticipation of being hit could be damaging: the teeth of some bodies excavated from the Battle of Bosworth Field, where Richard III lost his throne (and the back third of his head to a halberd blow) in 1485, had been flaked and chipped from being clenched so hard in combat.[12]

But standing in apparent contradiction to the previous paragraph about terror, death, and blood, close-range weapons and fairly effective armor made actually killing an opponent who was actively defending himself surprisingly difficult. Most of the killing in medi-eval battles, as had been the case in classical times, occurred in the pursuit stage when one side broke and ran: it is far easier to kill an enemy from behind when he's not trying to defend himself than when attacking him directly.

The difficulty of killing an armored opponent in a head-on attack accounts for the central importance in medieval battles of formation cohesion. A solid front of armed men supporting each other was hard to break, so keeping that front unbroken was vital, whether in defense against attacks or (what was far harder, at least for infantry) moving to the attack. The importance of maintaining formation and the strength of a united front also accounts for the key role attacks on the flanks and rear of a formation could be to breaking a strongly held position. The Mongol ability to coordinate the arrival of several units at a battlefield from multiple directions leveraged the vulnerability of an army's flanks and rear and probably accounts for the exaggerated impression of their numbers ("hordes") their victims had. Holding an army together in the face of non-frontal attacks that could turn an army into a panicked mob required resolute leadership and good overall morale on the part of the defenders.

Combining the effects of the battlefield environment with the importance of cohesion explains why more experienced troops, or at least troops with more training and discipline, almost always had a significant advantage in combat. The mass casualties at Visby, for example, were inflicted by the king of Denmark's professional soldiers

---

[12] An excellent catalog of excavated medieval war victims is Woosnam-Savage and DeVries, "Battle Trauma in Medieval Warfare," pp. 27–56.

on a much less experienced (and less well armored) group of peasants and freemen, a third of whom, the remains in the grave suggest,
were either old (which in medieval terms could mean over forty) or
under sixteen,[13] though this age range of victims was unusual. (The
excavated victims from the English Battle of Towton in 1461 were
all between about eighteen and thirty, for example.) But even in
hard-fought battles between relatively well-matched foes, experience
told, as it was not by inflicting mass casualties but by convincing the
enemy to give up and run that most medieval battles were won, again
often by managing to come at a formation from its flanks and rear:
the mere *threat* of such an attack could win the day. Two examples
illustrate both these points. The importance of flanks: in 1106, Henry
I of England won the Battle of Tinchebrai against his brother Robert.
It was a fight largely between two blocks of infantry, many of them
knights who had dismounted on both sides. But Henry hid a unit of
cavalry behind a nearby hill, and their surprise attack on the rear of
Robert's army decided what had been until that point an even fight.
That killing did not always decide a battle: at Brémule in 1119, noted
above, Henry's foot soldiers, again consisting of dismounted knights
deployed in several lines, first resisted the disordered charge of Louis
VI of France's cavalry, then managed to trap some of the French
cavalry between their lines, breaking their resistance. The number
of deaths in this battle between a total of about 900 knights on both
sides was three.[14]

    In what might seem like another paradox, in confused, sensory-
packed battles in which experience and morale played important
roles, individual leadership was central to the way armies functioned
in combat. This was true in a number of ways that had little to do
with what is often called "generalship," that is, with the "chess-
match" sequence of moves and countermoves each side made as
the battle progressed, a topic to which we will return in a moment.
Instead, leadership was largely a matter of the leader (king, general,
etc.) acting as the visible heart of the army, its center of morale and
emotion (to assign this heart its Aristotelian functions!). Leaders had
to be visible to play this role, marked out not just by position and
height (mostly on horseback) but usually by attire and above all by a
pennant, flag, or other dominant marker that could serve as a rally-
ing point. It was more important for a leader to be visible to his own

---

[13] Ohlén et al., *Från fars och farfars tid*, p. 402.
[14] On Tinchebrai, see Morillo, *Warfare under the Anglo-Norman King*, pp. 169–70.
On Brémule, see Morillo, "Kings and Fortuna," pp. 99–116.

side than to have an overview of the battle as a whole. Leading from the front, whether in attack or defense, was the most immediately visible but also (obviously) riskiest position for a leader to assume, and the one where the leader was likely to have the most restricted overview of the battle as a whole. There was in fact a permanent tension in combat using face-to-face technology between the "lead from the front" model of inspirational leadership and the "lead from the rear, control the chessboard" model of leadership – the leader as the brains, rather than the heart, of the army (though the heart and brain almost always coexisted in one leader).

John Keegan identified this tension and discussed it in terms of two western models of classical generalship: Alexander the Great (the quintessential leader from the front) and Julius Caesar, who consciously presented his role, in his histories of his own wars, as the brains directing the chessmen,[15] which established in European military historiography an emphasis on inspired genius as the height of generalship. But an even clearer tradition of the general as the brains of the army, with brains attainable not by innate genius but through education, can be seen in the Chinese tradition of military historiography stemming from Sunzi, where the ultimate brain behind the army was the written guidelines Sunzi (and others in the tradition) provided. There were military advantages to be gained by either mode of leadership: it is interesting that Mongol leaders, at the heart of battles that could be very fluid, given the cavalry armies involved, mostly chose the "lead from the rear" mode, for example. But the political ramifications of these styles should not be underplayed. Implicit in the Alexandrian model is the expectation that the mass of soldiers are themselves individuals who can be inspired to follow, voluntarily and enthusiastically, a leader who shares the risks and emotions of combat with his men. Caesar (whose histories were effectively campaign literature) and even more the Chinese tradition (which arose in the context of increasing autocracy among the competitive Warring States of that era) presented soldiers more as automata obedient to the will of the brainy leader (though Roman automata retained more individual thirst for glory and thus initiative than the Chinese tradition encouraged).

Medieval commanders worldwide found themselves having to balance the risks and rewards of these poles of leadership in ways that were shaped by both military advantage and political culture,

---

[15] Keegan, *Mask of Command*.

and usually exercised command in terms of both models at different times. The "brain" function of leadership usually took precedence before a battle, being exercised via prebattle dispositions of units and perhaps prearranged maneuvers such as Henry I's flanking cavalry attack at Tinchebrai, while the "heart" function took over once battle was joined. This reflected, again, the confused, sensory-overload nature of combat using medieval technology: even if most medieval battles were small enough that the entire field might, theoretically, be open to the general's view, the leisure to survey and assess would have been rare, and a leader's ability to influence the action was extremely circumscribed in any case, as we will explore in a moment, likely being most effectively exercised by a focused moment of inspiring heart-based leadership at a place and moment of crisis. In either model, however, the leader was the vital center of the army, so that killing the enemy leader was one of the surest paths to victory in combat, constituting (metaphorically) either a head shot or a stab to the heart.[16] The universality of the central role of leadership in these terms is illustrated by the Battle of Takkolam in 949, between a Chola (south Indian) army and the army of the Rashtrakuta king Krishna III: the Chola leader, the crown prince Rajaditya, was slain on top of his war elephant by one of Krishna's subordinates and the Chola army retreated as a result. Another Chola army lost its leader and king Rajadhiraja, also on his elephant, at the Battle of Koppam in 1054, but the king's brother Rajendradeva took command, rallied the army to victory, and ultimately succeeded his brother as king.[17]

The chaotic conditions of battle explain why "generalship" is an overrated concept in analyzing medieval combat: once a battle started, as we have noted, it was hard for a leader to maintain an overview of the board. But even if he did, conveying commands and exercising control (moving his pieces on the board) were also technologically constrained. In the din of battle, a leader's voice could only reach a tiny part of an army. Visible commands (using pennants or flags) and "amplified" sound-based commands (using drums, trumpets, and so forth) could only convey the most basic,

---

[16] William the Conqueror's bare-headed ride along his panicking lines at Hastings, in this metaphorical view, was an act of emergency CPR for his army: the heart had to be shown to be still beating. "Brain death," as it was more likely to occur away from the front lines, could be, at times, temporarily concealed if coherent orders kept flowing to the body; such "zombie armies" could even, though rarely, win the ongoing battle.

[17] Wagoner, "India," p. 481.

often binary instructions ("advance" or "retreat," "hold in place" being the assumed default). The larger the armies involved, the more difficult the problem. Orders could be conveyed to more distant units via riders, who obviously faced risks along the way, and the orders had to be conveyed via what was, in many medieval armies, a person-alized and ad hoc chain of command that might be broken as much by linguistic barriers (one of the problems Charles the Bold's com-posite mercenary armies faced) and personal jealousies or political maneuvering (which is what broke the Byzantine army at Manzikert in 1071) as by enemy action.

In short, medieval battlefield generalship involved the daunting task of controlling the uncontrollable while providing moral inspira-tion without getting killed. Put this way, the challenges of leading a medieval army are clear, and show criticisms of medieval tacti-cal generalship as based in the unrealistic expectations of different technological and social ages. (Though generalship as an analogy to chess is fundamentally flawed even beyond the Middle Ages.) We will return to generalship at the operational and strategic levels later in this chapter.

The Technology of Siege Warfare

Warfare on land consisted of campaigns, battles, and sieges. Campaigns – where the operational and strategic levels of warfare happened – were subject to technological limitations; we shall turn to those later. In terms of the arms and armor individuals could use, battles and sieges shared the technological environment outlined in the previous section. But siege warfare introduced technological considerations and techniques that were both more collective and longer-term than showed up in battle. It is to this technological envi-ronment that we now turn.

The fundamental fact to note is that the basic limitations of medi-eval technology in terms of energy sources for getting work done (wind, water, and muscle) gave the defense in siege warfare an advan-tage. This is because the process of building fortifications involved the builders being able to store up work-energy slowly over time, using basic work-multiplying technologies such as ramps, levers, and pulleys, in the defensive structures themselves. A fort, in other words, represents a significant accumulation of labor energy. Even the sim-plest forts, such as the motte-and-bailey castles of eleventh-century Europe, which consisted of a wooden palisade and tower erected on top of an artificially piled-up hill of dirt, took a week or more of conscripted labor to construct: after landing near Hastings in 1066, William of Normandy had a motte-and-bailey castle created in a week as a base of operations, using locally coerced workmen. Even simpler defensive positions could substitute the geological work of nature for labor energy, as when simple enclosures were placed on top of natural hills or, even more extremely, when stone fortifications rose from "naturally fortified" rock outcroppings that ensured the safety of the walls' foundations. Still, the essential principle was that fortifying a position meant the extended expenditure of energy to create structure.

On the attacking side, time was not the (nearly unlimited) resource that it had been for the defenders in the building stage. Thus, to match or top the energy accumulated by the defenders in their fort with energy expended for destructive purposes, the attackers had to expend that much energy in a much shorter time – something that the limits of medieval technology made very difficult – or find a way to avoid the accumulated work of the defensive position. It was this fundamental equation that shaped the patterns of siege warfare before, during, and after the Middle Ages. And it is this equation even more than problems of controllability, mobility, or rate of fire that explains why fire and gunpowder weapons were first and foremost deployed in siege warfare and in naval combat: only fire and chemical-combustion explosions could, in a usefully short time, concentrate an amount of energy adequate for destructive purposes against the accumulated energy stored in defensive structures, whether buildings or ships. We shall return to ships in the next section; here, we analyze the technology of building and besieging fortifications.

The first choice those constructing a defensive position faced was where to build. Such choices were shaped in large part by the sorts of geographic considerations explored in the previous chapter: fortifications were placed to control significant arteries of communication and protect vital locations, above all cities, which tended to arise at "natural" geographic foci preceding conscious military design. "Control" is the operative word, because fortifications always operated in two directions at once. First, to protect and defend what was inside the fort: this usually included both soldiers guarding the fort itself, and at different times civilian populations and the accumulated structures (including administrative "structures" like the bureaucracies and written records) often found in cities. In short, especially in grain states, forts protected the populations and the buildings people needed to survive and continue to generate wealth for their

Figure 11   The Theodosian Walls of Constantinople. The many miles of walls and towers that surrounded Constantinople represented a vast accumulation of labor power that made the city impregnable for centuries.
Source: Laima Gūtmane, via Wikimedia Commons.

rulers. Second, forts projected force beyond the fortification. This included the forts' armed forces going out to police the surrounding (friendly, civilian) countryside; interdicting enemy movements of troops and supplies; and symbolically projecting an image of the force and authority contained within the fort.

Thus, forts had to act as a safe base of operations, with an inherent tension existing between "safe" and "operations." This showed up in two ways. First, every wall had to have a gate, usually several, and gates were automatically the most vulnerable part of the wall. Second, in terms of terrain, a more remote, difficult-to-access location (such as a high rocky outcropping) would be safer from attack but less useful for projecting power outwards. More accessible sites could project power more readily but were correspondingly more vulnerable. Usually, the greatest, most imposing fortifications arose from attempts to make an accessible site highly defensible; probably the most successful instantiation of this sort of effort was the Theodosian Walls that protected Constantinople from the landward side (figure 11). These massive walls of accumulated labor, placed across a fairly narrow neck of land to protect a city guarded on all other sides by open water (and the walls continued along the water-front) and containing nine gates guarded by powerful towers, stood unbreached for over a thousand years, essentially throughout the medieval era. From 447, when Theodosius completed the expansion and repair of the original walls built by Constantine in the 330s, until Mehmet the Conqueror, the Ottoman sultan in 1453, who brought the world's biggest concentration of destructive energy, his massive artillery train of massive cannons backed by a massive army, to bear on the walls for weeks against a hopelessly inadequate supply of defensive labor (for defense, repair and rebuilding), the walls made the city impregnable.

Walls could be built from a variety of materials. Earthworks were simplest (the motte of a motte-and-bailey castle being essentially a small piece of earthen wall); often, the earth was excavated from what became a ditch in front of the piled-up wall, adding to its effective height. But the earth could also be "rammed": forcibly tamped down into containing forms to create a denser, more durable structure. Rammed earth walls were common around Chinese cities. Some were forty to fifty meters across at their base, narrowing thirty meters above to a top still wide enough to form a communications boulevard around the city. Earthen walls were highly resistant to deconstructive artillery bombardment, both from their thickness and as they could simply absorb bombardment without losing structural integrity, but were labor intensive and required constant upkeep especially against water damage. They could be faced in brick or stone to reduce such maintenance. Giant, brick- or stone-faced rammed earthen walls were the gold standard of medieval fortification (so much accumulated labor!): the walls of Constantinople were at heart of this type, though with extra brick and stone work added. But assembling that much labor was mostly unaffordable outside the imperial Chinese state and the capital of the Eastern Roman Empire.

At the cheap end were unrammed earthworks and wooden walls, the combination that went into motte-and-bailey castles (which were, furthermore, tiny, as their wooden palisades did not surround more than their own bailey, a small open area at the base of the motte, and the motte itself). But they were quick to build and surprisingly effective for the limited amount of accumulated labor they represented, which was still more than a small mobile force could bring to bear in many cases, unless they could set fire to the wooden walls, a tactic illustrated in the Bayeux Tapestry.

In the middle were walls of rammed earth, and brick or stone constructions (with all three sometimes combined in various ways).

Such materials were fire resistant, unlike wood, and more weather-resistant than earth, and interposed a small-weapons-proof barrier between attackers and defenders. It was easier to build stone walls up to a scaling-resistant height than it was earthworks, though high, thin walls were vulnerable to instability. It was this that made many medieval European walls such easy targets for early cannon, as the direct bludgeoning cannon could deliver to the base of a wall could topple it far more efficiently than the parabolic fire of trebuchets. Some stone construction mimicked the design of faced earthen walls: outer faces of worked masonry filled with dirt and stone rubble was a cheaper way to build depth into a wall. But cannon fire that damaged the retaining face exposed the wall to the destructive internal pressure of the contained rubble. Still, stone construction marked a significant improvement over wood and even rammed earth. The wooden parts of early motte-and-bailey castles were sometimes converted to stone, the outer bailey wall first, the tower on the motte later, as the earthen mound, unrammed, had to settle for decades before it was stable enough to bear a stone structure.

Note that, in the choice of fortification materials, no medieval society could afford metal (iron would have been the only possibility in terms of strength) even as a reinforcing material. The only other material available was water, as a moat could be added at the base of the walls to block various methods of approach.

With a fortification, from minuscule private castle to vast urban wall system, in place, it was the turn of the attacker to try to take or destroy it with the limited technologies available. There were, essentially, only a very limited number of ways to accomplish this: going over, under, or through the walls, or somehow getting the defenders out of still-intact walls.

Going over the walls was the simplest, when it was possible. All it took technologically was scaling ladders. Achieving surprise was undoubtedly the most important factor in most successful stormings of fortifications. Going through the walls could, in fact, be even easier, if the attackers managed, again through surprise, to rush through an open and unguarded gate. But most "normal" methods of taking fortifications involved far more hard work.

Going under the walls meant tunneling in, an option only if the fortification's foundations were not rock. As the tunnels would be dug from far enough away to be out of the defenders' sight, detecting tunnelling attempts sometimes called forth sophisticated technology. At the siege of Yu-pi in northern China in 546, the defenders may have detected approaching tunnels using an attested Chinese device, the geophone: a large ceramic pot with a thin hide stretched over the opening. Placed in a deep hole, the device amplified vibrations in the ground; a set of them could locate approaching underground activity with some accuracy.[18] The defenders could then dig counter-tunnels, potentially leading to underground combat, or try to smoke the attackers out.

Tunneling became mining, which was really a way to get through walls, when the tunnel was dug not into the interior of the fort but until it was under the walls and then parallel with them. The mine would be supported with timbers to bear the weight of the walls, but then filled with flammables and set ablaze. When the timbers burnt, the wall would, if the mining worked, collapse into its under-mined foundations. Walls could also be attacked directly and manu-ally with picks, or the application of individual muscle energy over time that was the exact inverse of the construction-accumulation process. Workers at the base of a wall were, however, wildly open to countermeasures as simple as defenders dropping heavy objects (or hot liquids) on them.

Getting through the walls, however, was most often attempted using siege artillery. Before gunpowder, the means of tossing large projectiles, almost always of stone, at the walls of a fortification dem-onstrate the limits of preindustrial power supplies excellently. The means of propulsion were limited in number and power. Tension, or the "giant crossbow" approach, rarely generated enough force to do damage to strong walls. Torsion, or the power stored in twisted strands (like rubber-band-powered airplane models), could power catapults that were more powerful, but were hard to construct and still of limited motive force. The levered-sling design of trebuchets, both traction (with the force applied by a set of men pulling down on the lever arm) and counterweight (the most effective of pre-gun-powder artillery, as it allowed greater energy to be accumulated and stored through loading a larger and larger container and cranking it slowly into position, and then to be released all at once) (figure 12), could throw significantly large objects a surprising distance, as anyone who has watched YouTube videos of pianos being hurled through the air knows (though piano-throwing trebuchets have significant iron construction; medieval trebuchets could not have thrown any-thing as heavy as a piano). A large number of such engines, set to work over a sufficient period of time, could ultimately apply enough

[18] Wallacker, "Siege of Yu-pi," p. 797.

Figure 12   Trebuchet. Counterweight trebuchets like this one were the most powerful siege engines before the invention of gunpowder cannon.
Source: Wikimedia Commons.

deconstructive energy to the stored construction-energy of a fortification to do serious damage.

But all the pre-gunpowder artillery, except for the tension-driven super-crossbows (which as noted were not terribly powerful), had a serious limitation: they lobbed their projectiles along a high-arc parabolic trajectory to achieve any kind of reasonable range (necessary in part to keep the artillerists out of range of small-arms missile fire from the defenders, and in part because of the mechanics of the engine itself). A lobbed projectile came down to hit a vertical target like a wall at an oblique angle, reducing the force of its impact. Even more than the application of a new, chemical-combustive form of energy to destructive purposes, it was the ability of cannon to send a projectile on an almost horizontal path (technically a much flatter parabolic path) directly into its target, converting far more of its motive force into destructive impact, that made guns such an improvement for siege work that they stimulated (in the post–1500 world especially) new designs for fortifications, and made inaccessible locations for forts more attractive.

The high-arcing fire of pre-gunpowder artillery was not useless, however, even if the walls of a fort were resistant, for it could play a role in the final method for taking a fortification, convincing the defenders, either physically or psychologically, that their continued presence inside the fort was untenable. Lobbing artillery shots over the walls and into the inhabited portions of a fort, whether that was the small area of a castle or the large, densely populated districts of a fortified city, could cause significant damage and misery (especially if what was lobbed in, as by the Mongols at Caffa in 1347, was plague-ridden corpses, creating a misery-spreading form of biological warfare). This remained true even when gunpowder dominated siege weaponry, as the continued use of mortars (high-angled cannon) demonstrates clearly.

Missile fire, as from bows, crossbows, and the like, could make manning the defensive walls dangerous. But the most direct and destructive technique along these lines was lobbing incendiaries into the fortified interior to set buildings, supplies, and men on fire. The effectiveness of this approach varied, of course, with the combustibility of the target, the design of the interior (open spaces reduced the danger of fire spreading), and weather and climate: a good rainstorm could literally dampen the impact of an incendiary attack. The other problem with using fire was that it could destroy much of the value of the target before the attacker could assume control of it.[19]

Beyond direct inflicting of damage, the most frequent techniques employed in medieval siege warfare all fit into the "convince the defenders to give up" category. The initial stages of an attempt to take a key fortified position could include isolating it from fresh supplies and from relief armies that might lift a siege. The Mongol campaign against Xiangyang and Fanchen began in exactly this way, with the construction of a set of counter-fortifications designed to cut off access to the cities. This sort of blockade had the advantage, furthermore, of not exposing the attackers to the hazards of close investment for a long period of time. The failure of the Song efforts to break up or disrupt this ongoing blockade – the "battle" portion of the Xiangyang campaign – not only maintained the blockade but advertised to the defenders that relief wasn't going to happen, which was usually a major inducement to surrender.

A blockade, carried more and more tightly against the target, became a close investment. At either distance, the main purpose was

---

[19] The same, of course, could be said of massacring the inhabitants of a besieged city after capture. Even if one accepts that there was a psychological benefit to be gained– "if you resist, you will suffer annihilation" – the frequency with which massacres happened compared to the utter destruction of the physical infrastructure of a city speaks to the value of the human labor force compared to the accumulated labor energy of built structures. It was easier to repopulate a city than to rebuild it, especially if slaves were one of the things to be gained from warfare.

to deprive the defenders of food and, if possible, water until stored supplies ran out and the defenders gave up. This usually became a logistical contest pitting stored supplies against the attacker's ability to keep the besiegers supplied in the field. Here, the defender's advantage of being able to store up labor energy over time was less decisive against the attacker's need to expend energy on the spot, because stored supplies were constantly consumed. Much depended, in specific cases, on the systems of transport a besieger could call on. If either side had recourse to water-borne transport, that constituted a huge advantage. Sometimes, as at the siege of Antioch in 1098, both sides effectively starved.

With both sides sitting in fixed positions and often running low on supplies of fresh food and water, the constant concomitant of siege warfare was the outbreak of diseases among both besieged and besiegers (note that the plague-infested corpses the Mongols lobbed into Caffa were *their own* plague victims). Diseases of poor sanitation, especially dysentery, were the most common, and contributed to the fact that disease caused far more deaths than combat in wars throughout the Middle Ages – and indeed until the Russo-Japanese war of 1905 in world history terms.

The difficulty and expense of breaking into a fortification or even of convincing defenders to give up account for the frequency with which sieges ended in negotiated settlements that had the added benefit of maintaining the usefulness of the accumulated labor that constituted the fortified site. Negotiations happened even across cultural divides that, in battle, might promote more ruthless slaughter. Garrisons or urban inhabitants would be offered terms that speak to the besieger's inherent difficulties: freedom to march out safely, even including doing so with their arms retained. If they will only *stop resisting, please.* The tendency for sieges prosecuted to the bitter end and ending with the besiegers getting into the fortification to result in wholesale massacres of the defenders *and* all the inhabitants of the site speaks not just to psychological policy – the setting of an example to encourage future surrenders on terms – but to the pent-up frustration of attackers forced to endure the dangers and hardships of a siege: massacres were revenge against those who dared to play the favored (defensive) side of positional warfare to the final turn.

The Technology of Naval Warfare

Geography

Naval warfare was the realm where technology made the biggest difference, or played the most determinative role in shaping conflict.[20] In large part this was inevitable: oceans, seas, and even large lakes and rivers were not open to armed conflict unless certain basic technological requirements (ships) were in place. Ships, in turn, as relatively large, expensive, and sophisticated technologies, were subject to differentiation by investment of capital and labor, which favored (though not exclusively, as we will see) states with access to both resources, including population, and capital in the prosecution of naval warfare, certainly more than in land warfare.

The technological limitations on naval warfare are most evident in the restricted realms open to it in the medieval world. The scope even of general maritime activity remained restricted for a long period even after the rise of hierarchical states and land-based warfare. Places that combined relatively calm, enclosed seas, friendly coasts (shoal-free and with suitable natural harbors or beaches), favorable wind patterns, and access to land areas with substantial populations and economic activity were not that common. Maritime trade and exploration spread only gradually in the wake of slow technological developments and the gradual accumulation of navigational and geographic knowledge. The gradual expansion of maritime and, to a lesser extent, naval activity was, it can be noted, a theme across the Middle Ages.

Naval warfare as distinct from maritime trade or troop transport arose even more slowly, because creating ships capable of acting as weapons or even weapons platforms required yet more specialized technology (and usually more manpower) than merchant marines did. Naval warfare required, furthermore, not just concentrations of people and economic activity near shores, concentrations that generated the sailing traditions and infrastructures of maritime activity upon which navies had to be built; it also required states capable of organizing military force, states for which sea lanes linked (but not too distantly) strategically important and contested locations. The medieval world inherited the Mediterranean as the premier arena

[20] A thorough survey of naval warfare from ancient times through the Middle Ages can be found in Morillo et al., *War in World History*, chs. 5, 10, and 15; chs. 20 and 25 take the story of naval warfare into the twentieth century.

of maritime warfare, facilitated by relatively calm sailing seasons, minimal tides, plentiful natural beaches and harbors, and a surrounding world of urban centers created in part by maritime connections.

Beyond the Mediterranean, the semi-enclosed but still stormy North and Baltic Seas, including the restricted waters of the English Channel, saw maritime and naval activity rise across the period with the increasing population and organization of the surrounding terrestrial realms. The same was true, to a lesser extent, in the South China Sea and the Straits of Malacca. The telling example of the limits on naval warfare is the oceanic region with the heaviest maritime usage outside the Mediterranean: the Indian Ocean. Transoceanic trade routes here developed early and were in heavy use throughout the medieval period, based on the predictable monsoon weather pattern that made round-trip circuits possible and obvious. But naval competition never arose on top of the Indian Ocean maritime world (at least until the Portuguese intruded from 1498). The open-sea nature of the routes, the decentralized, network-based nature of many of the polities around the ocean, and the sometimes shifting and diffuse nature of the main harbors combined to keep this maritime world trade-based, cooperative, and non-militarized. The key was that calm, enclosed waters where specialized warships could confront each other were rare, which brings us to the essential components of medieval naval technology.

Technology

Ships were, of course, the central technology for naval warfare, assuming the dual role of weapons platform, or the vehicle for carrying weapons, and weapon, especially in the Mediterranean where ramming other ships was an important mode of ship killing. It was, in fact, the multiple and often contradictory tasks that were required of ships as military technology that kept their effectiveness limited.

Ships had to act first as the "ground" for combat, keeping men, weapons, and supplies out of the sea. Seaworthiness tended to favor larger, rounder, and deeper hull shapes, with relatively high freeboard (height of the hull over the waterline), that could survive rougher seas. Such a shape was most efficiently driven by sail power, and was an economical means of transporting goods if its crew size was kept small (good merchant ships, in other words, were labor-saving devices). On the other hand, ships designed for naval combat favored longer, narrower hulls, for speed in either chasing down or ramming an opposing ship; power-on-command favored driving such hulls with oars, which meant lower freeboard, though if combat came to ship-against-ship missile fire or boarding, the advantage of height led to taller hulls or, in some cases, built-up areas (especially at the bow or stern) as firing platforms. Oared ships also had to carry large crews, while longer, narrower hulls provided little storage space: most would be taken up by water and food for the rowers in amounts that could last a day or two at most; oared ships could act as cargo vessels only for very high-value, low-bulk luxury goods.

The restricted range of medieval ships based on how much food and water they could carry for a crew were compounded by navigation technology that developed very gradually. Magnetic compasses, a Chinese invention, spread slowly in the latter part of the era; astrolabes, an Arab invention used to determine latitude, came only a bit earlier; and measuring longitude remained impossible until the late eighteenth century. Thus, most navigation consisted of "point-to-point" routes established over time, and laid out in charts, maps, and itineraries that gradually produced network-based knowledge about the main trade routes and how they linked up. Such knowledge was not, in most cases, militarily applicable.

Finally, in the same way that built-up, long-term investment in fortifications gave the defense an advantage over the limited forces of instant destruction available to attackers in land-based siege warfare, ships as built technologies had an advantage over the weapons that could be deployed to destroy them. Basically, only two methods were reliable for fatally damaging a well-built ship. First, breaking it using the force of another ship (ramming, which required skilled crews, specially fitted prows, and difficult tactics). Second, fire. Since ships were built of wood and outfitted with gear that was often coated in tar for weatherproofing, fire was more dangerous for ships than for fortifications, but was correspondingly unsafe to carry and difficult to project. Flaming arrows could not deliver enough fire, most of the time, to guarantee destruction, while siege engines capable of throwing larger amounts of burning material were generally too large and heavy for use aboard ships. Instead, ships were vulnerable to being burned in port, sometimes from land-based projectiles. But two medieval methods for lighting fleets ablaze stand out. First, a fleet in port or confined waters could, if the wind were right, be attacked with fireships – hulks filled with incendiary material, set ablaze, and set adrift into the closely anchored target.

Second, there was Greek fire, a combustible substance (or variety of substances – the composition of Greek fire is a matter of much historical dispute) made from some combination of petroleum,

Figure 13   Byzantine dromon (oared galley with two banks of oars) using Greek fire. Greek fire brought the destructive power of fire to bear in a focused way on the accumulated constructive labor of ships.

Source: Wikimedia Commons.

naphtha, and other ingredients that at the least could not be put out with water and perhaps was either spread or even ignited by contact with water. The substance itself, either pumped at high pressure out of bronze siphons mounted on the bows of galleys or lobbed, from on-board catapults, in earthenware pots that would shatter on impact, constituted a deadly weapon against wooden ships, and is often presented as the "secret weapon" that allowed Byzantine naval forces to destroy their foes repeatedly (figure 13). But in fact, Greek fire was a standard part of the weaponry of all eastern Mediterranean fleets in the period 700–1100.

It was, to be sure, an important and useful weapon, especially against more lightly built ships and against enemies trapped in confined waters or unprepared for its use, such as a Viking–Rus fleet destroyed on the Black Sea by the Byzantines in 941. But it was by no means surefire, so to speak, as the siphons had limited range and catapulted pots had limited accuracy. This, as much as effective Turkish countermeasures (vinegar was found to douse its flames) and the Turkish conquest of Byzantium, accounts for the disappearance of Greek fire from Mediterranean naval arsenals. Greek fire is thus an example of flashy but overrated technology that obscures the underlying bases of success in medieval warfare.

Finally, not only was ship killing difficult, but ships were valuable, and attackers therefore often wanted to capture rather than sink

Figure 14   Medieval cog. Cogs like this one, a fifteenth-century
sailing ship of Richard III of England, were essentially trading vessels
that could be fitted with "castles" fore and aft, loaded with archers and
men-at-arms, and so converted into warships.
Source: Ivan Vdovin / Alamy Stock Photo.

enemy vessels. Killing the enemy crew and soldiers was thus the more
direct and usual goal.

These various limitations produced several basic results for naval
warfare. First, throughout the medieval period naval warfare was not
fundamentally a separate sphere of military action, but a transport-
based adjunct to land warfare that in limited ways might become
"amphibious." Ships carried troops who for the most part would
fight on land after sailing, or attempted to prevent such transport,
as the Song navy patrolling the river at Xiangyang did. Or if there
was combat on water, ship to ship, it resembled land combat though
with a far greater emphasis on missile weapons. At the Battle of Sluys
in 1341, where an English fleet led by King Edward III defeated a
French fleet (with many Italian ships), the effectiveness of English
longbowmen played a large part in the outcome. In such board-
and-melee battles, troops on larger (especially taller) ships had the
advantage (figure 14). And in such battles, problems of ship-to-
ship communication that dominated later sailing-ship battles were

considerably reduced: a fleet might not maneuver much at all, and attempted to maintain a very close, mutually supporting formation. Sometimes, friendly ships were even chained together to provide coherence and a more stable fighting platform.

Maritime Strategies

The technologies of naval warfare (and maritime activity more generally) and the tactical patterns they generated affected strategic options as well. Fundamentally, three patterns of naval activity are visible in the medieval period: navies of imperial defense; predatory sea peoples; and a hybrid "proto-capitalist" model.

Navies of imperial defense were the technological pinnacles of medieval naval warfare, deploying the best, most expensive and innovative ships they could in defense of sea lanes and ports vital to their state. The Byzantine navy was one example of this model, deploying dromons, oared galleys with two banks of oars, armed with a ram, Greek fire, and marines capable of missile fire and hand-to-hand combat. The Arab fleets who constituted their main enemy were another variety of this model, though less vital to overall defense of the caliphate and used more often in offensive campaigns (which the Byzantine navy also undertook). The Song navy was the other example, patrolling not just the coasts of China but the major rivers, acting as we have seen as a vital part of the defense of the Southern Song against the Mongols. Song riverine ships included some human-powered paddle wheelers and ships mounted with catapults that threw gunpowder bombs. Tactically, imperial defense navies aimed at ship killing.

The other major model of naval activity was in many ways the opposite of navies of imperial defense: predatory sea peoples. These maritime raiders tended to be based in small independent social groups or emergent and decentralized states rather than being the product of centralized state policy; conducted offensively oriented raids against targets of opportunity; and were not technologically advanced, gaining their effectiveness from surprise and mobility at the operational level. Tactically, they aimed at capturing enemy ships (valuable in themselves and likely to be holding valuable cargo and people who could be sold as slaves). Examples include most famously the Vikings of northern Europe, Arab sea raiders after the breakup of the caliphate, the "thalassocracy" of Srivijaya (really a sort of piratical protection racket centered on the Straits of Malacca), about which little detail survives, and the Cholas of eleventh-century south

India, who raided around the Indian Ocean, including an attack that essentially destroyed Srivijaya. These groups were in some ways the maritime equivalent of the horse peoples of the steppes, and demonstrated (especially in the eyes of the navies of imperial defense) the close relationship or even equivalence between trading and raiding, between merchants and pirates.

Challenging this equivalence in some ways was the third model of naval activity, which arose with the emergence of independent Italian city-states in the eleventh century. Run by merchant oligarchies, cities such as Venice and Genoa developed navies as, in effect, an arm of their state-sponsored merchant marines. While in some ways simply a variation on the state-organized practice of armed violence in pursuit of political ends common to many medieval polities, the partnership between state and private merchant interests at the base of this model was unusual and pointed to future developments that bloomed after 1500.

Technology and War: Beyond Tactics

The technological world of medieval armed conflict that we have been exploring has had implications mostly at the tactical level of war: where metal met flesh, to put it most simply. But technology also shaped war at the operational and strategic levels, if less obviously and directly than in battle.

Communications Technology

The key technological realm to consider in these terms is communications technology. We have already seen some of the effects of how people could communicate at the tactical level: the need for visible leadership, the advantages of visibility in both directions that riding horses conveyed, and the organization of tactical units around standards, flags, and so forth speak to the fact that combat happened in a communications world of line-of-sight and audible communications. Banners and flags were more visible (and could convey information and orders in themselves) than individual commanders; drums and trumpets likewise could be heard from farther off (and so could convey information and orders) than a single human voice. Both audible and visual signals almost always depended on some prearranged set of meanings, which seriously limited their flexibility as command tools, as the world of sail-and-cannon warships would discover in following centuries, while the din and confusion of combat both necessitated and hindered such signaling.

Expanded to the level of campaigns – operations and strategic movements that might require coordinating widely dispersed forces – medieval communications technologies imposed even tighter limits on the militarily possible. Messages could be sent only by runners and riders, whose rate of travel barely exceeded that of the armed units they were trying to carry messages between, though an individual could move faster than a group, and the larger the group the slower it was. Faster means of sending messages, such as signal fires and beacons, were also severely limited. Probably the best-known version of this kind of system is the chain of fire beacons set up by the Kingdom of Gondor in Tolkien's Middle Earth, which Tolkien in fact based on Anglo-Saxon systems designed to warn of Viking raids. Such signals were, however, limited to a binary: either the orcs (or Vikings) were coming, or they weren't. These systems were of essentially no use in a mobile, fluid campaign.

Messages richer in information had to be delivered orally or in writing (writing itself being a communications technology not universally available across the medieval world, of course). Messengers and messages were then subject to interception, interdiction, or simple failure to arrive (often through the messenger getting lost). Even at short range, such as from one end of a battlefield to another, delivering such messages was difficult.

Thus, for a commander to coordinate the movements of widely separated units was usually an insuperable problem, which only got worse the larger the geographic scope of the campaign. The only armies to have succeeded at campaign-level coordination regularly, indeed with spectacular success, were the Mongols, those masters of rapid movement through vast spaces. That their entire lifestyle depended on making such coordinated movements seasonally undoubtedly enabled this ability to bring separate units – in effect corps-sized columns – together on an enemy position from several directions at once. It was, again, the heavily fortified riverine zone of defense in depth that the Southern Song created in the Yangtze valley that frustrated this *normal* mode of Mongol campaigning and led Kubilai Khan to instead launch a focused campaign on Xiangyang.

The Mongols made this kind of campaign work by using numerous fast messenger riders, but even more by, in effect, training their entire leadership corps and army in executing such movements. Large-scale animal hunts that slowly closed a huge circle around any prey in an area were the first training ground for this kind of coordinated maneuvering. When human enemies became the prey, the Mongols often added a psychological twist: they would leave an apparent gap in the great circle, encouraging the enemy forces to break and run for the escape route, which then turned into a deadly ambush of a panicked foe who had abandoned close order.

Clearly, Mongol-style mobile campaigns were beyond the capabilities of most medieval armies. In addition to messengers and training, the Mongol ability to execute such campaigns depended on two further factors. First, some prearranged set of targets and goals that the separate columns could aim for even without constant intercommunication. The single isolated cities of many of their foes provided exactly this kind of target (and again, the many urban centers of the Southern Song realm frustrated creating a clear focus). Second, their life of constant movement from pasture to pasture gave them a sense of the possibilities of movement across large distances that allowed reasonable calculations ahead of time of travel speeds and distances. Such knowledge could not be developed in the context of a sedentary society where operational movement was usually experienced in terms of "a day's ride." The dominance of this kind of calculation of movement is indicated by the "natural" placement of fortifications (especially semi-isolated castles in western Europe) at a distance of about twenty miles from each other – in other words, a day's ride, importantly from a known point to another known point. The steppes gave the Mongols (and indeed most horsed steppe armies) a different imaginative world of times, distances, and routes that often baffled their sedentary foes.

Mapping, Knowledge, and Formulating Strategy

Taking this conception up to the level of strategic planning alerts us to perhaps the most significant difference in the mental worlds of medieval commanders and those of us in our closely mapped, GPS-able modern globe. We are so used to thinking of geography (and thus strategy) in terms of accurate maps that it takes a leap of imagination to see the world as most medieval commanders must have: as a world consisting of a set of known connections, either of spatial itineraries ("how long do I have to go in which direction to get to Point A?" – think of constructing a national a map of a country from a set of step-by-step directions from one city to all important destinations) or, more importantly, in terms of resources (remember that armies could only march where they could find food to eat) and political allegiances that had to be constantly manipulated. Medieval strategists faced not a Risk board but a poker game that they had to play not just with the hands of military resources they were dealt, but with a limited pile of political chips that had to serve for any one hand and also through a whole night's betting. And the course of play in poker is subject to greater levels of chance than in Risk, though it's there in both.

As one example of medieval strategy in action, King John of England attempted to put a Risk-like strategy into effect against Philip Augustus of France in 1214. John put together a multiparty coalition that included the Holy Roman Emperor with the aim of launching coordinated attacks into Philip's realm from several directions at once, with the goal of regaining Normandy, lost ten years earlier, from the French king. The planned campaign still looks great when mapped out today: Philip facing concentric invasions from England, Germany, and English possessions in southern France. But making the pieces work together at the same time proved impossible, for both logistical and political reasons. Time and distance allowed Philip to play "interior lines of defense" against the multiple invasions, meaning that each hand of the game was played separately. When Philip won the decisive Battle of Bouvines at the climax of the campaign, he gathered the whole pot of chips, removing John permanently (as it turned out) from Normandy (as well as putting much of Aquitaine within his own grasp) and, crucially, cementing the prestige of the French monarchy for centuries afterwards.

This is not to say that medieval strategy did not exist, simply that it must be conceived of in different terms from the way that, say, the American Pacific campaign in World War II was planned and can be analyzed. The application of armed force and its associated tools and resources to achieving policy goals – the essential definition of strategy – was a constant across the medieval world, at levels from the relatively local to the imperial. But that application was not seen or planned as if on a Risk board: geography had a different meaning given the technologies of knowledge gathering and storage available in that world.

Similarly, Bouvines sat at the culmination of what might be called a Grand Strategy pursued for the previous century by the Capetian kings of France to reduce the position of their over-powerful vassals, the dukes of Normandy, who had also become, in 1066, kings of England. But can we speak of grand strategy in medieval warfare? Some historians have objected to seeing grand strategy in a world that had no conception of such a thing. Well, in fact, there was no medieval concept called "strategy," either. But just as military resources could be applied to political goals to produce strategy, if a succession (literally) of medieval political leaders pursued a consistent set of goals using their political, military, economic, and cultural resources over time, so it does no violence to the concept to see grand strategy in the medieval world. But in the context of medieval communications technologies, it didn't get planned or executed on a Risk board, but through a complex set of long-running poker games.[21]

Conclusions

Technology was a central factor in establishing the "Common Rules" of medieval warfare, not in a technological determinist way – technologies rarely produce unvarying outcomes in military history or any other aspect of human society – but by establishing constraints and limits within which medieval warriors had to operate. From weapons to communications technology, the tools people had to work with and the sources of energy they could draw on to power those tools provided a range of options that cultural choices and traditions worked with. The perspective of this chapter, as with the other chapters in this "Common Rules" part of this book, has been to focus on the underlying commonalities within which those choices were constrained, not on the vast variety of ways those choices were expressed. To sum up this part, medieval people inflicted violence on each other across the world using very similar tools, in a restricted range of places, and usually for a recognizable set of political reasons or within a limited set of political structures.

But not all medieval warfare was as alike as this initial set of chapters' essentially materialist perspective might suggest. In the second part of this book, we will explore the trajectory of medieval armed violence from a perspective that will focus not on political goals, or on grand strategy, strategy, operations, and tactics, but on reading wars for their role in the cultural construction of the medieval world by the participants in armed violence. What, in other words, did

---

[21] On grand strategy, see the debate about Edward Luttwak's influential *The Grand Strategy of the Roman Empire*, whose insights have been questioned primarily for being, in the terms set out here, too Risk-based, without recognizing the poker elements of the problem. For nuanced applications of Luttwak's concepts relevant to medieval and connected post-medieval worlds, see Hassig, *Aztec Warfare*, and LeDonne, *Grand Strategy of the Russian Empire*.

medieval wars mean, or perhaps more accurately, what meaning did medieval people create for themselves through resorting to armed violence? We shift, therefore, from a view of underlying stasis to changes over time.

PART II

Three Scenarios: Medieval Warfare in Changing Conditions

As we noted at the beginning of part I, historians are always concerned with two aspects of understanding the past that stand, if not in contradiction to each other, at least in a sort of paradoxical tension: continuity, and change over time. In part I of this book, the focus was very much on continuity: what, in this view, stayed the same over the entire history of medieval armed conflict. Now, in part II, we turn to the perspective of change over time.

The two views are not, in fact, contradictory, as can be seen by thinking of medieval armed conflict as an ongoing drama. Part I has outlined what the stage and the props for the action were like, and argued that they did not, in fact, change in any fundamental way over the course of the period. The unchanging nature of the stage and props (with the partial exception, just as the drama was reaching its last act, of the introduction of gunpowder weaponry as a new sort of prop) constrained what could take place on the stage: only certain kinds of actions were possible, and the actions taking place on one part of the stage were, in this view, directly comparable to those on any other part of the stage.[1] But constraining the kinds of actions people can take does not really constrain the number of stories that can be built from such actions. Even the variety of types of stories that can be told is infinitely larger than the kinds of actions that make them up.

---

[1] There are, admittedly, parts of the "stage," of the medieval globe – the Americas, sub-Saharan Africa, Australia and Oceania – that not only are not very visible from our modern seats, but whose actions were carried on in isolation and with fewer props, i.e. less developed suites of technology. But what they had was of a type with the technologies available everywhere, and the actions there comparable if slightly more restricted.

Thus, in part II, we turn to analyzing the stories that war and conflict in the Middle Ages tell us, and so we refocus our view toward change over time, in two ways. First, the very structure of stories – that they have a beginning, a middle, and an end – is about change over time. But change at the scale of individual stories is not really the subject of this part: there are too many stories, and it is not the purpose of this book to retell even a portion of them in any detail. We will instead consider groups of stories with similar themes, and examine whether the sorts of themes that many stories conveyed changed over time.

And as is often true of the analysis of stories, we will be concerned in some ways less with what happened in particular stories than with what sets of stories meant to their tellers and audiences.

5
The Early Middle Ages, 540–850: Wars of Medievalization

The Early Middle Ages, 540–850: An Introduction

We start, as we first saw back in chapter 2, with a "moment" of climate change and associated pandemic. The Late Antique Little Ice Age (LALIA) brought about changes to the world that demanded responses from human societies. Such changes are never uncontested, as change produces winners and losers. What was contested was how societies would change as they adapted to the changing world. Almost inevitably, "contested" meant fought over in armed conflict.

The argument of this chapter is that the wars and armed conflicts of the early Middle Ages, or the period encompassing the LALIA and the two centuries immediately following it, were primarily about reconstructing societies, or at times constructing new ones, in the place of the societies that had been disrupted by the LALIA and its effects. These constructions and reconstructions were not just practical adjustments to political structures and the distribution of power within and between different societies, but entailed the creation (or re-creation) of communal identities – again not just between societies, but within them. In other words, in addition to the standard processes of "state building" that have regularly attracted analysis, societies also engaged in what we might call "people building," or the construction of identities.

Thus, the wars and armed conflicts of this period were about the participants attempting to make their world meaningful. Armed conflict was not the only tool available for making meaning in this sense, but it was a major one, and was closely associated and used in conjunction with the other tools human communities usually deployed to such ends, especially religion.

The accumulated effect of the changes that war and conflict brought about in changed global conditions was, at least in (Afro) Eurasia and arguably, at least in some ways, in most of the world where complex human societies existed, to bring an end to the "classical" world and to give birth to the "medieval" world: in short, a global process of "medievalization."

Events

The LALIA

Geological and other scientific evidence suggests that a set of gigantic volcanic eruptions in different parts of the globe in 535/536, 539/540, and 547 caused a period of global cooling of about 2°C, easily enough to cause significant short-term weather events and to broadly disrupt agriculture, that lasted from about 540 to 660.[1] While the causal connection between this sudden climate variation and the spread of diseases remains speculative, the LALIA at least coincided with a set of Eurasian pandemics that included most famously the Plague of Justinian, almost certainly a bubonic plague outbreak, in the eastern Mediterranean world starting in 541.[2]

The evidence is that the LALIA was a global event. But climate events are inevitably expressed through local variations, and what was a challenge for some was an opportunity to others, as our first set of wars demonstrate.

The Paradigm: The Islamic Explosion

Muhammad died in 532. Even before he died, the new community he created had begun to push outward, looking to expand its base. The result, over the next hundred years, exceeded anything anyone

---

[1] Büntgen et al. "Cooling and Societal Change." While the climate effect was most extreme in the northern hemisphere, ice cores from Antarctica form part of the evidence for the volcanic eruptions, demonstrating at least some global scope. See also Newfield, "Global Cooling Event of the Sixth Century." The best overview of climate history is Lieberman and Gordon, *Climate Change in Human History*. See also White et al., *Palgrave Handbook of Climate History*, esp. ch. 32, "The Climate Downturn of 536–50," which offers a balanced assessment of the onset of the LALIA.

[2] On the "first plague pandemic," see Green, "When Numbers Don't Count."

could have imagined beforehand. By the 730s, an Islamic world stretched from Spain to deep in central Asia. This new Islamic civilization was one of the defining features of the medieval world that emerged with it.

We outlined some of the background to the Islamic explosion in setting up the Battle of Qādasiyyah, a key moment in the early expansion.[3] The Arabian Peninsula, home for centuries if not millennia to Arabs divided into tribes that had persisted nearly as long, saw Muhammad create unity under the banner of his new religion. He managed, from his initial base at Medina, to co-opt the leading Quraysh tribe based in Mecca, partly by negotiating a reconfiguration of Mecca from pagan pilgrimage site to holy center of Islam (and thus continuing pilgrimage site). The united Arabs then turned outward.

Muhammad's state- and people-building efforts undoubtedly benefited from an influx of wealth from Rome and Persia in the form of subsidies stimulated by competition between the Roman and Sassanid Persian Empires for allies. That wealth also came with institutional inducements to create larger groups with stronger leaders so as to stabilize the alliances formed. But to tie this to the LALIA, the global drop in temperatures did not simply disrupt agriculture in the sedentary empires; it had the opposite effect in the deserts of the Arabian Peninsula. The century-plus between 540 and 660 brought cooler and wetter weather there, and therefore the wealth Arabia generated internally, from limited agriculture (and scrub growth suitable for feeding camels), from trade, and simply in numbers of people, rose notably. More people and more wealth are always a condition for greater political organization, and Muhammad's Arabia proved no exception.

The two great empires were the first to feel the effects of Muhammad's reconstruction of Arabia. He'd started to lead campaigns northward, but died just as they got underway. His disciple Abu Bakr assumed control of the *umma*, or Muslim community, taking the title caliph, or successor, and suppressed revolts by rivals. He continued the campaigns; successful campaigns of conquest and booty taking often followed succession disputes, in polities as widely separated as the early caliphate, central Asian Turkish empires (see below), and the Aztec Empire, as a way of demonstrating legitimacy. Decisive victories in battle against the Romans at Yarmuk (636) in Syria and against the Persians at Qādasiyyah (638) in Mesopotamia

---

[3] See ch. 1 above and the references cited there for the early Muslim campaigns of conquest. See also Gordon, "Early Islamic Empire."

cemented and advanced both conquests. The Eastern Roman Empire eventually survived, though barely and in truncated form – the provinces of Syria and Egypt (conquered in a campaign ending in 642) were two of its richest possessions – mostly because its capital at Constantinople, sheltered across the Bosporus and surrounded by its massive walls (noted in chapter 4), resisted capture successfully in 669, 672, and after a major siege in 718. The Persian capital at Ctesiphon fell months after Qādasiyyah exposed it to a direct Arab advance, and the entire Persian Empire had been conquered by 650. Once Abu Bakr's caliphate controlled, in particular, Mesopotamia and Egypt, two of the world's greatest grain-producing regions, it was effectively a superpower, capable of launching further campaigns of conquest westward across north Africa and eastward into southwest Asia and western central Asia. By 751, an Arab army was contesting the latter, successfully, with a Tang Chinese army at the Battle of the Talas River.

Here, we need not trace the course of these conquests in detail. Rather, it is the character of these wars, the story the conflicts told, that concern us.[4] Two initial conditions are important. First, Islam itself was, as far as we can tell, not fully defined as a religion or "civilization" when its armies first emerged from Arabia. It was clearly a product of Bedouin Arab culture, however. In this, it was remarkably egalitarian in its views of people – Muslim emissaries to the Persians made it a point to stress their own egalitarianism over against the rigid hierarchy of the Persian court, which the Arabs perceived as servile – including having a bias against hereditary leadership (figure 15). Its tribal identities were also as ancient and fundamental to its peoples' identities as any cultural traditions it would encounter. Second, its first two mortal enemies were mostly its polar opposites: intensely hierarchical, sedentary and urban centered, and deeply hereditary at most levels of society. (One of the developments in the Roman world at this time, in reaction to the labor shortages caused by the LALIA and the Plague of Justinian, was to increase and broaden requirements that labor be hereditary, a typical "decline in labor freedom" reaction to labor shortage meant to guarantee labor availability.)

The immediate result of this cultural clash was that the Islamic community, or at least its leaders, began to define the *umma* in a classic construction-of-identity way: by contrast (and combat) with Others. The caliphate's Others were East Rome and Persia, the great

---

[4] The interpretation that follows owes its essence to the argument presented by Crone in *Slaves on Horses*.

Figure 15 Moorish soldiers. Muhammad I of Granada leads his army in 1264. Muslim warriors were drawn from and adapted to a wide variety of social and cultural bases.

Source: Wikimedia Commons.

empires. Religiously, this pushed Islam toward being Not Christian (and Not Jewish); though the genealogical connection to the earlier "Abrahamic" religions was always central, other differences – what the earlier incarnations got wrong, from the Muslim perspective – were highlighted. Being Not Zoroastrian was much less of a problem, first because there was no direct genealogical connection; second because Zoroastrianism, as the "religion of the Persians," did not really make universalist claims that competed with Islam's, though it is not clear that Islam started out as universalist as it became, perhaps having been initially shaped by Muhammad as the "religion of the Arabs."

One piece of evidence for this last view is that the Arab armies that conquered the old empires were not then spread among the new people (as might be expected were mass conversion the aim), but stationed in isolated "garrison cities" meant to keep them separate from and in control of the subject population in an almost colonial arrangement, reinforced by the policy of taxing non-Muslims but otherwise remaining tolerant of the beliefs of "Peoples of the Book" (Christians and Jews). As the Pact of Umar, the "contract" (forged later but nonetheless accurate for its supposed date of 637) by which the Muslim rulers guaranteed the safety of the conquered, specifies: "We [the conquered] shall not seek to resemble the Muslims by imitating any of their garments, ... the turban, footwear, or the parting of the hair. We shall not speak as they do ... . We shall not mount on saddles, nor shall we gird swords nor bear any kind of arms nor carry them on our persons."[5] Conversion of the subject populations in such conditions happened slowly and organically, usually through relationships of patronage between Arab soldiers and locals.

In short, the Arab conquests were wars that consciously aimed at creating and defending the cultural identity of a people. The remaining wars central to the Islamic world before 850 were about working out this identity.

The problem was, the conquests succeeded too well. Building an identity around the notion that "we are not sedentary imperialists" sat very uncomfortably, almost immediately, with possession of a vast, mostly sedentary, empire. In "low and slow" conditions of political structure, heredity (even if the heredity was sometimes fictive, as among the Augustan emperors of Rome) is an almost irresistible principle of succession, as anything else requires too much gathering and in-person communication.[6] Even the hypermobile Mongols, who did require (and manage) gatherings of all their notables to settle the succession to rulership of their empire, did so to confirm the hereditary lines emanating from Chinggis Khan. The early caliphs faced this problem starting in 656, when Ali, cousin and son-in-law of Muhammad, became caliph, and revolts followed.

Ali lost the ensuing civil war, and Mu'awiya became the first Umayyad caliph. The civil war was deep enough to create the split in Islam between the Sunnis, the majority, and the Shi'as, the minority party of Ali. But despite Ali's claim having been based on heredity,

[5] Lewis, *Islam*, p. 218.

[6] Indeed, no other reliable and morally defensible principle for succession existed until the creation of modern democracies and the concept of "sovereignty of the people" in the eighteenth century. Arguably, no other principle has ever emerged, as modern autocracies repeatedly demonstrate. Even the Chinese Communist Party has retrofitted a "people's sovereignty" kind of principle into an authoritarian system, as the Soviets did in Russia ... until that didn't work either. Whether "people's sovereignty" will survive today's wave of authoritarian attack remains a sadly open question; if it doesn't, succession disputes are sure to follow.

this was not a fight between heredity-defending Shi'ites and egalitarian Sunnis. It was really a dispute between different hereditary claims: the "direct descendants of Muhammad" party of Ali, and the "hereditary" claims of the Sunnis, who represented the interests of the Quraysh, the tribe that had controlled Mecca before Muhammad and thought of themselves as the "natural" leaders of the Arab world.[7] The real anti-heredity voice that had emerged came from among the educated *ulema*, or interpreters of Islamic law: scholars, mostly located in urban Mesopotamia, but who saw themselves as the defenders of Bedouin values, including being Not Sedentary Imperialists and thus pro-egalitarian and anti-heredity. They asserted their control over the meaning of Islam through legal and literary means. Given the hereditary claims and rich trappings of rule inevitable to the masters of what was, at that point, the world's richest empire, the Umayyads proved vulnerable to the *ulema* casting them as less-than-faithfully Islamic. Through still clearly the rulers of their empire, the caliphs lost some ability legally to impose taxes and conscription on their subjects and lost some hold on their legitimacy as rulers.

A century later, in 747, this contributed to the revolt of the Abbasids, descendants of Muhammad's cousin al-Abbas based in Khorasan in northeastern Persia, who aimed to reclaim the mantle of true Islam from the Syrian-based Umayyads. The Abbasid caliphate, establishing a new capital at the newly built city of Baghdad (on the frontier between Arab and Persian heartlands), attempted to wrest control of the meaning of Islam from the *ulema*, but failed, and so ended up facing the same problem as the Umayyads, only without their historical aura. By the early decades of the 800s, the structural problems of medieval Islamic rule – questionable central legitimacy, the directly related lack of any real aristocracy, of birth or service, to buttress central rule, adding up to a serious disconnect between state and society – had led the Abbasid caliphs to rely on foreign (mostly Turkish) slave soldiers for their military forces. Separated from society by both ethnicity and slave status, such soldiers were supposed to be dependent upon (and thus loyal to) their caliphal

---

[7] The largest lasting impact of the Sunni/Shi'a split was directly related to this period of wars of identity. Having been swallowed whole almost instantly by the Muslim explosion, the Persians reasserted their separateness from the Qurayshi-Syrian-Arab rulers of the caliphate by predominantly adopting the Shi'a version of Islam, though it was several centuries after the conquest until the majority of the population of Persia had converted to any form of Islam.

employers. While their central Asian origin indeed made them effective soldiers, they also, like many similar "praetorian guard" forces, became kingmakers who controlled their masters as much as they were controlled.

This in turn resulted in the steady fragmentation of the Islamic world into many small pieces, theoretically under the rule of the caliph but effectively independent. Each invariably reproduced the structure of the caliphate, right down to armed forces centered on a force of slave soldiers, a pattern that would continue through the Mamluks of Egypt to the Janissaries of the Ottoman Empire. The outcome for the Islamic world was fairly dire: Muslim states ruled over their own societies as, in effect, colonial administrations, deploying foreign armed forces to maintain their hold on power over an alienated populace. Given the widespread demilitarization of Islamic society, the only challenge came, periodically, from frontier warriors for the faith, or *ghazis*. Such home-grown "barbarians," in effect, could replay the role of Muhammad himself by sweeping in from the margins to the center of power to reestablish True Islam, succumb to the inevitable trappings of power, and in their turn be ousted, a pattern that inspired the great polymath Ibn Khaldun's view of the structure of world history.

To sum up, the Arab explosion of 630–750 established, through war and conquest, a post-LALIA identity for an entire civilization. But continued internal arguments and armed contests over that identity down through 850 rendered the Muslim world problematic, at least for governance. The Dar al-Islam was still capable of carrying on wars around its borders and did so regularly, as we shall see in subsequent sections. But those "normal" wars, while they often had implications for the survival and identity of Islam's neighbors, were essentially irrelevant to the development of Islam itself. It was in the ongoing wars between the fragments of the caliphate, in other words, that a discourse about legitimacy and identity in the Islamic world continued.

The Roman World

The fate of the Persian Empire, swallowed if not completely digested by the sudden violent emergence of Islam, shows the truly existential stakes involved in this age's wars of reconstruction and identity. Fail, cease to exist. The other great classical empire embroiled in the birth of Islam, the Roman Empire, shows the possibilities for reconstruction of identity and consequent survival, at least temporarily.

There was more to the Roman world than the eastern Mediterranean portion, of course, so after examining the fate of the eastern (continuing) half of the old empire, we will turn to the western half, already by the time of the LALIA no longer The Roman Empire, unlike the eastern half, but a set of successor kingdoms mostly run by Germanic war leaders.

Unlike the challenge Islam faced in constructing a new civilization and identity, the challenge for the different regions of the Roman world was to defend or reconstruct what the crisis had shaken.

The Eastern Roman Empire

As we have already noted, the Eastern Roman Empire was involved in a life-or-death struggle with the Sassanid Persian Empire in wars from 602 to 628 – the Persians besieged Constantinople in 626 before a series of campaigns by the emperor Heraclius into the heart of Persia turned the tide. These wars left both sides exhausted, on top of the economic contractions caused by the LALIA and plagues of the era. The Muslim conquests of Syria and Egypt, as well as north Africa, left the Eastern Roman Empire seriously reduced in size and resources. Faced with a vast, rich, and expansionist caliphate, East Rome entered into a period lasting into the 800s when it struggled simply to survive. It did so due to the defensive strength of Constantinople, to the military, administrative, and economic coherence the capital city provided to a reorganized provincial structure of the empire, especially in its core possessions in Asia Minor, and to a complete reorientation of its cultural identity.

In the contraction after the losses of the 630s, the Roman field army withdrew to Asia Minor. To help support it, the state settled its units in four divisions of the region called "themes"; over time the themes multiplied in number with each home to a unit also called a theme. What held this potentially decentralizing arrangement together was that taxes in the themes were assessed in gold, and the soldiers were paid in gold drawn from the taxes and used in turn to pay the taxes, creating a sort of gold circulation system that ran through the capital city, keeping the system tied together.

Militarily, the much-reduced Roman army this system supported had little chance of meeting major Arab invasions (which happened nearly yearly) head on, so they perfected practices of harassment, retreat to fortified positions, attempting to minimize damage, and avoiding open battle. The invaders would be harassed and (sometimes) attacked when they were on their way home laden with booty.

The empire also did what it could to buy off attacks and divert the caliphate using allies and diplomacy. This left much of the empire open to periodic plundering but proved effective at preventing permanent conquests by the caliphate until its fragmentation in the mid–800s took the pressure off.

The multiplication of the number of themes, achieved mostly by subdividing the first four, aimed partly to increase flexibility in responding to invasions, but was also designed to reduce the power of the major theme commanders, who posed a potential political threat to the emperor. To further counter this threat, by the 750s new units, called *tagmata* and based in the capital itself, were established under the emperor's command. More full-time and professional than the somewhat militia-ized thematic units, the *tagmata* also gradually assumed the role of spearheading offensive campaigns as they became possible.

These developments make up the material reorganization forced on the Eastern Roman Empire by the climate and plague crises and by the Arab explosion. Even more important in some ways, however, was the accompanying cultural shift in identity that has caused historians to refer to the empire after the losses of the 630s as the Byzantine Empire rather than the Eastern Roman Empire (the empire's own historians and writers continued to refer to themselves as Romans – *romaioi*, in the Greek that had become the main language of the state). In place of the old Roman conception of a universal empire, a conception that transferred itself to the Christianity that became the official religion of Rome in the 350s (thus the *Catholic*, or universal, Church), emerged a "Byzantine" self-image of a Chosen People, playing a special role in history: isolated and under siege but resisting the tide of Islam from their fortress centered on Constantinople.[8]

This shift was closely associated with the Iconoclast Controversy that shook Byzantine internal politics from the 720s to the 840s, the details of which need not concern us here except in so far as the controversy, on the surface about the orthodoxy of using icons, or portrayals of the divine in human form, was almost certainly influenced by Islam's opposition to representational art, and, though settled in favor of the pro-icon position, deepened the growing cultural division between eastern (Greek, Byzantine) and western (Latin, Roman) forms of Christianity, a division that increasingly threatened to spill over from the religious to the military sphere of conflict.

[8] See Whittow, *Making of Orthodox Byzantium*; see also Haldon, "Byzantium to the Twelfth Century."

The eastern half of the Roman world in the period 540–850 therefore presents us with a long and complex set of armed conflicts through which the East Romans/Byzantines reconstructed their political and military world, and built a new identity that motivated their wars of survival and reconstruction. The continuity of the Byzantine world from the original Roman Empire – most visible in the continuity of unit names and numbers in the central institution of the polity, its army, and in nominal self-identification – is certainly there, but structural, especially military, change and new foci of identity dominate. Yet the ongoing Constantinopolitan-centered unity of the empire also stands out.

The Western Roman Empire

Significant change had come earlier to the western half of the Roman Empire, which had ceased to have nominal or administrative continuity in the fifth century; the last western emperor was deposed by the Germanic war leader Odoacer in 476. The unified (half-)empire had been replaced by 500 by several kingdoms, each led by a war leader of Germanic origin. Franks, Visigoths, Ostrogoths, Burgundians, even Vandals – each successor kingdom faced the challenge of attempting to claim part of the mantle of *Romanitas*, the legacy of an empire gone but certainly not forgotten, while constructing its own identity among its rivals. Warfare was central to both of these tasks.

But the fragmentation of political power in the former Roman realm meant that none of the successor kingdoms could deploy anything close to the resources of the whole. Furthermore, the onset of the LALIA in the mid–500s and the impact of the plagues that accompanied it further reduced state-building resources, economic and demographic, and the kingdoms struggled even to maintain a facade of *Romanitas* and to manage conflict within their societies, never mind with their political rivals. Conflict became increasingly privatized as it fragmented, and the possession of and ability to use arms gained in importance in the construction of social identities within the kingdoms. In some ways, people building replaced state building as the "central" (albeit decentralized) goal of western European warfare.

One result was that participation in military activity became a central determinant of male identity, completely replacing an older Roman civic ideal of masculine leadership.[9] Second, in the context

---

[9] This point and the following section owe much to the analyses of Guy Halsall: *War and Society in the Barbarian West* and "Western European Kingdoms."

of recruitment of "barbarians" to fill the ranks of the Roman army, "barbarian" ethnic identities became a sought-after perk of military service. *Barbarian* came to mean *warrior*, or freeman, and *Roman* came to mean *taxpayer*, which in the context of labor shortages and hereditarily imposed vocations increasingly meant unfree person. Barbarian identities inevitably spread through the kingdoms' populations (which were thus "Germanic" only by cultural construction, which is why Latin remained the language from which modern European languages in the area of the empire descended). Competition for the privileges of warrior identity then helped produce the dominance of aristocratic families as a military elite surrounded by retinues of armed dependents. The corresponding disappearance of "Roman" (taxpaying) identity meant that rulers, deprived of income, came increasingly to rely on these aristocrats and their retinues to produce armed forces for the realm, with rewards for service consisting of land grants rather than cash payment. The rulers' ability to coerce any particular part of their realm declined, and politics became a privatized game of persuasion and competition, making for a world of constant armed conflict through which political and social structures were defined, personal identities were earned, and "states" as institutions that transcended personal conflicts disappeared. In short, a very different path of development from the state-centered one followed in the eastern half of the Roman world, but one no less dependent on armed conflict – pervasively through a militarized society – as a central force in the (re)construction of this civilization after the LALIA.

The major components of this socio-cultural evolution – armed forces raised from privatized aristocratic retinues, supported from landed estates that tended to become hereditary possessions that further entrenched the warrior elite that dominated this society – culminated in the Carolingian dynasty of the Frankish polity. Rising to dominance in the 700s under Charles Martel, his son Pepin, and his grandson Charles the Great (Charlemagne), the early Carolingians came to control most of western Europe outside Iberia and Britain. Constant campaigning built an experienced, successful army that brought new areas, above all Saxony, under their control. But the cultural marker of Carolingian dominance was their association with the papacy, which had emerged as the center of western, Latin Christendom. This involved both defense of the papacy as a landed power in Italy, made necessary by the decline of Byzantine ability to project force into the peninsula, and the defense of papally sanctioned orthodoxy against heresy. Both roles infringed on what Byzantium saw as its proper imperial role. But taking advantage of the reign of the empress Irene, of questionable legitimacy (to the Franks) because of her gender, Charlemagne cemented the alliance by being crowned Emperor of the Romans by the pope on Christmas Day, 800.

This marriage of empire and papacy proved a momentous but far from straightforward moment in the construction of western European identity. It put Latin Christendom on an increasingly divergent path from the Greek Orthodoxy of the Byzantine world. It also allied state power to religion, making "Christendom" both a political and cultural identity whose frontiers became a site of culturally charged political conflict. But the primacy of emperor or pope (later developed as "church" and "state" as separable spheres) in this marriage remained uncomfortably vague.

The potential dominance of the emperor in the marriage failed to develop in part because after 800, political developments seriously reduced the power of the Carolingian state. Expansion, limited by the size of the empire and its underdeveloped economy and communications (that is, by "low and slow" constraints), ceased; service in the army became less attractive and harder to enforce; and at the same time the empire faced new waves of incursions from Vikings, Magyars (central Asians who had settled in the Hungarian Plain), and Saracen (Islamic) raiders. Combined with the Frankish tradition of partible inheritance, which tended to split estates and realms, local and imperial, among sons, the Carolingian world after 800 fragmented politically even as it achieved cultural unity and prestige.

Warfare among the fragments of the Carolingian world was endemic, but tended to move away from territorial conquest and toward performance of legal legitimacy of landholding and reinforcement of social identities, especially among the emergent warrior aristocracy and in contradistinction to the priestly class and the peasants beneath them both. The medieval European conception of society as a triad of "those who fight, those who pray, and those who work" expresses this in large terms. The beginnings of the emergence of notions of chivalry as the defining ethos of the warriors was a more focused aspect of the same process of self-definition through warfare.

Both Islam and Byzantium are examples of how the wars of (re)construction and identity that characterize the early Middle Ages produced unified polities in conjunction with cultural identities. Western Europe may seem, by contrast, to have failed at the task of (re)construction. But this ignores the at least temporary (and influential) success of the early Carolingians, and places too great a state-centric emphasis on political unity as a marker of "success." If we take political fragmentation as part of the structure of the western European world constructed in response to the challenge of the LALIA and the end of the Roman Empire, the region's wars fit perfectly into our thesis, and even emphasize the fact that the Islamic world in fact followed the same pattern: cultural unity constructed through warfare in a world that, after 800, fragmented politically. And in both the Islamic and western European worlds, fragmentation generated a class of warriors probably larger, in aggregate, than had existed before, supported by their dominance over agricultural producers and an agrarian economy that, once the conditions of the LALIA began to ease in the 700s, began to expand. Thus, fragmentation from this perspective can be read as a sign of worlds that had grown richer and politically more complex. And from this perspective, it is the continuing unity of Byzantium that stands out. Unified hunkering down in Fortress Byzantium was not necessarily a path to a richer (and more complicated) world.

The Steppe World

The potential problem with fitting the fully horsed steppe world into this part of this book, whose thesis highlights changes created by climate and demographic challenges, is that the military history of the central Asian region is often written with a stress on continuities. That is, once the horse-and-bow combination that made steppe armies so formidable was established sometime in the second or first millennium BCE, as exemplified in the emergence of the Scythians in the western steppes and the Xiongnu in the east, there wasn't really further development. The essentials of hit-and-run tactics, nomadic raid-trade-tribute strategies in their relations with their sedentary neighbors, and even decimal-based unit organization remained the basis of steppe success thereafter, limited only by the political fractiousness of the various steppe tribes, which meant that the majority of steppe military activity was inward-directed in endless tribal warfare and reshuffling of power. In terms of cultural identities, the paradoxical outcome of this political-military stasis was constant flux, itself a form of stasis: tribal identities came and went with the evanescent success of certain groups, but nothing essential was transformed.

It is not that there is no truth to this picture, but it seriously exaggerates the continuities of this world and consequently underplays the cultural and political creativity generated from within steppe societies. The fact that this view downplays the ability of steppe societies to adapt and change as circumstances did hints at some of the origins of this view. As usual, our knowledge of the "barbarian" steppes originates in the perspectives of their sedentary neighbors, who were the writers of history. Inability to change and resulting stasis are characteristic qualities projected onto "primitive" Others by societies who view themselves as more advanced – compare the supposed stasis of the "medieval" world as imagined by the "moderns," whether of the Italian Renaissance looking back at the European "Dark Ages" or the colonial west constructing the unchanging "medieval" stasis of The Rest (see chapter 2). The unchanging steppes are, in other words, an illusion created by the cultural chasm separating the horsed steppe worlds from their literate neighbors.[10]

This was particularly true of political structures and traditions, where several landmarks and the traditions stemming from them reveal that the steppe world was indeed an integral part of the connected and emerging medieval world. After the foundational steppe cultures, the Scythians and Xiongnu, had established the steppe-nomadic presence in central Asia, the rise of the Turks and the First Turkic Khaganate, established in 552, marked a major turning point and had significant influence on all its successors through the early Middle Ages, especially in terms of political structures. It also marked a notable increase in the interaction between the steppes and the surrounding sedentary worlds. Then, the rise of the Mongols under Chinggis Khan[11] marked another turning point that shaped steppe polities, particularly with respect to succession and legitimacy, as well as again reshaping their relations with the sedentary world through the high and late Middle Ages. We shall return to the Mongols in chapter 6. For now, we turn to the Turks.

The First Turkic Khaganate and the LALIA

The Turks rose to prominence when the Ashina clan of the Götürks, one of many tribal confederations in the eastern steppes,[12] rose

---

[10] A linguistic indication of this perspective is provided by the Byzantine use of the word "Scythian" for any central Asian nomadic group, long after the Scythians had ceased to exist. But to be fair, Byzantine writers applied such classicizing language to most of the peoples they dealt with: western Europeans remained "Franks" long after the disappearance of the Carolingians as the dominant rulers in western Europe, and the Byzantines themselves remained "Romans" to the end of the empire.

[11] Note that the Turkish title *khagan* and the Mongolian form *khan* are simply different transliterations of the same word, with the former sometimes written as *qaghan*.

[12] As always, tribal identifications were politically constructed identities, not ethnic ones, though Turkic peoples occupied a good deal of the steppe region in the 500s.

up under the leadership of Bumin Qaghan against their overlords, the Rouran khaganate, in 546, defeating the Rouran and making themselves the dominant power on the Mongolian plateau by 552, when Bumin died. They then expanded rapidly under Bumin's son Muqan Qaghan, extending their rule from Manchuria in the east to the Black Sea in the west, the first central Asian empire to span the continent.

What lay behind the sudden rise to dominance of the Götürks? Answers are hard to come by, not least because the details of central Asian politics are often opaque due to the source difficulties we have already mentioned. And periodic upheavals were endemic among steppe polities. But the rise of the Turks was, even by these standards, sudden and carried much further than usual, suggesting at least something unusual about its context.

The answer offered here can be no more than a suggestion, one already hinted at by Büntgen et al.[13] If the initial political disturbances that the Turks took advantage of indeed date to the 540s, they coincide closely with the onset of the LALIA in central Asia. Harsh winters were always a stimulant for competition over grazing grounds; a sudden climate shift of the intensity indicated for the LALIA must have both heightened such conflict and destabilized the established political structures within which that conflict usually occurred. This could account for both the timing of the Turks' rise and the unusual breadth of their conquests once they got started. (It does not seem that the climate shift benefited the steppe economy directly, as was the case in Arabia, which saw increased rainfall and thus fodder for camels and supplemental agriculture for people. But the adaptability of steppe pastoralism probably meant that, aside from heightening conflict over the best grazing grounds and generally destabilizing politics, the climate shift damaged economic activity less than it did in sedentary agricultural areas.) In short, the sixth-century restructuring of the steppes looks like a LALIA effect as much as the better-documented cases of its impact on the rise of Islam, the Roman world, and the Persian Empire.

The khaganate came into conflict, as it spread westward, with the Sassanid Persian Empire, who had earlier been supporters of the Götürks. Contact with the Eastern Roman Empire in the Black Sea region led to trade embassies and eventually a tense alliance against the Persians that proved significant in the recovery of East Rome

---

[13] Büntgen et al., "Cooling and Societal Change," p. 1.

under Heraclius, and thus in the severe weakening of Persia, just before the Islamic explosion. Turkic expansion probably also played a role in the movement of other steppe groups into Europe, including the Avars, who came into conflict with (and were conquered in the 790s by) the Carolingian Franks, and then the Magyars. To the east, the Turks became major players in Chinese warfare, attempting to intervene in the wars through which the Tang dynasty replaced the Sui in 618. The Tang in turn conquered the eastern Turk khaganate in the 630s and the western khaganate in 657. The fall of the eastern khaganate resulted in part from further LALIA effects: a series of especially harsh winters in 627–30 led to massive die-offs of Turk herds, destabilizing the khagan's rule.

The Second Turkic Khaganate

The fact of an *eastern* Turk khaganate resulted from the khaganate splitting into eastern and western halves after a major civil war in 584 (the khaganate was already divided into eastern and western halves for administrative purposes). After the Tang conquests a period of Chinese dominance in central Asia followed, but the Turkic khaganate reemerged, in the east from 682 until 742, in the west from 699 until 766,[14] though both halves struggled to maintain coherence against internal rivalries and external threats. They were succeeded in the west by the Khazars and in the east by the Uighurs.

Under both the First and Second Turkic Khaganates, the central Asian steppe world assumed a new importance in connecting eastern and western Eurasia. The opulent luxury of the Turk rulers at their height impressed rulers from all the major sedentary powers, and central Asia became even more a meeting ground for the spread of the religious traditions that accompanied the rebuilding character-istic of this era. Military and religious expansion were closely inter-twined (along with trade caravans). The Turks themselves worshiped the central Asian sky god Tengri, but were constantly open to other influences. Though Persian Zoroastrianism made no inroads into the region, and was then swallowed by Islamic expansion as we have seen, its bastard child, dualist Manichaeism, spread widely, and Nestorian Christianity also followed the Silk Road through Turkic-controlled lands. Buddhism continued its spread, and by the mid–700s Islamic expansion was reaching into the Turkic realm just as Turkic soldiers

---

[14] Golden, *Central Asia in World History*, p. 40.

were becoming the backbone of Islamic military forces. In 751, growing Arab-Islamic and Chinese-Buddhist spheres of the Abbasid caliphate and the Tang dynasty met in battle at the Talas River, a battle decided in favor of the Muslims and their Tibetan allies when the Karluk Turks, an offshoot of the Götürks, defected from their Chinese alliance. As a result, Islam, not China, would dominate southern central Asia for the remainder of the Middle Ages.

The Chinese World

Like much of the Eurasian world around the year 500, China looked back on a past characterized by imperial unity and influential constructions of Chinese identity tied to that imperial past. After the fall of the Han dynasty in 220, the Jin managed to reunite the realm and maintain a fragile unity until 317. But the fall of the Jin initiated a period of political fragmentation. Beneath the state-level breakup, locally powerful families built up retinues of armed followers who gradually carved out the outlines of a new identity as military specialists. The similarities of this process of social differentiation based on armed conflict to what had happened in western Europe after the breakup of the Roman Empire demonstrates how fundamental war and conflict were to how medieval societies organized and defined themselves, especially in the absence of a strong and *accepted* (that is, *legitimate*) central authority. Even when the existence of such an authority remained the ideal, as it did in both western Europe and China, what that did was push military competition among successor polities toward the goal of reestablishing unity.[15]

In the nearly three hundred years of disunity that followed the fall of the Jin, two further major dynamics shaped armed conflict in the Chinese world. First, China's relations with the nomadic, "barbarian" horsed world of the steppes assumed even greater centrality than they had attained under the Han, when the northwestern frontier had first become a major issue with the rise of the Xiongnu. Second, the geographic divide between northern China and southern China gradually rose in importance. These two factors intersected in ways that had lasting implications for Chinese identity.

North China, above the Yangtze River and including the Ordos region enclosed in the great loop of the Yellow River, remained the

---

[15] For Chinese warfare in this era, see Graff, *Medieval Chinese Warfare*; Graff, "China," pp. 181–210; and Lorge, *Warfare in China to 1600*.

economic and population center of China in this period, though the south was beginning to gain as Han colonists moved southwards, often displacing non-Han populations in the process. This facilitated the main southern states coming under the rule of émigrés from powerful families in the north. Colonists and émigrés alike often moved south fleeing from the military insecurity of the north: the major northern states in the centuries of disunity were ruled by nomadic steppe invaders who then created hybrid Sino-Turkic polities whose leading families were of mixed Chinese and nomadic origins. It was in this mixed and increasingly militarized society of the north that the most important battles for Chinese power and identity would be played out in the early Middle Ages, though with paradoxical results.

The north was crucial because no southern state had the military, economic, or bureaucratic capacity to conquer the north. The northern states had greater capacity in these ways, in part because their access to (or alliance with, or ruling class made up of) steppe manpower meant that all the best cavalry forces were there. The north still, at this point, had larger populations and richer economies, though that was beginning to shift in favor of the south. It was also in the north that a class of professional military personnel developed. But the northern states had to face each other before turning south, and for a long time no one northern state could dominate. Even when northern powers turned south, the Yangtze formed a barrier that developing southern riverine naval forces reinforced. Beyond that, the warmer, wetter climate of the south made sustaining cavalry forces there difficult. Thus, would-be northern conquerors had to succeed quickly or risk getting bogged down, opening them to threats in their rear from northern rivals. The result for two and half centuries after the breakup of the Jin was division and stalemate.

The timing of the end of this stalemate, with the unification of the north under the Northern Zhou dynasty in a series of wars from the 550s culminating in 577, after which their successors, the Sui, conquered the south and reestablished a unified Chinese Empire in 589, is suggestive of some sort of influence by the LALIA on breaking the stasis that had prevailed. We know China was affected: there are reports of snows in August of 536 at the initiation of the climate event. But beyond that suggestive timing, it is not clear what effect weather and climate had on the events leading to the Sui reunification. Nevertheless, the Sui came to power looking to (re)construct Chinese imperial identity with the Han past as a model.

Sui Unification

The Sui faced this task with important tools that differed from what the Han had to work with. In order to eliminate their rivals and defend the northern frontier, the Sui leaders had increasingly drawn on the armed followings of the local strongmen who had come to dominate society in the period of disunity, co-opting the militarization of society for imperial purposes. The conscription of the farming population that the Han had inherited from the first unifying dynasty, the Qin, ceased to be a significant tool of central power.

Unlike the strongmen, who had attained a level of aristocratic permanence and status through their mastery of local conflict, their armed followers had not managed to convert proficiency in arms into social status, and had instead become something like a hereditary class of cultivator-soldier families, only semi-free and dependent on their superiors. (This stands in contrast to the fate of "barbarian" populations in the fragmented western Roman world, whose possession and use of arms were the basis of their legal status as free persons.) Under imperial control, this class became the foundation in the succeeding Tang dynasty of the *fubing* system of raising armies: Tang manpower came from possessors of military lands who were thereby obligated to serve in imperial armies. Spearheaded by the cavalry forces of the northern semi-barbarian aristocracy and their relatives in fully barbarian allied steppe tribes, the *fubing* system proved an effective and cost-efficient way of defending the barbarian frontier and guarding against internal challenges. Though differing in its origins, the end result is comparable to the thematic armies of the Byzantine Empire.

Also, in a process comparable (though not identical) to the linking of barbarian warriors and Christianity in western Europe and the emergence of the caesaro-papist structure of Christianity in Byzantium, the Sui promoted Buddhism, which had already been spreading among the militarized aristocracy as well as other groups. The spread of Buddhism reflects the influence of steppe networks of cultural exchange reaching into China, and gave the Sui a new ideological tool for reinforcing imperial legitimacy that augmented (but did not replace) Chinese conceptions of legitimacy grounded in Confucianism.

The Sui needed additional tools, however, to attempt to recreate Han dominance, because they faced a more complex world than their predecessors had. In addition to the threat of steppe barbarians, which had not even arisen until the Han were already well established, the entire east Asian world had grown in state-level organization and cultural sophistication in part because of the success of the Han model. A key example of this was the emergence of the kingdom of Goguryeo (Korea) at the northeast corner of the Chinese world. The Sui, attempting to rebuild central power and bring the world to heel at the same time, in the context of an ongoing climate shift, walked into a disastrous overextension of their efforts.

Many of their efforts succeeded, it should be noted, even if the Sui were not the ultimate beneficiaries. Sui initiatives included new systems of administration, new coinage, and massive public works projects. The Sui expanded the Great Wall facing the steppes and, most consequentially in the long run, constructed the Grand Canal that linked the political-military core region in the north, including the reestablished Han capitals at Chang-an and Luoyang, with the growing economic breadbasket of the Yangtze valley. But these projects depended on massive amounts of conscripted labor. The new military system, which drew on aristocratically controlled military labor that otherwise might have fallen beyond central control, probably made such levels of labor conscription possible, demonstrating the essential equivalence of conscripted soldiery and conscripted labor. But the Sui also drew massively on their military manpower in a series of invasions of Korea from 598 to 614. The perhaps predictable result of drawing resources maximally from the agrarian population in the context (probably) of climate-induced economic contraction was serious peasant unrest. When the invasions of Korea failed, stripping the coercive efforts by the central government of any corresponding benefit in terms of legitimacy and identity formation, the dynasty almost immediately suffered multiple rebellions and fell into chaos.

The Tang from 618 to 750

Those rebellions turned rapidly into a military competition for the mantle of imperial legitimacy. The winning faction, who established the Tang dynasty, won in large part because Li Shimin, the second son of their leader, was a terrific general who won all the major battles he fought. This both attracted followers to his side and made the pacification of hostile areas easier. He was an astute diplomat who avoided an early crisis with Turkish intervention as the rebellions were getting started, then used his familial connections to maintain a Turkish alliance that safeguarded his rear and supplied needed cavalry forces. He was also, it must be said, a ruthless politician who became the second Tang emperor after killing his older brother and pushing his father out of office. He took the reign name Tang Taizong.

Tang Taizong embodies the main elements and paradoxes of Tang Chinese identity as it developed under his rule and in the rest of the dynasty's history. His familial connections to the "barbarian" steppe peoples, backed by military success, in effect expanded the realm in which Chinese identity formation could operate while making that identity more complicated. Those family connections were also representative of what had emerged as a military aristocracy in China during the period of disunion. Both the barbarian and military elements of Tang Taizong's identity were potentially problematic against the background of the model of the Han, who had been "purely" Han Chinese (indeed, the dynasty established the identity, as the name shows!) and had stressed civilian control of the military and the superiority of civilian over military values.

Tang Taizong himself successfully exploited his "barbarian" connections, as we have already noted, in terms of alliances and diplomacy among the steppe tribes. Once he had secured the domestic side of Tang rule, he turned to aggressive management of the northern frontier. A series of offensives in the 620s, 630s, and 640s carried Tang dominance into the steppes with the conquest of the eastern Turks noted above. The Tang usually managed these conquests through a combination of diplomacy, bribery, and the use of allied or already subjugated Turkish tribes against other hostile tribes. Diplomacy did much of the work of turning the Turks against each other, after which the Chinese could intervene at the request of one side or the other.

Tang Taizong's self-presentation is a fascinating study in the projection of identity. He was clearly proud of and anxious to burnish his military exploits: accounts of his victories often exaggerate (or at least highlight more than might be completely accurate) his own role in planning campaigns and leading in battles.[16] But he could not single-handedly redirect the established values he inherited from the Han, and indeed displaying the values established in the past enhanced Tang legitimacy. Thus, his official portrait shows him not as a military hero but in the yellow robes of a Confucian scholar (figure 16). And like the Sui, Taizong and the early Tang rulers continued to promote Buddhism, popular among the aristocracy, as a spiritual buttress for the intellectual values promoted by Confucianism.

---

[16] Graff, "Battle of Huo-I."

Figure 16   Emperor Tang Taizong of China. A talented military commander of mixed Han and central Asian ancestry, Li Shimin (who took the reign name Tang Taizong) presented himself in his official portrait in the yellow robes of a Confucian scholar.

Source: Wikimedia Commons.

But both from this perspective and in practical military terms, the contradictions buried in the Tang projection of identity eventually caught up with the dynasty. The successful offensives against the Turks pushed China's frontiers far into central Asia. Locally supported and essentially part-time forces such as made up the *fubing* were not well suited to offensives beyond China, and were much harder to maintain and deploy in defense of distant frontiers. As a result, over the century after 650, especially after the 670s when the Turks revived as an independent force, the burden of frontier defense was shifted to increasingly long-service, full-time professional armies, themselves made up mostly of troops (and generals) of barbarian origin. This was a shift in force profile that exactly paralleled not only the increased Byzantine emphasis on *tagmata*, full-time professionals, as opposed to the militia-like thematic forces, when Byzantium went over to the offensive against the fragmented Abbasid caliphate after 850, but also the western Roman reliance on recruiting barbarian troops.

This shift certainly increased military efficiency, but at the cost of creating forces that posed, potentially, a greater threat to central authority. Oddly (but probably under the influence of the semi-barbarian military aristocracy), the state at the same time fell off in its efforts to prevent the generals in charge of the professional armies from turning their commands into personal power bases. Rotating assignments, mechanisms of civilian oversight, and so forth were all gradually abandoned. The almost predictable result came to pass in 755, when, four years after the defeat the Tang suffered to the Abbasids at the Talas River, the frontier general An Lushan rebelled against central control.

His rebellion lasted from 755 to 763, was suppressed only with help from the Uighurs, the successors to the Turks in central Asia, and nearly ended Tang rule. Even when the dynasty recovered, its power was never the same. After a century of tentative rule, the country effectively broke into competing warlord realms of which the central state was only one. In the century between 850 and 950, armed conflict decisively finished the remains of classical Han China and cleared the field for a new economic-political-cultural construction under the Song dynasty, which came to power in 960. The key elements of this ground-clearing era of conflict were that the military aristocracy essentially killed each other off while destroying any legitimacy or prestige attached to military service. This was certainly *not* a productive discourse about legitimacy, power, and identity for most of those involved in it.

Meanwhile, the fragmentation of state authority in a period when the climate was warming again led not just to rising economic activity, especially in the south, but to much more of the economy escaping the state control and regulation it had been under since Han times. The imperial state would reemerge after 960 under the new Song dynasty, but the transformations of the period of Tang fragmentation meant the Song would be a very different sort of state and society than had existed when the Tang came to power.

The Indic World

In India, a "classical ideal" of imperial unity and cultural model setting resulted from a combination of two empires. In terms of the unity of the subcontinent under one ruling power, the early classical Maurya Empire (322–185 BCE), which had united virtually the whole subcontinent including the Indus valley in the northwest, had set the standard. But the late classical Gupta Empire (mid–200s–543), while not as extensive as the Maurya, being confined to the northern half of the subcontinent, established a cultural Golden Age that subsequent Indian empires would look back to for inspiration. Particularly in terms of social and political structures, including military manpower and practices, and their links to Hindu religious identity, the Gupta are the relevant model for the purposes of this analysis.

There is not a strong consensus among historians regarding the reasons for the decline and disappearance of the Gupta Empire. Standard accounts date the decline to the mid–400s, with increased invasions by central Asians, possibly related to the Huns, after 500 contributing to territorial losses and increasing fragmentation. If this timing is correct, then the decline of the Guptas is difficult to connect to the LALIA, which did not begin until c.540. And perhaps it is unrelated.

But a recent archaeological study claims that instead of gradual decline, sudden massive flooding in the heart of the empire in the Bihar region brought the empire to a catastrophic end around 550.[17] Deeply contrasting accounts of the state of major Buddhist monasteries by the traveling Chinese monks Faxian (from 399) and Xuanzing (630) lend support to this view. The timing of this catastrophe is

---

[17] Telegraph Online, "Deluge Drowned Mighty Guptas."

suggestive ... but not more than suggestive, especially since the impact of the Late Antique Little Ace Age (or even the better studied Little Ice Age) in the Indian subcontinent has received almost no attention,[18] and the monsoon weather system of the region differs from the usual patterns of continental Eurasia. Could the volcanic events that brought sudden hemispheric cooling across Eurasia have triggered massive floods in northern India? At the moment, we do not know.

Nevertheless, we can say that, for whatever reason, including a possible push from the effects of the LALIA, the classical Gupta Empire fragmented into a multiplicity of warring princely states after 550. In characterizing the wars of the period 540–800 in India, we are on somewhat firmer ground. The successor states followed the Gupta model of military organization, with the key warriors, often mounted, supported by land grants. Elephant corps and masses of ill-armed infantry rounded out the armies. The princely Hindu rulers conducted warfare against each other on a basis whose politics, if not the battles themselves, contained a large element of ritualistic maneuvering based on the concept of *mandala* outlined in the *Arthashastra* of Kautilya, a Maurya-era text. This resulted in "conquests" in which the losing side submitted to the winners and became subject tributaries, remaining in power locally. Larger imperial aggregations thus tended to be ephemeral, breaking up after the death of the "conqueror."

While such warfare might appear somewhat pointless in "real" political terms, it certainly acted as a discourse about legitimacy and identity among the participants that, unlike the wars in which the Tang dissolved, did not endanger the existence of the participants. It was instead an arena in which kings could assert their *kshatriya* (warrior caste) status and legitimacy, demonstrate the efficacy of the endorsement their *brahman* (priestly) caste gave them (the *brahman–kshatriya* alliance being the key to the power structure of these kingdoms), and perform deeds worthy of being recorded in the annals and other cultural displays created under their patronage.[19] The military weaknesses of this world of warfare, including serious deficiencies of Indian horse breeding and thus cavalry, would be exposed, however, when armies from the neighboring Muslim world with substantial central Asian elements began raiding in the 800s and turned more systematically to conquest in the 1100s. Before that intervention,

[18] White et al., *Palgrave Handbook of Climate History*, p. 205.
[19] Avari, *India*, pp. 728–41.

however, post-Gupta Indian warfare was a classic discourse about power and identity that reinforced the coherence of the world in which it occurred.

Other Worlds

Including the Americas in a global survey of medieval warfare poses some difficult problems. These did not show up in part I of this book, because American warfare in the Middle Ages was clearly operating by the same "rules," that is under the same physical constraints, and thus the same structural tendencies those physical constraints produced, as the rest of the world did.

Even in looking at the medieval world from the perspective of climate challenges, we may be able to discern similar processes of reaction and reconstruction at work in some places. But the isolation of the Americas from the Afro-Eurasian societies that were connected to each other by networks of migration, trade, and conflict means that some factors are simply out of the picture. For example, the LALIA in Eurasia was closely connected to the first Eurasian plague pandemic, even if the direct causal mechanisms connecting them are not agreed upon. But the Americas were not part of the Eurasian disease-sharing pool (until, of course, the Spaniards arrived in 1492, at which point the American populations faced catastrophe).

The question this raises, therefore, since we are defining The Middle Ages, globally, in terms of climate changes and the challenges associated with them, is: are the Americas really part of a "medieval" world? Based not just on the Common Rules of the first part of this book, but on an at least roughly similar pattern of challenge and reaction that can be seen as a basis for periodization, a positive answer can at least be defended.

The center of "classical" civilization in Mesoamerica was clearly the great city of Teotihuacan in the central valley of Mexico. It is not clear if the city was the center of an imperial polity or simply the dominant city-state in the region, but in its prime from 0–500 CE, Teotihuacan at the least set the cultural patterns for Mesoamerican societies and was probably one of the largest cities in the world. Its fairly sudden decline began in 535 with the first of the great volcanic eruptions that initiated the LALIA. Climate change led to droughts, famine, and population decline, triggering serious unrest. Around 550, Teotihuacan's major monumental buildings were all burned in internal conflicts.

Because it is not clear that the great city actually exercised direct imperial control over much of Mesoamerica, it might not be technically accurate to say that the Mesoamerican world "fragmented" after the decline of Teotihuacan. But the post-Teotihuacan politics of the region were at the least "polycentric," especially in the Mayan Yucatan, where numerous city-states that had been under the cultural influence of Teotihuacan competed militarily during the "classic" Mayan period down through about 800. Much of that warfare is comparable to the wars of the Hindu kingdoms after the Gupta in being relatively ritualized (though plenty of people died in both cases) and not fundamentally about territorial conquest but about hierarchical primacy, identity, and religious legitimation. As in India, it bound together a coherent cultural world.

"Medievalization": A Process

The various sets of wars outlined thus far in this chapter may be read as defining a process that we might call "medievalization." This was a patterned process whose steps are visible in almost all our sets of conflicts. Although it did not always lead to exactly the same result, even the exceptions can tell us something valuable. The steps in this process were, to sum up, as follows.

First, each set of wars began with an established model of classical unity and identity: the Roman Empire, the Han dynasty, the Guptas (combined with the Mauryas), Teotihuacan, and even the Persian Empire, both as an "anti-model" for Islam (along with Rome) and as an actual model or provider of later administrative structures in the Islamic caliphate. The influence of these imperial models, it should be noted, often extended well beyond the areas that they actually controlled politically. Roman influence, for example, was felt well into "Germania," beyond the Rhine; Persian influence extended well into central Asia.

Second, this imperial model and its underlying socio-economic structure were put under stress by the onset of the LALIA, in many places accompanied by widespread disease events rising to the level of a pandemic. This is not to say that the LALIA created a catastrophe that brought "classical" civilizations automatically to an end. Human societies are usually more adaptable than such a reading implies. Yes, high-level state structures in the agrarian era were often fragile, as a result of being built, of necessity, in a way that was unfair and coercive. But too much focus on state mechanisms at the highest level fails to capture the richness and flexibility of human communities underneath the state. The "collapse" or fragmentation of a major empire often meant better conditions for those under its rule, not chaos and misery. At the least, collapse and fragmentation offered more opportunity for more people to try to define their own ways of living. Admittedly, such opportunities were often pursued via armed force. This is, indeed, the underlying point of this book: war and conflict were not just a matter of major state confrontation, but a pervasive tool of social construction and cultural formation.

It is true that armed conflict as a major tool of social (re)construction often favors those who already possess power, wealth, and armed followings. This accounts in part for the third step in this process: that in many places, there was an apparent reconstruction, militarily led, of classical unity and prestige in the context of the economic downturn of the LALIA or its immediate aftermath. Examples include the Umayyad caliphate (which, though culturally new, built upon structural foundations laid by both the Persians and Rome), the Carolingians, and the Tang. Both the ongoing power of old elites and their ability to project cultural images of imperial prestige, which in turn helped legitimize the power they were (re)claiming, helped this stage of attempted reunification. Although it did not happen everywhere, the attempt was pervasive.

Then, in a fourth step, that imperial reconstruction fragmented into competing pieces, with those pieces drawing on a post-LALIA expansion of economic activity that supported more widely spread militarization below the state level. This stage is clearly visible in post-Carolingian Europe, in the fragmentation of the Abbasid caliphate, in the warlordism of the late Tang and the fragmentation that followed, in post-Gupta northern India, and in the classic Mayan period after the decline of Teotihuacan.

A focus on that last step shows what an interesting, complex, and important set of processes was going on under the state-centric guise of "collapse" or fragmentation. Widespread military conflict and competition were central. All of that military competition acted to tie together the worlds in which it happened culturally: widespread military activity acted, in other words, as a major channel of intracultural discourse about values and legitimate power. This had two further consequences.

First, the cultural competition among warrior leaders for legitimacy accounts, in part, for the close association of this stage of the larger process with the spread of major religious traditions, especially those that in world history terms may be seen as the "salvation religions":

Christianity (in both its western Latin Catholic form and its eastern Greek Orthodox form), Islam, Hinduism, and Buddhism (the last of which, in China, stimulated new developments in Confucianism that would bear fruit under the subsequent Song dynasty). Even in Mesoamerica, where the major salvation religions would not penetrate until the coming of the Spanish, Mayan warfare had a distinctly religious tone, as each Mayan city-state was in fact less a city-state than a "portal" state built around its own unique entryway, or portal, to the spirit world, which in turn legitimized the ruling family of the state.

Second, competition among warriors at the structural level, in the absence of an overarching state mechanism to control the production and distribution of wealth, encouraged the development of local resources. This was certainly facilitated by the general improvement of agrarian conditions with the end of the LALIA in the mid–600s, but climate-driven improvements in productivity (which may not have been as global as the downturn itself was) were not the only mechanism here. Instead, it was fragmentation itself, which tended to force greater self-reliance on local areas, especially in terms of producing the wealth that could support the local military personnel, that played a major role here. This sort of local agricultural activity inevitably connected via regional networks to produce greater economic activity at the level of trade and manufacturing, a process visible in China, western Europe, the caliphate, and out into the peripheries of all these areas.

The end result differed in each area in many ways, but the *process*, again a process that we can call "medievalization," looks remarkably similar. To repeat a point we made earlier, fragmentation should not be taken, from a state-centric perspective, as a sign of failure. Medievalization built deeper, culturally more coherent (more religiously connected and connectedly religious), and economically richer societies. It was the process, in short, that created the cultural worlds that continue to lie at the roots of much of today's world.

The key aspects of this process of medievalization and the importance of the results it produced may be highlighted by contrasting the trajectory of Byzantium. The Eastern Roman Empire, as we have seen, actually managed not just a reconstruction of imperial unity, but to avoid its initial disappearance. An imperial state remained in charge through the entire period. That the "Byzantine" state was different from the old East Roman state is undeniable, but the coherence and continuity of the state, especially compared to its contemporaries, are notable. Remember, the "East Roman"/"Byzantine" distinction is one imposed in retrospect by historians: the people themselves were, to themselves, always Romans.[20] Byzantium then avoided the subsequent fragmentation and militarization that happened elsewhere. Indeed, between 850 and 1100, much of Byzantine society was gradually *demilitarized* as the thematic military system declined. With an imperial state remaining firmly in charge of the economy, Byzantium did not see the level of economic growth of its neighbors. And while Byzantine culture was, like its neighbors', pervasively religious, the structure of the religion remained caesaropapist – that is, under central imperial direction – with implications for the coherence of its religious identity in the provinces. Ultimately, the fate of the Byzantine Empire, as we shall see in the next chapter, was not as "successful" as its western, Islamic, and Chinese rivals.

Conclusions

This chapter argues that the wars of the early Middle Ages, from the mid–500s to the mid–800s, were the discourses through which the societies of the post-LALIA, post-"classical" world defined their social and economic structures and cultural identities. Those identities – militarily shaped and often deeply militarized, heavily religious in ways intimately connected to the structures of (military) power, often politically fragmented, and economically decentralized in ways that frequently produced (or at least coincided with) growing prosperity – constitute the fundamentals of "medieval" worlds. When connected to each other, these worlds combined to form a medieval world which, if not fully global, encompassed a substantial majority of humanity.

Each medieval world, of course, had its own values and identity. Thus, their connections to each other, which grew more intense as each developed in the early Middle Ages, were by no means unproblematic. The stories of warfare in the next period of the Middle Ages are about meetings, encounters, and the clashes that ensued. We turn to those stories in chapter 6.

[20] To return to a metaphor from ch. 2, late-career Elvis was still *Elvis*, with all the reputational prestige but also limitations that metaphor implies. Byzantium had Asia Minor; late-career Elvis had Las Vegas.

6

The High Middle Ages, 850–1300: Wars of Encounter and Connection

The High Middle Ages, 850–1300: An Introduction

The wars of the early Middle Ages, which we surveyed in chapter 5, were predominantly "internal" to the societies engaged in them. That is, they took place between polities, or military actors, who shared a cultural world, and the wars they engaged in were critical in defining what that world was, who was important and mattered in it, and what it meant: what its values were and who shaped those values. This is not to say that none of the wars of the early Middle Ages crossed cultural boundaries. Clearly, many did, as for example when Islamic armies invaded the Orthodox Christian world of Byzantium. The claim is rather that in terms of creating and defining a "medieval" as opposed to a "classical" world, the internal wars mattered more, overall.[1]

The result, by around the middle of the 800s (in the major, connected, Eurasian worlds; as always, the Americas and other separate worlds are harder to shoehorn into the Eurasian chronological scheme), was that these internal wars had progressed a long way toward forging fairly coherent, culturally self-conscious, and eco-

---

[1] This claim could be accused of displaying "survivor bias," especially in the case of the Persians, whose (independent) cultural realm disappeared. And the survival of the Byzantine world was certainly at stake in some of its wars with the caliphate, so external wars obviously still mattered. But in the case of the Persians – in ways very comparable to the fate of the Saxons when the Carolingian Empire incorporated them – they did not, in fact, "disappear," but entered into the "internal" wars of the world they had become part of.

nomically expanding worlds. They were often or even usually politically fragmented, but this was part of their richness and vitality, and
fragmentation did not prevent many of these worlds from expanding
around their frontiers.

Political and economic expansion, then, inevitably brought these
various early medieval worlds into increasing contact with each other.
Contact then led, as might be expected between worlds who were in
the process of aggressively defining themselves, to conflict, conflict
that was pursued militarily. The discourses about meaning and legitimacy that had shaped the early medieval world therefore tended to
join into a larger "discussion" about the shape of the greater medieval world and the identity of its members. That larger discourse or
discussion is the topic of this chapter. Its end result, I will argue, was
the creation of a connected, global medieval world, even if the "globalization" of that world would only be completed after it had to face
a new climate-and-disease challenge after 1300. One measure of the
depth and significance of the transformation brought about by the
early medieval wars of "medievalization" and their competitive combining in the high Middle Ages is the difference in how the medieval
world responded to climate challenge compared to the classical world
it replaced. But that will be the topic of chapter 7. For now, we will
examine the wars of the high Middle Ages through which the various
early medieval worlds forged a combined medieval world.

Warfare and Culture

The shift from internally focused warfare to warfare that increasingly
crossed cultural boundaries was not simply a change in the political
focus and goals of armed conflict. It carried serious implications for
how warfare was conducted. In short, enemies who shared a culture
treated each other differently from enemies who were divided by
culture. We need to understand the dynamics of warfare and cultural boundaries in order to understand the wars of this period. This
requires first that we define more precisely what we mean by *culture*.[2]

This is not an easy first step, given the multiple vectors along which
personal identity can be and historically has been constructed, and
is especially problematic for the Middle Ages, an era long before
nationalism in its various guises appeared to dominate the stage of

[2] This section is based on Morillo, "General Typology of Transcultural Wars."

(international) identity formation. Pragmatically, we can make a distinction between *Big Cultures* on the one hand and *subcultures*, component segments of Big Cultures, on the other. The former consist of broad areas sharing major cultural features ranging from basic ecological and subsistence patterns and material culture to broadly shared aspects of worldview – religion, philosophy, perhaps even cultures of war. The early Middle Ages, as we saw in chapter 5, witnessed the emergence of a number of medieval Big Cultures, in large part through what we will now call *intracultural* warfare, or war that did not cross cultural boundaries.

Subcultures will share some (perhaps many or most) of a Big Culture's features with other subcultures of the same Big Culture but differ from them in a few respects that (at least in some contexts) appear crucial to the members of the different subcultures. Subcultures may themselves be made up of their own subcultures, and the boundaries between subcultures cannot be conceived of as fixed. Rather, subcultures must be seen as malleable socio-cultural constructions whose boundaries shift constantly in response to political, ecological, and other circumstances, sometimes through slow processes of identity formation across large parts of the local population, but sometimes in response to active construction of local cultural identities by community leaders or would-be leaders. Big Cultures were undoubtedly less subject to conscious manipulation due to their scope; still, they too should be seen not as "natural" entities but as the sum across time and space of local culture formations interacting in ways that tended toward convergent acculturation; this, in technical terms, was the process involved in medievalization.

Thus, transcultural war was war in which perceptions of cultural difference influenced the conduct of war, altering it significantly from the patterns of intracultural war. This definition depends crucially on the notions of cultural identity expressed by the participants, whether in actions or words. It also implies that not all cultural differences mattered in generating transcultural warfare. Two societies might have different cultures in many respects, including language, ethnicity, and so forth, but if they shared a common diplomatic and military culture, warfare between them was not transcultural.

Given the divisions of cultures outlined above, there are two types of transcultural wars, in addition to the "base" category of intracultural wars. First, *intercultural wars*: wars between Big Cultures. Second, *subcultural wars*: wars between subcultures of the same Big Culture (or indeed between subcultures of a larger subculture). The impact of these types of war on the way wars were waged may be understood by comparison with the usual patterns of intracultural wars.

Intracultural Warfare

The opponents in intracultural wars understand each other and by definition share a common culture of war. Intracultural war therefore tends to demonstrate agreed-on conventions of conflict, limitations on war, and perhaps even ritual or ritualized elements of warfare. Not that the conventionality of intracultural war need make war less bloody; rather, participants' expectations of slaughter (of whom, by whom) or lack thereof are generally predictable in intracultural war. Thus, absent an external shock to the system or broader cultural or social shifts, intracultural warfare tends to be stable and to reinforce, through performance of expected roles, notions of cultural identity embedded in the culture of war. Shifting cultural or social contexts can move intracultural war toward subcultural war, however. Intracultural wars have usually been the assumed context of analysis of specific cultures of war.

Intercultural Warfare

In intercultural war, or war between members of different Big Cultures, by contrast, the lack of shared cultural assumptions about conflict means that at least one side simply does not understand the other, and often this is mutual. In such situations, tacit assumptions about the limitations or customary practices and patterns of war necessarily disappear, replaced by a pragmatic feeling-out process. Again, the lack of tacit limitations or rituals does not necessarily produce bloodier-than-usual conflict, though it can. Instead, pragmatic limitations, which in conditions of agrarian logistics and communication outlined in the first part of this book could be considerable, tend to assert themselves. As the parties to an intercultural conflict become acculturated to each other, either through warfare or through broader channels of cultural exchange, the conditions for intercultural war dissipate, and such conflict moves toward either intracultural war or, if an irresolvable cultural difference emerges from the process of acculturation, subcultural war. The sorts of misunderstandings and the issues around which acculturation occurs in intercultural conflicts can reveal some of the tacit assumptions underpinning a culture of war, assumptions otherwise hidden from view in accounts of intracultural wars.

Subcultural Warfare

Subcultural war sees not mutual comprehension or non-comprehension between the parties to conflict, but instead what might be called mutual anti-comprehension: the parties understand but demonize each other on the basis of the cultural rift that divides them, a rift usually interpreted as central to cosmic order at some level. In the context of an otherwise shared culture, subcultural warfare thus often produces a heightening of ritual elements deployed now in a competition for legitimacy or mythic power. On the other hand, heightened ritual is accompanied in subcultural warfare by an abandonment of limitations or customs that mitigate violence. Subcultural warfare thereby usually becomes the bloodiest form of warfare, as each side aims to annihilate the other in order to restore order to the universe. Should neither side be able to eliminate the other, subcultural war can result in long-term, low-level but destructive, irresolvable conflict, though mutual exhaustion or larger cultural shifts may produce a resolution into intracultural conflict. Subcultural warfare can thus expose very clearly the fundamental cultural assumptions underlying a wider culture of war in ways that may not be clear in either intracultural or intercultural war.

War as Discourse: Acculturation

This discussion of warfare that crossed cultural boundaries has referred to the process of "acculturation" that often occurs in warfare. This concept highlights the way in which warfare acted as a form of discourse – a discussion, albeit a violent one – between the combatants. War was, in other words, one of the ways in which groups that encountered each other exchanged information (about technologies, behaviors, values, and so forth) and therefore came to understand each other better, perhaps constructed new behaviors and values that they might share, and ultimately forged new connections between their worlds. It was this process – essentially the same process of world building that constituted what we called "medievalization" in chapter 5 – that was at work, on a much vaster scale and across much larger gulfs of cultural difference, in the formation of a more global and connected medieval world in the period surveyed in this chapter.

Given the scale of the world and the depth of the divisions in it, multiple cases of mutual acculturation certainly did not produce "one world," culturally or militarily, in this period. But this process did create connections that worked and endured even across the significant remaining divides. Nor was this process exclusively military. In conjunction with connections forged via warfare, the medieval world grew more connected by economic exchange – trade routes and the like, including economic exchanges such as slave taking that remained a significant part of war in many places – and the exchange of ideas through religious encounters and other intellectual means, such as mapping of trade routes by merchants and sailors or the spread of technology, including military technology.[3] The argument here is simply that warfare was one (significant) way that the medieval world became more closely tied together.

We may now turn to the military events of this process in the period 850–1300.

Events

The Middle Ages, as this book has defined them, began with the LALIA, a climate event that challenged the agricultural basis of the classical world, calling forth responses that reconstructed the world along "medieval" lines. The serious global cooling of the LALIA began to abate by the mid–600s, and by the mid–800s, at least in many parts of the northern hemisphere, the climate began to enter into a period that climate historians refer to as the Medieval Climate Anomaly. This brought warmer temperatures and thus longer, more favorable growing seasons. The Medieval Climate Anomaly, which lasted until about 1300, defines the central, or "high," portion of the Middle Ages, a period defined, therefore, more by opportunities than by challenges.

Expanding Worlds

In large part because of a more favorable climate, the worlds of the high Middle Ages tended to expand, starting at the basic level of agrarian economic production and consequently in terms of

---

[3] And to repeat a point from part I of this book, arguing for the *significance* of military encounters in this process is *not* an argument for the efficiency, and certainly not the humanity, of militarily influenced acculturation. The only thing military activity was best at, among the processes of acculturation, was getting people killed; and for those with military power, it usually proved a good way to maintain their (coercive, hierarchical) power throughout the process of acculturation, certainly a more controllable method than economic exchange (trade) provided.

population. This growth was especially strong at the opposite ends of medieval Eurasia, in China and western Europe. Though the rate of growth was not large enough to show up significantly on the logarithmically based chart of global population that we presented in chapter 2 (figure 4, p. 34), this population growth was plenty enough to drive territorial expansion, expressed both by growing internal settlement density and elimination of wild areas, and by external "colonial" expansion.

In China, just as the Song dynasty was getting established, new strains of rice developed in Champa (modern southern Vietnam) in the Mekong delta, strains that were more drought-resistant and ripened more quickly than established forms. This allowed two rice harvests a year in some regions and the expansion of rice cultivation to terraced hills. Food supplies (and the rice available for wine brewing!) expanded dramatically. Population growth followed, and Song economic activity, including iron production, ceramic and silk industries, and trade, both internal and external, also expanded. Song China was the world's richest society in this era. On the other hand, most of the economic and population boom took place south of the Yangtze. This intensified an emerging and potentially problematic characteristic of China: that its military and political center of gravity remained in the north, while its economic and demographic center of gravity was increasingly in the south.

Much of the Islamic world was already in warmer, drier regions of southwest Asia that benefited less from the Medieval Climate Anomaly than cooler, wetter areas such as northwestern Europe and parts of China. But the Islamic world still saw agriculturally led economic and demographic growth based on the trade connections and cultural unity of the vast Islamic world. Between 700 and 1200, new crops from newly connected parts of that world diffused everywhere within it, along with improvements in irrigation techniques, animal husbandry, and farming knowledge spread via Arab scientific networks. This set of developments has been called "the Arab Agricultural Revolution,"[4] which probably exaggerates its overall impact (note again our logarithmic graph of total human population), but it was nonetheless significant.

Finally, western Europe also saw dramatic improvements in its agricultural economy. Warmer weather certainly played a central role here, but so too did other factors. A new form of heavy plow

[4] Watson, *Agricultural Innovation.*

that could turn and aerate the heavy, rich soil of the region opened new lands to cropping, and competitive estate management among warrior and religious landholders whose income depended directly on the productivity of their holdings encouraged investments to open new settlements.

This last factor shows that economic expansion was not simply a product of a more favorable climate or improvements in agricultural "technology," broadly conceived. Instead, the socio-cultural structures constructed by the processes of medievalization described in the preceding chapter contributed in important ways. First, the internal warfare that followed political fragmentation generated larger classes of warriors, who in turn required support. While there is a certain "chicken and egg" problem with deciding whether an improving economy allowed this expansion or the expansion stimulated a search for more economic support, it does seem that there was an element of conscious investment by estate holders, including not just warriors but religious establishments founded in the medievalizing drive for religious legitimation of power. Second, the political fragmentation that characterized the emergence of the various medieval worlds probably played a direct role. Smaller, fragmented polities could not exercise the same level of regulatory and restrictive control over economic activity – could not, to put it more bluntly, constrain as effectively the activities and influence of merchants – as the classical empires had. This is clearest in the case of the differences between the economic policies of Han and early Tang China and those of the Song (and every subsequent dynasty). Simply reestablishing unity proved inadequate to bring burgeoning economic activity back under hierarchical control. But it also is visible in the Islamic world (especially when compared to classical Roman and Persian economic management), in western Europe, and in certain ways in the Indic world. In short, medievalization both drew on and encouraged economic growth that tended to outpace the (re)construction of central authority. And once again, only in Byzantium did the old classical pattern of an economy firmly under central state control remain.

In addition, the processes of medievalization contributed directly to the expansionism of medieval worlds. The militarization of medieval societies tended to create an outward push when the expanded warrior class redirected their energies (or had their energies redirected by renewed central authorities) against external foes. These externally directed energies often brought religious justifications along with them once internal legitimacy for wielders of armed force had been secured.

Set in a finite world, the expansion of the various medieval worlds brought them into closer, more regular contact with each other, contact that regularly expressed itself in military conflict, especially given the expanded role of warriors in these militarized societies. It is to the instances, cultural patterns, and consequences of these conflicts that we now turn.

The Paradigm: The Mongol Conquests

Interpreting the Mongols, whose conquests and empire creation are the most important events of the high Middle Ages, has been a fraught exercise for medieval historians for some time now. For much of the twentieth century, the Mongols, like most central Asian nomadic groups, went underreported and under-analyzed. Since they were not a "major civilization" – that is, a sedentary society that generated its own written records – they did not qualify for significance as it was traditionally measured. But with the rise of world history in the second half of the twentieth century, the fact that the Mongols had had an impact became harder to ignore, and by now their significance is generally undisputed.

But "significance" is a pretty neutral term, and more recently historians have tended to divide along a boundary that is not exactly "moral," but that has definite good/bad overtones. Basically, the Mongols are seen as significant for the vast amount of destruction they wrought (a sort of scientifically updated view of them as uncivilized barbarians, never mind the vast destructive swathes civilized peoples have cut through the fields of history); or they are reassessed as significant for forging a new, more highly connected world that formed the foundations of a globalized modernity (as well as for being just kinda cool).

At the risk of being the stereotypical historian for whom "the truth lies somewhere in between," the argument here is that the Mongols and their conquests and empire were, in fact, significant in both ways, and that the two views of them not only are not contradictory but are complementary. The Mongols represent, in ways that are major and significant, the often destructive processes of cultural encounter and clashing that characterized the high medieval world of expanding societies, on the one hand, and the ensuing processes of acculturation and connection that transcultural warfare as a form of discourse inevitably entailed, on the other. Indeed, it can be argued that the Mongols pursued both of these paths consciously and effectively.

The Mongols arose from the steppe world of central Asia and began, with the rise of Temujin, a local leader who overcame much adversity to become Chinggis Khan, one of the greatest conquerors in history, by continuing the reshaping of that world that had begun after the LALIA and the rise of the Turks.

The Steppe World

Temujin, whose father was murdered when Temujin was a boy, took lessons from the loyalty of the close allies and kin who aided his rise to leadership. This rise, including the uniting of the steppes under Mongol leadership, was probably the more difficult half of his career – he was already about forty years old when he achieved mastery of the steppe world – and the way he shaped that world provided most of the tools with which he created the largest land empire in history.

Temujin proved an able war leader and politician, so his initial rise to steppe leadership followed paths already well trodden by earlier nomadic leaders for building a large steppe coalition of tribes. The Uighurs, Qara Khitai, Alans, and Cumans were each in turn defeated and incorporated into the Mongol system. It was at this point, however, that Temujin diverged from established norms to forge better tools of conquest and rule. Schooled by betrayals and the uncertainty of tribal alliances of his youth and early career, by the time he achieved hegemony over the Mongols in 1204 he began to institute changes. In the *yasagh*, or law code, that he issued that year (already something of an innovation), he formalized systems that he had already started to implement. Instead of assembling a federation of extant tribes, Temujin, now holding the title Chinggis Khan, or universal ruler, broke up each new tribe that joined his growing coalition, creating new "tribes" under the leadership of his closest and most loyal supporters, who, if not actual relatives, became Temujin's fictive kin. He thus used the fluidity of steppe identity to his own advantage, rebuilding Mongol society in a way that focused all loyalty on him. He reinforced this with prohibitions against feuding, or private conflict and killing of Mongols by Mongols, appropriating the legitimate use of violence into his own hands.

Thus, while linguistic divisions remained between the Turkic western steppes and the Mongol-speaking eastern steppes, in terms of cultural identity Chinggis forged a more unified horse world under the banner of Mongol identity (figure 17).

Though the Mongols would prove to be religiously tolerant as conquerors, they worshiped the sky god Tengri, as was common on the

Figure 17 Mongol warrior. Mongol warriors, combining horsed mobility
with firepower and united under the leadership of Chinggis Khan, created
the largest contiguous land empire in history.
Source: Sergio Momo / Getty Images.

steppes, and used Tengri to legitimize world conquest. After all, they
could claim rulership of everything under the sky!

By unifying the horsed world of central Asia, Chinggis brought into
focus the cultural chasm between that nomadic, pastoralist world
and the sedentary, agrarian worlds that surrounded it. But the cross-
cultural conquests he then led in those worlds created connections
across the great divide and tied much of the world closer together.

East Asia

Northern China was the first target for Chinggis and served as a sort
of cultural bridge from the steppe to the sedentary world. This was
because, as we saw in chapter 5, northern China was ruled by barbarian kingdoms, the western Xia and the Jurchen Jin, whose rulers'
origins and military style were steppe-nomadic. But as hybrid realms,
they also drew on Chinese infantry and siege engineers. They fell
rapidly to Chinggis' armies – the Xia in 1227, the Jin in 1234 – and
were incorporated into the empire, bringing the Mongols infantry and
siege warfare capabilities that could not have been developed on the
steppes. These proved important starting in 1219–21, when Chinese
siege engineers assisted in the Mongol conquest of the Khwarezmian

Empire in southwest Asia. In east Asia, they played a role as early as 1235, when the Mongols first invaded Korea. The mountainous, heavily fortified peninsula was not an easy conquest; it was not until 1259 that the Goguryeo kingdom surrendered. In 1244 Tibet submitted to Mongol rule and Tibetan Buddhists assumed a significant role in the eastern half of the empire as spiritual advisors.

The conquest of north China and northeastern Asia was followed by a pause while the Mongols focused their attention westward. But as we recounted in chapter 1, in 1268 Chinggis Khan's grandson Kubilai, as Great Khan and thus the overall leader of the empire, which by then had split into four pieces, initiated the conquest of the Song dynasty in south China. This clash of titans, with the Mongols sending the largest invasion force they mustered for any campaign against the largest, richest military establishment in the world, ended with the surrender of the last Song emperor in 1276. Kubilai had declared the new Yuan dynasty during the Xiangyang campaign in order to attract Song defectors, and the Yuan after 1276 ruled all of China, made Korea a vassal state in 1270, and launched further invasions around the periphery of China into Japan, Vietnam, and southeast Asia.

In all of those peripheral campaigns, Mongol armies faced problems of geography that blunted the effectiveness of their usual campaigning style even more than the heavily fortified and wet geography of southern China had during the Xiangyang campaign. The difficulty of transporting troops across the sea to invade Japan was driven home by the fact that both invasions, in 1274 and 1281, were undone by storms wreaking havoc with the Mongol (essentially Song Chinese) fleet – the *kamikaze* (divine winds) that were central to the Japanese account of their triumph over the invaders. Vietnam and the rest of southeast Asia were even wetter and more humid than south China and were covered in heavy jungle in many areas; Vietnam (the Dai Viet kingdom) also benefited from advice and assistance provided by Song refugees. There was a certain irony to this, as Dai Viet had only thrown off Chinese rule in the region around 1000, and China, whether under Han or Mongol rule, remained the key threat to Dai Viet independence. What this demonstrates is that even more than geographic barriers, Mongol expansion crossed cultural boundaries in ways that cast the Mongols as outsiders and barbarians.

This negative view prevailed even when (as was true in most instances) the military superiority of the Mongols either was obvious or was demonstrated in the course of a particular campaign. One of the most famous examples of this was that in the first Mongol invasion of Japan, the Kamakura warriors who met the Mongols on the beaches opened the fighting in the style that was crucial to Kamakura internal warfare as an expression of cultural identity and performance of internal hierarchy: with loud proclamations by leading Kamakura warriors of their names, clan connections, and famous deeds, and with the ritual firing of "whistling arrows" to announce the commencement of hostilities. Reportedly, the Mongol response to these acts was to burst into gales of laughter. The cultural ("lifestyle") basis of Mongol military superiority – in other words, their steppe origins – is demonstrated by the fact that no one other than other steppe peoples could adopt Mongol ways of war. Steppe origins, given the cultural fluidity of steppe peoples, also account at least in part for the Mongol openness to adopting effective non-Mongol military techniques and technology, including siege weapons and the engineers who built and operated them.

On the other hand, "military superiority" was never a basis for a cultural identity that lent legitimacy to the rule of militarily superior conquerors. Might makes right, but might also engenders resistance, or at best only grudging cooperation, making for an inefficient tool of rule, especially in terms of economic extraction. The Mongols, who were in fact fairly pragmatic and wealth-obsessed, rapidly learned the tools of legitimation, which usually included adapting to the religious and philosophical traditions of rule already extant in the regions they conquered. (This was, again, a long-standing pattern among cultur-ally fluid steppe conquerors, who had been adopting the trappings of their sedentary victims for centuries. It is worth pointing again to the contrast between this steppe-nomadic pattern and the deeply entrenched tribal cultural identities that prevailed among the desert-nomadic Arabs, identities that shaped the course of the Islamic explo-sion and the evolution of Islamic identity in enduring ways *against* the influence of long-established Roman and Persian traditions.)

This cultural adaptability, which inevitably ran somewhat counter to the cultural foundations of steppe military superiority, helps explain the patterns of Mongol cultural evolution throughout their empire, and thus the apparently contradictory patterns of cultural clash and acculturation that characterize the Mongol impact. In east Asia, it perhaps shows most clearly in the tension within the Mongol world over Kubilai's declaration of a new Chinese dynasty, the Yuan. Kubilai saw the move as a necessary and beneficial part of allow-ing and making the most of the conquest of Song China. It pro-vided an ideological basis for the legitimacy of Mongol rule grounded in Chinese concepts of governance. It therefore enabled Kubilai to attract to his service not just defectors from the Song military (for whom "military superiority" was probably the most persuasive argument) but bureaucrats and officials from the Song administration, who were vital to the Mongol ability to benefit from their conquests economically.

The problem was that Sinicizing moves such as declaring a new dynasty alienated some of the most steppe-based and nomad-identified of the Mongols themselves. As a reminder, before he could launch the Xiangyang campaign, Kubilai had to defeat a rebellion by his younger brother Arigh Böke, who represented the "purist," steppe-oriented side of Mongol cultural interests. Such tensions would play out in every part of the vast Mongol Empire. What underlies the paradoxical Mongol impact is that even while they split culturally along the lines of their various conquests, the Mongols remained united by their sense of being Mongols and especially by their fidelity to Chinggisid legitimacy – that is, by their loyalty to the family ties that led them to greatness. This cultural paradox can be discerned in the history of the Mongols in the Islamic world, and can in certain ways be seen in the Mongol impact in Russia, where pre-Mongol cultural traditions were much less firmly established.

Islam

Mongol relations with the Islamic world started out on the wrong foot because the Khwarezm shah, suspicious of Mongol intentions, executed a Mongol trade caravan and subsequent ambassadors sent by Chinggis Khan. Chinggis was probably not looking for war, as he was engaged in the subjugation of the Jin in north China, but considered ambassadors sacrosanct. A rapid and devastating invasion followed in 1219. Chinese siege engineers enabled Mongol forces to take all of the major cities, including Bukhara, Samarkand, and Urgench; the civilian populations were massacred to make an example for potential resistance elsewhere. The shah ended up fleeing to an island in the Caspian Sea, where he died. The entire Khwarezmian Empire was under Mongol rule in two years, and a generation of Mongol rulers held Islam in particular contempt: during the invasion, Chinggis had the besiegers of Bukhara trample pages from the Koran under their horses' feet.[5] Still, Chinggis remained focused on north China; invasions of the western steppes, leading into Russia, the Caucasus, and eastern Europe, then occupied Mongol attention into the 1250s.

---

[5] Juvaini in Rossabi, *Mongols and Global History*, p. 76.

But under Chinggis' grandson Hülägü, the Mongols turned to southwest Asia and the core areas of the Abbasid caliphate. The key to their conquest was the siege of Baghdad in 1258, which lasted a mere twelve days, after which the conquerors massacred much of the population and, probably more significantly in the long run, did severe damage to the vast and vital irrigation systems that made central Mesopotamia a breadbasket.[6] Their hostility to Islam played out in their treatment of the caliph. Not wishing to shed the blood of a religious leader and echoing Chinggis' symbolic trampling of the Koran years before, the Mongols wrapped the caliph in a carpet and had their cavalry trample him to death. All of Iran, Iraq, and major parts of Anatolia came under Mongol rule. But they also suffered the first crack in their reputation for invincibility when a small Mongol detachment was defeated by the Mamluks of Egypt at the Battle of Ayn Jalut in 1260. This section of the empire, under Hülägü and his successors, came to be known as the Ilkhanate.

The cultural contradictions came to the fore in the Ilkhanate. Despite the initial hostility to Islam with which Mongol rule began, the Ilkhanate became the first section of the empire to convert to Islam, which became the dominant religion in the western half of the Mongol realm. And for centuries after the conquest, Chinggisid descent became a central tenet of legitimacy throughout much of the Muslim world.

The Caucasus, Russia, and Eastern Europe

The Mongols conquered the Caucasus region, including Armenia and Georgia, almost in passing as a side effect of their conquests in the Islamic world. The two main invasions happened in 1220–3 and sporadically after 1235. This was a largely Christian region under Muslim rule, so the inhabitants were not automatically disposed to hate the invaders. But the impact of the Mongols on the whole region, as well as on Islam – that an invasion of aliens had happened, such was the distance between the horsed world and the sedentary societies around it – is perfectly captured by the Armenian historian

---

[6] The siege of Baghdad also saw the first impact of the Mongol expansion on disease spread, a gigantic part of their lasting impact. It was during the siege that bubonic plague, carried by the conquerors out of central Asia, broke out among the besiegers and spread to the city, contributing to its rapid fall. Ninety years later, the same set of vectors launched the Black Death into far vaster areas of southwest Asia and western Europe. See Fancy and Green, "Plague and the Fall of Baghdad."

Grigor of Akanc in his *History of the Nation of Archers*. As we have seen before, he describes the Mongols as follows:

> They were terrible to look at and indescribable, with large heads like a buffalo's, narrow eyes like a fledgling's, a snub nose like a cat's, projecting snouts like a dog's, narrow loins like an ant's, short legs like a hog's, and by nature with no beards at all. With a lion's strength they have voices more shrill than an eagle. ... They give birth to children like snakes and eat like wolves. Death does not appear among them, for they survive for three hundred years. They do not eat bread at all.[7]

This expresses the cultural chasm that defines intercultural warfare and the initial impact of the coming of the Mongols in many areas. Notable is the dehumanization of the Mongols, in their many animalistic characteristics, mixed with a certain awe of their inhuman capabilities (living three hundred years). Yet Grigor himself illustrates the effects of his own acculturation later in his chronicle, when he describes Hülägü as a just ruler who only shed the blood of the wicked (albeit copiously) and gleefully relates how he "favored" Arabs by ordering them to eat pork on pain of death.[8]

Mongol invasions of Kievan Rus began in 1236, and after hugely destructive campaigns most Rus land was under Mongol rule by 1240. In addition to the expected cultural divisions between Mongols and Rus (religion, economic base, language, and so forth), Mongol operations in Russia show an interesting and specifically military cultural clash. The Rus were accustomed to withdrawing to their cities over the winter, as the freezing weather made campaigning too difficult. The Mongols, by contrast, preferred winter campaigning because the major rivers froze over, increasing the range and mobility of the virtually unopposed invaders.

From Russia the Mongols then launched exploratory raids into eastern Europe, dealing crushing defeats to armies of Poland, Bohemia, and Hungary and causing panic throughout the rest of Europe. But they withdrew from the gates of Venice and Vienna to attend a *kurultai* to choose the next Great Khan after the death of Chinggis' son Ögedei, and never returned.

They remained as rulers in Russia, however, and historians have argued about the impact of what some have called "the Mongol

---

[7] Grigor of Akanc, *History of the Nation of Archers*, in Rossabi, *Mongols in Global History*, pp. 25–6.

[8] Grigor in Rossabi, *Mongols in Global History*, p. 100.

yoke." The "yoke" version sees the period of Mongol rule as having
isolated Russia from contemporary developments in western Europe,
including the Renaissance and related economic development,
accounting for centuries of Russian underdevelopment and sowing
the seeds for growing hostility between Russia and western Europe.
This view, however, seriously underplays already extant divisions
between Catholic Europe and Orthodox Russia, represented by the
"Battle on the Ice" (or the Battle of Lake Peipus) between the forces
of the Republic of Novgorod, not yet under Mongol rule, and the
Crusading forces of the Livonian Order. This would be simply the
first of centuries of conflict with western European forces that always
threatened to become a fully subcultural clash.

The "yoke" version of history also underplays the constructive
role of Mongol rule in shaping the emergence of Muscovy as the
dominant power in former Kievan Rus territories, as well as the links
the Russians gained through Mongol imperial connections. It does
nationalistically emphasize the key role of Muscovy in throwing off
the Mongol yoke. Yet the Novgorod victory under Alexander Nevsky
was immortalized in Sergei Eisenstein's 1938 movie about Nevsky,
so there is plenty of anachronistic Russian nationalism to go round
on either side of this controversy.

Assessing the Mongol Legacy

The historiography of the Mongols in Russia represents a particularly
divisive piece of the larger historiographical question of the impact
of the Mongol conquests and empire. Did the Mongols have a negative, destructive impact on the world, or a positive, creative one? The
simple but unsatisfying answer is "Yes." The problem is that this is
not an argument that could easily be decided by adding more facts.
The basic facts on both sides are both known and acknowledged.

On the side of destruction, the Mongols clearly, in some places
more than others, did major damage of exactly the sort one would
expect from history's most formidable steppe-nomadic military
power rampaging through the sedentary worlds that surrounded it.
Massive numbers of people died: the tales of skulls being piled up
outside cities that resisted are too numerous and well attested to dis-
count. Longer-term impact on global demography stemmed from the
initial preferences of pastoralist conquerors. The destruction of the
irrigation systems of central Mesopotamia prevented Baghdad from
resuming its place as a center of the Islamic world for centuries; some
estimates say that the damage was not fully overcome until some time

in the nineteenth century. In other areas, including parts of north China, the Mongols turned productive farmland into pastureland, a policy already pursued on a far smaller scale by the Turks when they took over Byzantine Anatolia in the eleventh century. The scale of this impact can be seen in climate records: the rise of the Mongols coincides with a small and brief but statistically significant moment of global cooling in the midst of the Medieval Climate Anomaly.

On the other hand, it is true that the most destructive episodes in the Mongol record are concentrated in the first fifty years or so of their expansion – roughly 1210–60. What this suggests is what other records also tell us: that almost as rapidly as the Mongols brought destructive intercultural disaster, they adapted, learned how to make their depredations more sustainable in the mode of the sedentary rulers they displaced ... in short, they acculturated (and their subjects adapted to Mongol rule: the process went both ways); local, management-level intracultural conflict took precedence; and the positive effects of the Mongol Empire began to take hold.

The code word for this side of the Mongol impact has long been "Pax Mongolica": the Mongol Peace, a phrase modeled on and perhaps more justified than the original "Pax Romana," the Roman Peace. (As one contemporary critic of Rome put it, the Romans make a desert and call it peace.) And the Mongols did not just suppress conflict among their varied subjects, reserving legitimate use of force to themselves. They positively encouraged merchant activity, providing safety to trade caravans across the Silk Roads that crossed their realm (they knew the economic and information benefits merchant networks could bring); often removing institutional barriers and lowering tax and tariff costs (if only by removing many of the separate borders where they usually obtained), and generally lowering the cultural hostility to merchants and their activities within lands under their rule.

The result, after the initial period of destruction, was the flourishing of a trans-Eurasian world of trade and cultural exchange, including the exchange of human talent directly instigated by the Mongols' propensity for recruiting ("capturing" is in many cases more accurate, admittedly) human talent and deploying it to their best advantage around their realm. This included siege engineers, bureaucrats, philosophers, and religious sages, as well as craftsmen and other specialists in the production and distribution of things and ideas. Marco Polo, son of an Italian merchant family who served the Mongol administration in China for decades before returning home and publishing a wildly popular account of his travels, is the best-known (in the west) example of a broad category of people whose world was created by the Mongol conquests. Muslim counterweight trebuchets, Chinese gunpowder weaponry and ceramics, Islamic textiles, all are examples of cultures and technologies whose spread resulted from the Pax Mongolica.[9] All of which resulted in a more connected world, and indeed a world whose constituent parts *expected* to be more connected. The Mongols, therefore, stand as the fountainhead of the western-European-led explorations that aimed at reestablishing the trade connections disrupted by the fragmentation and fall of the Mongol empire. In other words, it is possible to credit the Mongols with initiating a period of globalization that still continues.

To complicate the question further, it was the expansion of the Mongol Empire, based on the movement of vast numbers of troops and animals across the deserts and steppes of the Silk Roads, that brought the Black Death, the second great bubonic plague pandemic, from the northern Himalayas to a vast swath of Eurasia. Visible as early as in the siege of Baghdad in 1258,[10] and certainly in China in the 1330s, then most famously in the eastern Mediterranean and western Europe from 1348, the connection of the Mongols to the Black Death is an aspect of this assessment that we will put off to the next chapter of this study.

Adding up a balance sheet of positive and negative effects from such a huge, messy ledger is an impossible task. But as we said at the beginning of this section, we need not decide which side was more important. Both were important, and both stand within the framework of analysis for this chapter: war and conflict in the period 850–1300 were about the medieval worlds that emerged in the previous era encountering each other, often in ways that led to armed conflicts, which in turn established "discourses" (often armed) through which connections were forged and the larger medieval world was welded together. The Mongols were a central part of that single, continuous history of war and armed conflict as a world-building process.

The Worlds of the Crusades

The other classic case of cross-cultural conflict that characterized the high Middle Ages, almost a second paradigm, is the Crusades. While

---

[9] See for example Allsen, *Commodity and Exchange.*
[10] See note 6 above in this chapter.

the Mongol case is unified around the Chinggisid-led explosion with the Mongols always at its core, the Crusades are a more multipolar, complicated set of encounters, confrontations, and resulting connections that brought at least three major sets of societies, each itself far from unified, into contact and conflict. The trigger was actually a late wave of the Turkic expansion out of central Asia, as the Seljuks first established themselves in the eleventh century as the dominant power in the Islamic world of southwest Asia, then, almost by accident, dealt the Byzantine Empire a catastrophic defeat at Manzikert in 1071. In the process of attempting to recover its heartland in Anatolia and reestablish itself, the empire sent a request to Catholic Christendom for mercenaries with which it could fight the Turks. The resulting Crusade surprised everyone, indicating how much the internal dynamics of each of the three societies involved had dominated developments up to that point. The Crusades were not, in other words, the culmination of a long "civilizational" struggle. But they would have serious implications for each of the societies involved: western Europe, Islam, and Byzantium. We will consider the Crusading era from the perspective of each in turn.

As with most of this book, this section will not present a detailed history of Crusading warfare. There are enough books on the Crusades to fill many library shelves, many of them excellent.[11] The purpose here is to interpret Crusading warfare in terms of the perspective of this section, seeing the wars of the Crusades within our larger global perspective as cross-cultural conflicts that played a role, perhaps counterintuitively, in connecting the medieval world more tightly together. The cross-cultural aspect of the Crusades may seem obvious, but can be overemphasized. Especially once western Crusader states had been set up in the wake of the First Crusade, a context was established in which wars worked along with other processes of interaction and exchange as a discourse through which the sides, at least sometimes, came to understand each other better; if the discourse was not terribly broad, it at least acted to create a shared military culture, seriously reducing the transcultural nature of Crusading warfare in southwest Asia, at least. But the echoes of the Crusades reverberated through subsequent centuries and arenas of conflict, right down through the present day.

---

[11] Among many others, see Smail, *Crusading Warfare*; France, *Victory in the East*; Marshal, *Warfare in the Latin East*; Tibble, *Crusader Armies*; and the extensive bibliographies in each of those works.

Western Europe

In 1095, Pope Urban II called upon the knighthood of western Europe to go to the aid of their fellow Christians in the Byzantine Empire. This was in response to Emperor Alexios Komnenos' plea for mercenaries as he was attempting to rebuild his empire after the disastrous Battle of Manzikert in 1071 had led to the Seljuk Turks taking much of the empire's heartland in Anatolia. Urban's preaching catalyzed a response that took a somewhat unexpected form: an armed pilgrimage. The pope, if the various accounts of his sermon at Claremont can be trusted, had in fact not suggested mercenary service. He had promised remission of sins for those headed to Jerusalem, and had urged Europe's warriors to turn their violent energies against an external infidel foe instead of continuing to fight with each other – an attempt to assert church leadership over this fractious society. The knights in turn probably heard a plea not to aid Byzantium but to reclaim Christ's patrimony, the Holy City – the sort of warfare for landed estates they had become accustomed to. In other words, the internal forces that had shaped this society in the previous era of wars of identity exploded outward, not exactly coherently led, but certainly enthusiastic for both religion and revenge.

Thus, in terms of the motivations of western European Crusaders, the function of Crusading warfare in building connections across the medieval world may seem obvious; indeed, one school of interpretation has tended to see the launching of the Crusades as part of an attempt by western Europeans to hook themselves into the lucrative trade networks of southwestern Asia that led eastward to the riches of India and China. But this is almost certainly wrong. Crusading was, for almost all western Crusaders, an expensive and money-losing proposition. Only a select few leaders, already rich, saw gains by being able to create new states under their control. Nor were the Crusades a stimulus to Italian merchant activity to the eastern Mediterranean, beyond activity directly related to transporting and supplying Crusaders and their states. The deeper development of trade routes that connected western Europe to the trade networks of Asia is more plausibly seen as an effect of the Pax Mongolica discussed in the previous section. The Crusades were, in other words, what they claimed to be: Holy Wars.

The First Crusade, though not at all what Alexios wanted, succeeded beyond expectations, capturing territories in Palestine from unprepared and divided Muslims. A set of Crusader states was formed around the central Kingdom of Jerusalem, and Crusading became a central, if sporadic, activity for Europeans for the next several centuries. Crusades were aimed, generally, at three different targets. First, against Muslims in the Levant (and secondarily in Iberia as a continuation of the Reconquista, the reconquest of the peninsula from Muslim rulers who had taken the region in the 700s as part of the Islamic explosion). Second, against pagans on the eastern frontiers of Europe, an effort led mostly by Germans against Slavs and other people in the Baltic and eastern European area. Third, against heretics within western Europe itself. Each set of these wars displayed different military and cultural characteristics.

The Holy Land In the Levant, the Crusaders faced Turkish foes who were certainly their equal, both militarily and culturally (indeed, the Muslim world held a low opinion of the rustic rubes from the west). But radically different styles of warfare posed problems for both sides that had both cultural and technological roots. European soldiers were generally more heavily armored, rode bigger horses, and emphasized melee combat, especially the battle-winning charge of their heavy cavalry. The Turks, with their roots in the horsed world of central Asia, were more lightly armored, rode smaller, faster horses, and emphasized the classic steppe combination of mobility and firepower. If the Europeans could bring the Turks to blows they could defeat them, but if the Turks could avoid close combat they could wear down and demoralize the westerners, especially as the Turks were better equipped for the heat and dryness of the Levant. Often, a tactical standoff resulted. European infantry, armed with crossbows, could hold Turkish light cavalry off far enough to neutralize Turkish archery and protect their own knightly cavalry, but the Turks could also avoid the deadly European heavy cavalry charge at that range (figure 18).

This led to cultural perceptions on both sides that disparaged the other. The Europeans disdained the Turks as cowardly and deceitful; the Turks in turn saw the Europeans as stupidly rash and unsophisticated, an opinion shared by Emperor Alexios' daughter Anna Komnena in her history of her father's reign. But in fact both sides adapted rapidly to the other's strengths and weaknesses, and most Crusading warfare after the First Crusade can most accurately be described as intracultural, at least in terms of military culture. Battle outcomes in this context often depended on generalship and the discipline to wait for the enemy to make a mistake, a discipline both sides regularly displayed; outcomes therefore also depended on the strategic imperatives around the battle.

Figure 18 Crusading warfare. Battles between mostly Turkish Islamic soldiers and western European knights were challenging for both sides. At the Battle of Ager Sanguinis (The Field of Blood) in 1119, depicted here, the Turks came out victorious.

Source: Wikimedia Commons.

Once they were established in the Holy Land, the Crusaders were almost always short on manpower. Strategically, they depended heavily, therefore, on two things. First, Crusading orders – essentially armed "monks" unique among the world's military[12] – provided a constant source of manpower, though one that fell outside the direct control of the political leaders of the Crusader states. The Knights Templar and the Knights Hospitaller emerged as the two main orders. The orders developed a Europe-wide organization of recruitment and landed economic support that fed supplies and men steadily into the Holy Land. Second, the states depended on a network of strong fortifications to defend their territories. Faced with a Muslim invasion, they would gather their castle garrisons, with

---

[12] Monastic orders with armed forces also developed in Japan in this period, but the monks and warriors constituted separate categories of personnel in those Buddhist organizations.

Crusading order support, into a field army that would shadow the invaders, limiting their ability to forage or settle in for a siege. This army would avoid a battle that, if it went badly, would open all the now nearly empty fortifications to an easy mop-up. When the harvest season approached, the Muslim armies, consisting of a core of slave professionals but mostly of warriors who held *iqta*, landholdings that supported them, would head home to manage their land. This was in large part a classic sedentary pattern of strategy, even if the initiative rested mostly with the Muslims except when a major Crusade reached the Holy Land. The limit on the Muslim ability to reconquer the Crusader states was mostly their own lack of unity. When the Kurdish leader Saladin defeated his rivals and united Egypt and Syria, the Crusader states came under much more consistent and threatening pressure. This resulted, in 1187, in Saladin forcing the army of the Kingdom of Jerusalem into a critical campaigning error. Saladin's resulting victory at the Battle of Hattin was followed by his rapid conquest of all of the Crusader territory but a coastal strip of fortifications that were saved by the Third Crusade and continuing naval support from Italy. As a notable sign of how intracultural warfare in the Holy Land had become by Saladin's time, Saladin was widely portrayed by his European foes as a "chivalrous" opponent.

Once the coastal strip was stabilized after 1187, the rump of the Crusader states survived for another century as a European outpost in the western Mediterranean. But to emphasize a point we made above, it was largely not through these territories that Europe connected to Asian trade networks and the Mongol Empire, which emerged too late, despite diplomatic missions to the khans, to provide the Europeans with an ally behind their Muslim foes.

Crusades continued to be launched into the Holy Land, variously aiming directly at Jerusalem, at Egypt as the strategic key to the region, and once, disastrously, misdirected at Constantinople, which we will consider further below. Except for that ill-fated Fourth Crusade, none had any lasting success; ironically, the multicultural Holy Roman Emperor Frederick II actually regained Jerusalem in 1229 via a negotiated treaty. His reward was a mixture of prestige and vilification (he was excommunicated on Crusade), illustrating the continuing importance of power and identity struggles internal to Europe for external relations.

Eastern Europe The fragmented, militarized society of western Europe, with its social structure, military organization, and cultural identity having been consolidated under Carolingian leadership, survived a period of external siege in the first century after 850. Invasions by Vikings from Scandinavia, Magyars from the Hungarian Plain, and Saracen naval raiders in the Mediterranean furthered the breakdown of unified imperial authority and stimulated the spread of small private castles. But economic activity began to revive at the same time, so towns multiplied and expanded while townsmen emerged as an unaccounted-for and somewhat uncontrolled element in terms of social structure (townsmen worked, but not as peasants), military organization (urban militias, often self-organized for self-defense against local lords, became a major source of crossbow- and spear-armed infantry beside the knightly cavalry), and cultural identity (towns and cities became the leading centers for church construction). The tense combination of knights, castles, and urban infantry, often as likely to oppose each other as to cooperate, generated a demand for land and labor, whether to support knightly estates or to feed urban commercial activity, and so in turn generated a steady force for expansion on the frontiers of western Europe.

In Crusading terms, the two key frontiers were Iberia (which we will consider further below as part of the Islamic world) and eastern Europe, where waves of German settlement ran into established pagan societies of Latvians, Lithuanians, Estonians, and other Baltic peoples. Crusading orders modeled on the ones in the Holy Land, such as the Teutonic Knights and the Livonian Order, led much of the military effort to convert and colonize this region. Though forced conversion was not technically allowed in canon law and these orders often operated with only sporadic papal approval, forced conversion of the area was the result (except for Lithuania, whose nobles led a voluntary conversion for their own benefit[13]). The mixed, decentralized economy of the region was also converted to sedentary estates. The whole process was thoroughly colonial[14] (more so even than in the Holy Land, where the agricultural and religious substructure of the Crusader states remained much more Islamic than Christian) and brought Latin Catholic Christianity up against the emerging Russian Orthodox world – we noted the great Battle on the Ice between the Livonian Order and Novgorod's Alexander Nevsky above.

Internal Crusades The consolidation of western European Christian identity in the period before 850 produced one final set of Crusades: those against heretics. Here's how that process unfolded.

---

[13] See ch. 3, p. 68 and note 11 there.
[14] The entire dynamic is well described in Bartlett, *Making of Europe*.

In the period from 540 to 850, the chief concern of church leaders was Christianizing the population of Europe (Christians were probably still a minority in 540). Since most of the converts would be pagans of one variety or another, and since syncretism provided an important path of conversion, dogmatic or theological consistency was not a primary concern, especially once the Franks adopted orthodox Nicene Christianity and defeated the Goths and Lombards, who were Arian (a non-Trinitarian heresy). But after 850, certainly by the later 900s when the most threatening non-Christian peoples such as the Vikings and Magyars had begun to convert, the dynamic shifted. Rivalries internal to Christian Europe came to the fore, and religious identity became implicated in these rivalries. The emergence during the church's rivalries with secular leaders of a legalistic style of theological controversy (many popes after 1050 were trained canon lawyers) actually then generated heresy by defining the circle of orthodox belief more precisely, drawing boundaries that excluded some previously tolerated beliefs. When Crusading was added to this mix after 1100, the result was internally directed Holy Wars.

The best-known (and paradigmatic) of these subcultural wars was the Albigensian Crusade of 1209–29.[15] This was called for by Pope Innocent III, the pinnacle of papal legalism, against the heretical Cathar population of southern France. Catharism, with centers in the city of Albi (hence the name of the Crusade) and the County of Toulouse, was a dualist heresy with origins ultimately in Persian Zoroastrianism. It formed part of the politically independent cultural complex of southern France, also known as Languedoc for the different French dialect/language spoken there.

The military details need not concern us beyond the fact that the conflict showed all the brutality of a subcultural conflict whose stakes were seen as cosmic. The slaughter of Cathar populations, sometimes described as a genocide, is summed up by the words attributed to the Abbot of Cîteaux when the forces under his moral leadership stormed Béziers in 1209. Told that the Crusaders could not distinguish Catholics from heretics, he is said to have replied, "Kill them all, God will know his own."

[15] For the Albigensian Crusade, see, among many others, Sumption, *Albigensian Crusade*; Pegg, *Most Holy War*; Marvin, *Occitan War*.

Islam

Western Europe's internal development between 540 and 850 produced a kind of warrior-led fragmentation that generated violent
energy outward as well as inward. Similarly, the Islamic world in
the territories of the Umayyad and Abbasid caliphates, from Iberia
to central Asia, also fragmented into pieces that spent much of
their energy fighting each other. The major Islamic power when the
Crusades began was the Seljuk Turk sultanate; the Seljuks, moving
from the steppes, had taken advantage of Islamic fragmentation to
create their own empire. (As we have noted, it was Seljuk victory
over Byzantium at the Battle of Manzikert in 1071 that had triggered
the Crusading movement in the first place.) But already by 1098
the Seljuk Empire, in typical Turkish fashion, had begun to frag-
ment. Islamic fragmentation, however, did not translate into external
expansion as European fragmentation did, except in India, a case we
will deal with separately below. Or it did not until after 1300, when
the Ottoman Turks rose to prominence.

One explanation for the difference is that while Europe's warrior
class led their society as landed aristocrats with a major share of
governance, particularly at the local level as (land)lords and officials,
Islam's warriors remained detached from their society as a whole in
several ways. First, the core of most Muslim state's military forces
was slave soldiers who were intentionally separated from the society,
by both slave status and foreignness, in order to make them loyal to
rulers whose legitimacy was questionable in Islamic terms defined by
the scholarly class of the *ulema*. Second, even the warriors who held
iqta, landed estates superficially similar to European fiefs, did not
have a strong connection to peasant society. The *iqta* were essentially
grants of revenue rights, not land management arrangements that
carried rights and responsibilities for local governance via courts or
entrepreneurial expansion of economic mechanisms such as mills and
markets. And many *iqta* holders were also, culturally, transplanted
Turks from the steppes, as foreign to their peasant populations as
the slave soldiers. Thus, Muslim warriors did not form an aristocracy
who could organize and synergize their society. Instead, they related
to their society in the way of colonial masters. One result was that
outside the military establishment, Islamic society had become thoroughly demilitarized and politically uninvolved, which suited their
military masters just fine.

The eruption of the Crusades into this society in 1098 had a whole
series of interesting and sometimes unexpected effects. Viewed in

terms of the initial state of Islamic fragmentation and rivalries, the success of the First Crusade becomes somewhat more explicable. An iconic example: the Crusade nearly foundered at the siege of Antioch in 1098. After nearly starving before the city, the Crusaders finally took it via suborning an Islamic defender into opening a set of gates. But then a major Turkish army arrived and threatened to besiege the starving Crusaders in turn in a city denuded of supplies. The Crusaders sallied out to attack. From the Christian perspective, God miraculously intervened and caused their desperate charge on starving horses to succeed. Islamic chronicles reveal the truth behind the miracle. Kerboga, the Turkic leader, had alienated most of his subordinates and allies, who decided en masse to abandon him at the first Christian attack.[16] The recovery of the Christian conquests over the next century depended crucially, as noted above, on Saladin's ability to eliminate his rivals and unite the Islamic world of southwest Asia.

The military success of the Crusaders also, however, made the Turks, the only Islamic warriors who could meet the westerners on something like even terms, yet more important to Islamic military organization, entrenching the pseudo-colonial character of Islamic societies in southwest Asia even more. The fact that the Crusaders could take over an Islamic peasant population without much trouble is in part explained by this.

More counterintuitively and perhaps in contradiction to this effect, the Crusaders brought with them an ideological tool that Islamic leaders such as Saladin adopted happily: the idea of Holy War. Islam, of course, had its own conception of Holy War: *jihad*, which literally means "struggle." But after the early days of the Islamic explosion, the civilianization of Islamic society meant that *jihad* had come to mean the individual, internal struggle to become a better Muslim as much as or more than it meant armed struggle against the infidel. The sudden and unexpected success of the First Crusade spawned a reaction. Successful Islamic leaders could now reclaim *jihad* against the Christians, not only as an offensive tool but even more by being able to claim the title "Defenders of the Faith," a valuable addition to their aura of legitimacy. Defending the faith emerged as an enduring basis for claims of legitimacy in the Islamic world, even after the Mongol conquests made Chinggisid descent a requirement.

Thus, in the end, the impact of the Crusades on the established Islamic polities of southwest Asia was simply to reinforce the

---

[16] See Peters, *First Crusade*, pp. 221–8 and 233–5.

pattern of developments that had emerged before 1100. In three other cases, however, the Crusading intervention had more significant effects.

Egypt Egypt was ruled by the Shi'a Fatimid caliphate when the First Crusade arrived and conquered its possessions in Palestine. Egyptian armies at this point were Arabic, not Turkish, and found themselves at a severe disadvantage against the Crusaders because they fought melee-oriented battles with lances and swords, but with much lighter equipment and horses than the Crusaders. But the Fatimids survived into the mid–1100s because Egypt was not a target of the Crusaders until the latter decided in the 1160s (not unreasonably) that taking Egypt was the strategic key to holding Jerusalem. A series of invasions in the 1160s weakened the Fatimids, who then fell to Saladin, who founded the Sunni Ayyubid dynasty and proved the Crusader strategic insight correct by using Egyptian resources to dominate Syria and then retake Palestine.

But Crusaders continued in the 1200s to see Egypt as a strategic key to retaking the Holy Land, and Crusades led by King Louis IX of France (St. Louis) failed miserably at conquering the Nile valley (Louis himself was captured during the Seventh Crusade in 1249 and had to be ransomed) but seriously destabilized the Ayyubid dynasty. In 1250, the death of the ruling sultan led to a takeover of the kingdom by the sultanate's elite slave soldiers, the Mamluks, who were of Turkish and other steppe-nomadic origins.

Though the Mamluks had cultivated a pseudo-noble status for their corps, despite their technically servile standing, the legitimacy of rule by a group with servile origins (as well as the almost required ethnic division from the mass of the population) put the Mamluks on the usual tenuous footing occupied by many Islamic ruling groups. But Crusading and Mongol history then intersected. In 1260, as we noted above, the Mamluks, under their Sultan Baybars, defeated a small Mongol expeditionary force at Ayn Jalut in Syria, a victory whose cultural impact was all out of proportion to the actual size and immediate military effect of the battle, but which was reinforced by Mamluk victory at the much larger Battle of Homs in 1281 over the Ilkhanid branch of the Mongols. In addition to dealing the first blow to the image of Mongol invincibility, the Mamluk successes against the destroyers of Baghdad gave the Mamluk sultanate the aura of being Defenders of the Faith. This reputation faded over time, but the Mamluks survived as rulers of Egypt until they were conquered by the Ottomans in 1517.

The Ottomans It was the Ottoman Turks, a group descending from a local leader named Osman (again, terms such as "Seljuk" and "Ottoman" are markers of political identity, not ethnicity), who emerged as the ultimate "winners" of the Crusading and Mongol eras in southwest Asia. Taking advantage of the power vacuum created by the fragmentation of the Seljuks, the chaos created by Mongol incursions, and the decline of Byzantium (below), the Ottomans gradually built up a base first in Anatolia, then also in southeastern Europe, and in the 1400s created one of the largest and most dynamic empires in the world. In effect, they were the winners of the "Defenders of the Faith" competition that the Crusades had initiated. But the Ottomans' story is for the next chapter.

Iberia The final arena of the Islamic world affected by Crusading and related expansion by western Europeans is Iberia. The story here is interesting for the interplay of war, state building, and cultural frameworks of development.[17] Muslim rule in Iberia dated back to the Ummayad conquest of Visigothic Spain in 711, with only a few small Christian kingdoms in the far north of the peninsula left unconquered. But they resisted further offensives by the Cordoban caliphate, and by the 780s, when Charlemagne intervened south of the Pyrenees, Muslim and Christian Iberia settled into an uneasy coexistence. The pattern of conflict between 800 and the final Christian conquest of Granada in 1492 demonstrates how fundamental cultural values can shape armed conflict. The unified caliphate of Cordoba on paper held all the advantages of wealth, manpower, and organization over its small and divided opponents. Yet the frontier between Christians and Muslims moved steadily southward over the centuries, interrupted only sporadically by incursions of new Muslim powers based in north Africa. Why?

The social and cultural structures each society had constructed in the early Middle Ages hold much of the answer. The Christian society had evolved around a central cultural value based on the primacy of law going back to Roman (and to some extent Christian) origins. Militarized law, but law nonetheless, which carried an implicit recognition of the legitimacy of the state. One result was that when Christian states called upon their subjects for the money and manpower necessary to prosecute war, the society could negotiate such demands from a foundation of legal rights, which produced

---

[17] This analysis draws on Morillo, "Sword of Justice." See also Powers, *Society Organized for War.*

agreements whereby the society contributed in exchange for further rights. Such negotiations ended up building up the legal mechanisms of the state, so that, in the words of Charles Tilly, "states made war and war made states." In this context, private groups found it profitable to carry on frontier warfare at a low level constantly, and the Christian states steadily grew in their functionality.

By contrast, the evolution of Islamic society had produced a central cultural value that did not recognize the legitimacy of state power. The result was that when the caliphate, or its various successor states, demanded money and manpower from its subjects to prosecute a war, there was no basis for negotiation. Either the society refused, leaving the state to depend on its central resources, or if the state pressed, the population of the state's cities simply avoided the request, often by leaving. In other words, over the long run the equation for Islamic states was "states made war, and war unmade states." Hence the slow but steady movement in favor of the Christians. This was interrupted only when the Almoravids and then the Almohads, Islamic powers that arose outside Iberia under the banner of renewing "true Islam" (another pattern that originated in the early Middle Ages), invaded to overthrow the "decadent" existing power and in the process pushed the frontiers back temporarily. After a Christian coalition created in part by Innocent III calling a crusade against the advancing Almohads defeated the Muslims at the Battle of Las Navas de Tolosa in 1212, however, no further revivals emerged. By 1252 only the Kingdom of Granada survived under Muslim rule, and it fell to the Catholic Monarchs, Ferdinand and Isabella, in 1492.

Byzantium

Before the Crusades By 850, the rump of the Eastern Roman Empire, by then transformed enough that historians refer to it as the Byzantine Empire, had survived the explosive expansion of Islam and repeated invasions by the powerful caliphate. The caliphate, by that point under the Abbasids, then fragmented, taking the pressure off Byzantium. For a century after 850, in fact, the empire managed to go slowly onto the offensive against the fragmented and fractious statelets along its border with Islam in Asia Minor and northern Palestine. Moving from defense to offense had a number of important consequences and revealed the nature and limits of the transformation that had turned Rome into Byzantium.

That transformation was not, as we saw in chapter 5, like the ones that had "medievalized" Latin Christendom, Islam, and even

China, India, and in some ways the steppe world. Byzantium never fragmented politically, but remained an empire tied together administratively by the civil aristocrats who ran its bureaucracy from the capitol at Constantinople. Its government therefore remained in firm control of both social and economic activity, approaching economic regulation as an aspect of its "Fortress Byzantium" mentality. And this mentality was accompanied by the development of a cultural self-identity as a Chosen People whose role was to defend the Christianity centered at Constantinople.

Expansion brought this entire construct into question.[18] Offensive campaigns accelerated the move from *thematic* armies to *tagmatic* ones. Counterintuitively, it also raised the status and potential influence of the aristocratic military families of the regions outside the capitol at Constantinople, who provided the officer class for the army and who benefited from the new lands taken from the Muslims. The rise of the provincial military aristocracy posed a threat to the dominance of the central civil aristocracy. Expansion even brought the centrality of Constantinople into contention, especially when old regional centers such as Antioch, which had pre-Constantinopolitan prestige (and were associated with alternative/heretical versions of Christianity such as Monophysitism), came back under Byzantine rule. All of this set up a growing conflict between the (civil, Constantinople-centric) conception of being Byzantine as being a Chosen People tied to a particular land, and a (military, provincial) conception of Byzantine identity as a true continuation of *Romanitas*, of an older Roman-ness that had pretensions to universalism and far more inclusiveness than a Chosen People construct could accommodate.

By 950, this clash was moving the empire toward civil war, especially when representatives of the military aristocratic families gained the throne in the persons of first Nikephoros Phokas and then John Tzimiskes. The conflict came to a head during the reign of Basil II, who came to the throne in 960 at the age of two – he was junior emperor to the two generals and became senior emperor in 976 when Tzimiskes died. He fought civil wars against the military families until emerging victorious in 989. And though he has a deserved reputation for military success and glory, he settled the deeper conflict in favor of the civil aristocracy and the capitol. He rounded off and in effect closed Byzantine expansion to the south and east, redirecting (and thus controlling) the military aristocracy toward wars against the

---

[18] For this section, see Whittow, *Making of Orthodox Byzantium*.

Bulgars in the Balkan Peninsula. His victories there earned him the nickname "the Bulgar Slayer" and expanded the empire's frontier to the Danube without threatening Byzantine identity, since the region lacked a non-Constantinopolitan tradition. He married a daughter to the ruler of Kiev, leading to the Christianization of Russia. Using Rus (originally Viking) soldiers, he created a tagmatic unit known as the Varangian Guard.[19] By the time he died in 1025, the empire was at its largest extent in centuries, its treasury was full, and its prestige was at an all-time high.

But he was followed by a series of weak successors, and the structural toll of the internal conflict between civil and military interests turned out to be dire. The thematic army having already withered away, the tagmatic forces were steadily disbanded as a threat to the throne. The price of Byzantium's successful maintenance of centralized rule was that when the center was weak, the entire structure was weak. In 1071 the edifice met disaster. Norman invaders in Italy defeated a Byzantine army at Bari.[20] Even more catastrophically, the Seljuk Turks defeated a treachery-ridden Byzantine army at Manzikert in Anatolian Asia Minor and then overran the heart of the empire. This set the Crusading era in motion.

Byzantium and the Crusades The reconstruction of the empire after Manzikert, under the Komnenos dynasty, saw many elements of what we might call a belated medievalization of the Byzantine world. Military aristocrats came to the fore, starting with the ruling house. Militarization of society followed, with land-based military service providing military manpower beside the extensive use of foreign mercenaries. And the economy slipped out of central control, especially as Venetians took over much of the empire's lucrative foreign trade. But it was still a far smaller, weaker empire that had to deal with the Crusades and their consequences.

Foremost among these was the increasingly hostile relationship between eastern and western Christianity. The basic misunderstanding about the purpose of the Crusade (or from the Byzantine perspective, what Emperor Alexios had asked for, a dispute that came down to the question of agency: who was in charge of this thing?) gener-

---

[19] A later captain of the Varangian Guard, the Norwegian Harald Hardrada, would die invading England in 1066, falling to Harold Godwinson before the latter fell to William the Conqueror.

[20] The Byzantine force included many Anglo-Saxon refugees from the events of 1066 in England who had joined the Varangian guard.

ated further misunderstandings and suspicions in its course, especially when the Crusade took Antioch, which the Byzantines thought should go to them as their *recently* previous territory. Although the mid–1100s emperor Manuel Komnenos worked hard to rebuild the Greek relationship with the westerners, it fell apart again after his death and culminated disastrously in the Fourth Crusade.

In brief, the leaders of a prospective Crusade contracted with Venice for naval transport to Palestine. But far fewer Crusaders showed up than anticipated, leaving the Crusaders owing the Venetians more money than they could raise. The Venetians agreed to have the debt pay for Crusader help in taking the Byzantine port city of Thessalonika for Venice, which controlled Byzantine trade. When this dynamic intersected with a Byzantine succession dispute refracted through the lens of east–west hostility, the Crusade ended up at Constantinople. The Crusaders assaulted and took the city with some inside help, looted it mercilessly (enriching Venice in the process), and turned it into the capital of a Latin kingdom. The outlying regions of the empire survived and the Greeks retook the city in 1260, but the empire never recovered any real power or wealth. It survived as an echo of a memory until the Ottomans finally took the city in 1453.

It is perhaps a bit of an interpretive stretch to see the decline and fall of Byzantium from 1071 onwards as a result of the fact that East Rome never underwent the militarily led process of medievalization that we have defined and described here. But it is striking that of all the major societies that emerged from the transformations of the LALIA in the period 540–850, East Rome/Byzantium left the smallest, shallowest direct imprint on the post-medieval world. It survived most clearly only in the foreign territory of Moscow, the Third Rome, under the rule of the caesars (czars). The cultural confrontations and military competition of the Crusades proved fatal to the empire itself, and the Ottomans took over the growing network connections that tied formerly Byzantine territory to the wider medieval world. Late-career Elvis had left the building.

Islam in India

Our final example of the encounter of cultural worlds is the incursion of Islam into the Indic world. This developed over two chronological phases. From roughly 800 to 1100, Islamic forces raided into northwest and north-central India; after 1100, the raids increasingly turned to conquest, and by 1200 a major Islamic polity, the Delhi sultanate, dominated the northern half of the subcontinent.

On the surface, the encounter between the Islamic world and the Hindu states of India looks like a classic case of transcultural warfare, even more than the clash of Muslims and Christians in the early Crusades. After all, Christianity and Islam were cousins religiously: both were Abrahamic, religions "of the Book" who recognized each other's traditions. Hinduism, by contrast, presented the Muslims with what appeared to be a polytheistic, idolatrous religion that was anathema to everything central to Islam, virtually inviting an emphasis on *jihad*, or intercultural Holy War. The encounter in the subcontinent was, indeed, more culturally divisive than that in Palestine, but not for the apparent reason.

As a reminder, what mattered in transcultural warfare was differences in *military* culture – other cultural differences might have no appreciable effect on how opponents conducted warfare. In the Crusades, the various participants brought different religious motives and military cultures to the arena, but acculturated to each other rapidly in military terms, with the result that much Crusading warfare was essentially intracultural. The same was even more true in Iberia, where structural-political culture differences led to different political outcomes despite a culture of war that was shared across the peninsula even more than in Palestine. By contrast, in the cultural encounter in India it does not appear that religious hostility or ideas of *jihad* motivated much of the conflict.[21] Instead, particularly in the period dominated by raiding, economic motives – plunder – came to the fore. India presented raiders with rich collections of precious metals, often at undefended centers such as Buddhist monasteries and Hindu temples. While economic raiding lasted as the primary form of interaction between the two cultures, this raised hardly any real cultural issues.

When the Muslim polities neighboring India turned toward conquest more than raiding, it was largely to make the collection of wealth more permanent and efficient, and so still didn't raise deep cultural conflicts. But warfare for conquest exposed the real differences in military culture between Islamic and Hindu rulers, and the intercultural warfare that resulted significantly favored the Muslims. As we explained in chapter 5, Hindu warfare before 850 had been about "symbolic" conquests, performance of identity, and shifting alliances. The Muslims who entered into this "game" did not play by

[21] Wagoner, "India," esp. pp. 484–5.

the rules. Their victories were deadly for the losers, who were dispossessed of their realms at the least and often killed. And the Muslim "players" won consistently because of their central Asian slave soldiers. India was bad territory for breeding horses, so Indian cavalry had small, undernourished horses, primitive saddles, and minimal training. The Turkic Muslim cavalry dominated, and Muslim armies were generally more professionally trained and experienced than their Hindu foes. The Muslims also imported improved fortification designs and more powerful siege machinery, including the counterweight trebuchet, from southwest Asia. Finally, the Indian culture of shifting alliances meant that Hindu princes rarely if ever allied with each other to oppose Muslim invaders, each looking instead to play for his own advantage. This was also another indication that the wars were not motivated by hostile "ideologies."

The Muslim move toward conquest resulted in the foundation in 1206 of the Delhi sultanate, whose first dynasty was, as in Mamluk Egypt, of slave-soldier origins. The sultanate, which ruled much of northern India, was a culmination of many of the dynamics of raid and cultural incomprehension that led up to it. The result was not happy.[22] It imposed a whole layer of Muslim regional rulers above Hindu society, effectively institutionalizing cultural conflict through the intentional destruction of Hindu temples and centers of learning, imposing a form of colonial rule familiar to other Muslim polities. It systematized economic exploitation by imposing ruinous tax rates on peasant production. And it rapidly fragmented, in typical Turkish fashion, into effectively independent statelets subject to very little central control, thus offering no improvement in terms of endemic local warfare. But in terms of creating a more connected world, Delhi did connect north India to the wider Islamic and central Asian worlds, initiating a synthesis of Persian and Indian languages, art, and architecture that would flower under the later Mughal Empire. The sultanate may not have been a *good* part of the connected medieval world, but it was a part of it.

Conclusions

The High Middle Ages, from the mid–800s to the early 1300s, saw the internal discourses that had formed the various early medieval

[22] Jackson, *Delhi Sultanate*, is the best overview.

worlds expand and increasingly meet each other, coming into what we can see as sets of argumentative discourses that crossed cultural boundaries rather than creating them. Still, arguing proved to be a way for the various early medieval worlds to learn about each other, connect, and thus forge a more unified medieval world. As in the early period, warfare and conflict were central to this process. Military conflict remained closely connected to religion – religious differences were usually the most visible marker of cultural boundaries in this period, so that conflict, both external and internal (as with the Albigensian Crusade or various Sunni–Shi'a wars), was usually seen in terms of religion even if religious difference was not the ultimate motivation for conflict.

But the connections formed across this world mattered as much or more than its visible divisions. From this perspective, warfare became increasingly tied to growing networks of economic exchange. The friendly global climate provided by the Medieval Climate Anomaly stimulated this growth at its agrarian base, and merchants extended it steadily. Sometimes, warfare contributed directly, as when the Pax Mongolica stimulated cross-Eurasian trade and cultural exchange, or on a different scale when landholding warriors encouraged agricultural expansion and the founding of markets to enhance their own income. Sometimes, it followed economic growth; Muslim raiding into India can be seen in this light.

All of which means that around 1300, when the Medieval Climate Anomaly began to cool into a new Little Ice Age – not a Late Antique one but a longer, even more global cold period that would last until well past 1800, a cooling once again accompanied as it began by a massive plague pandemic – it was a more connected and thus resilient medieval world that faced a new environmental challenge. War and conflict would once more be central to how the various pieces of the connected medieval world responded to this challenge. We turn to those wars in the next chapter.

7
The Late Middle Ages, 1300–1500? Or 1800? Wars for New Worlds

The Late Middle Ages: An Introduction

On the surface, the conditions that brought the Middle Ages into being – the suddenly colder climate event called the Late Antique Little Ice Age, or LALIA, and the Eurasian plague pandemic that accompanied the onset of the LALIA – recurred to bring the Middle Ages to an end. The warm period known as the Medieval Climate Anomaly, which had enabled and even encouraged economic growth starting at the level of agricultural production in the period 850–1300, came to an end. The first signs of this shift in western Europe came in the summers of 1315 and 1316. The sun didn't shine, it rained incessantly on the cold land, and crops failed. Famine followed, if only regionally. Rather than this being a temporary "weather event," the global climate began to descend into what has long been known as the Little Ice Age. (The LALIA was named after its better-known successor.) Thirty-three years later, in 1348, the second plague pandemic erupted into western Europe. Within three years, as many as one third of the western European population, or about 20 million people, was dead. The toll was similar in China, the Islamic world, and central Asia.

By most measurements, the recurrence of climate change and pandemics was worse the second time around. The Little Ice Age certainly lasted longer than the Late Antique one did: the LALIA cooled the world for just about a century, whereas the cooling that set in around 1300 lasted well into the nineteenth century. And the Little Ice Age was colder at its depths: this was the period during which Shakespeare's Thames regularly froze over. In addition, the

second plague pandemic, known best in European history as the
Black Death, killed far more people, probably a higher proportion
of the population of the world in its time, and was more widespread
than the earlier outbreak of bubonic plague in the 500s, and would
recur regularly, at least in Europe, for centuries. The last outbreak of
plague in London happened in 1665; the last in Europe in Marseille
in 1720–2.

And yet, their combined impact was arguably less dramatic than
the sixth-century impacts had been. The relative importance of
change versus continuity in historians' views of the past is a matter of
constant argument, which is why periodization, the dividing up of the
past into periods marked (theoretically) by more significant moments
of change against a background of continuity, is also a matter of constant argument. Comparing the two cold and plague impacts runs
headlong into this argument.

The cold and plague of the 500s, as we argued in chapter 5,
brought an end to the "classical" world of vast empires and glitter-
ing cultural glory. The empires broke into pieces, their economies
and cultures were transformed, through a process dominated by the
discourses of armed conflict and religious interpretation. Classical
worlds were "medievalized": fragmented, yes, and the results thus
often less impressive, on the surface, than their classical ancestors
with their imperial reach. But economically richer, politically and
culturally more deeply rooted in their societies, and consequently
more resilient, surviving in a more occupied and competitive world.

The argument of this chapter is that the cold and disease that
struck the world in the 1300s had one of two effects. Either, first,
they transformed the medieval world in a way that brought that
world to an end by 1500 or so, in a manner comparable to the transformation after the 500s. This is the standard argument about the
period and is explained thoroughly and well, especially for western
Europe, by Bruce Campbell in his book *The Great Transition.*[1] Or,
second, cold and plague challenged the medieval world in ways that
were certainly significant, but posed a challenge that the medieval
world met successfully using the tools and structures that had built
(and had been built during) the medieval world. In this second
view, building on some of the arguments made in chapter 2 about

---

[1] For the purposes of my argument, the choice of the word "transition" – rather
than, say, "transformation" – in Campbell's title is interesting, as it implies (in my
reading) a change that still contained significant levels of continuity.

periodization,[2] the Middle Ages continued on through the Little Ice Age, as the medieval worlds built in the period 850–1300 continued to expand (truly globally after 1492), encounter (each other and new worlds, including the New World of the Americas), and engage in armed conflict (still according to the Common Rules laid out in part I of this book). And thus, in this view, what brought "the Middle Ages" to an end was, to paraphrase Campbell, the Great Transformation: the Industrial Revolution and its globalizing empire of capital and industry.

In an attempt to have it both ways, this chapter will explore the wars of 1300–1500 (thus recognizing the standard periodization) and the stories they tell about adaptation, about maintaining, defending, and expanding the worlds built in the previous period in the face of new challenges. In doing so, it forms the third "scenarios" chapter of part II of this book: the cultural interpretation of war and conflict in the Middle Ages. But it will do so with an eye always on the question of whether, and if so when, the medieval constructions built earlier came to an end. If they did not (until the age of Steam and Speed), then the Middle Ages can rightfully swallow and digest the chimeric "early modern" monstrosity, banishing it from historiography to the refuse pile of outdated concepts.

Themes

Like the societies that existed in 540, the societies of 1300 faced crises of major proportions. But whereas the crises of the sixth century broke classical societies apart and prompted wars of reconstruction that entailed the creation of new cultural identities, the crises of the 1300s challenged but did not break the more resilient societies of the fourteenth century. The wars of the late Middle Ages were therefore partly wars of reconstruction, but instead of the creation of new cultural identities, they tended to reaffirm the identities created centuries earlier.

Shock and Change: Mongols, Cold, and Plague

The climate change and pandemics that began in the 1300s were not alone in shocking the major societies of Eurasia, at least. The

---

[2] See above, ch. 2, "The Making of the 'Middle Ages'."

eruption of the Mongols out of the steppe world, discussed in the previous chapter as the paradigmatic case of wars of expansion and encounter, came as a vastly destructive surprise to almost all of the Eurasian world, including (in Egypt) parts of Africa and certainly including areas such as western Europe that did not even suffer any occupation by (and only minimal direct contact with) the whirlwind of nomadic conquest.

And while the Mongols themselves ended up suffering from the effects of climate change and pandemics – their rule over China fell apart essentially because of these factors, for instance – their empire also contributed to the combination of crises, not just directly through their conquests, but by creating the connections of trade and travel that spread the bubonic plague to so many areas from the regions of central Asia where it was endemic and touched some of the routes of the Silk Road. Indeed, as we have seen, one of the earliest outbreaks of plague carried by Mongol armies and their followers seems to have been at the siege of Baghdad in 1258.

Dealing with Shock and Change

Two themes stand out in the reactions of the world's societies to the combined crises of Mongols, plague, and changing climate. First, the well-established cultures of the societies facing these challenges, especially the differing frame values each society had developed over the course of the early and high Middle Ages, significantly shaped their responses – far more, in most cases, than the crises altered or reshaped those cultural values. Second, the role of armed conflict in societies' responses to crisis remained central. But one aspect of armed conflict, namely the development and application of technical knowledge to further the goals of competition and conflict, assumed new importance in a number of ways.

One interesting result of the cultural variety that characterized the world that met this period of challenge is that, unlike the Arab explosion for the early medieval wars of (re)construction and identity and the Mongol conquests (and secondarily the Crusades) for the high medieval wars of encounter and cross-cultural conflict, there is no easy paradigmatic case for the variety of late medieval wars.

Culture: Framing Responses

One of the cultural tendencies that characterizes agrarian societies is that they usually saw the world in terms of an idealized past when things were better (and, in the Biblical case, when people lived far longer) – a Golden Age view of history. What counted as the Golden Age varied from society to society: sometimes a mythical distant past (as with the Greek Golden Age), sometimes a more historically based period, as with the time of the Prophet in Islam or the early model rulers of Confucian ideology. The constant corollary of this Golden Ageism was that agrarian societies saw improvement, or adaptation to new problems, in terms of a return to past ways and values – what Confucianism called a "return to virtue." Reactions across Eurasia to the catastrophes of the Mongol conquests and the Black Death[3] usually exhibited some version of this cultural construct. This is not to say that such societies could not or did not innovate. Innovation and inventiveness are spread pretty evenly across human groups, with the number of people networked together often constituting the key to the emergence and spread of innovation. But these societies tended to frame innovation as something like "rediscovery of an old truth," not as innovation per se. In modern advertising terms, "Old and Tested" was good, "New and Improved" was suspect. This cultural framing shaped military reactions to the challenges of the age.

The Role of Armed Conflict: Knowledge and Application

Again, "Golden Age" framing does not mean that innovation did not happen in medieval societies. Indeed, advancements in knowledge and technology that were militarily applicable characterize the late Middle Ages, as the many connections forged by the encounters and conflicts of the previous era allowed the accumulation, spread, and improvement of useful knowledge across Eurasia, in particular. Two examples stand out, one "military adjacent," one specifically military and connected in important ways to the first.

The first was that the growing network connections of the high Middle Ages fostered a set of maritime technologies grounded in trade but with many military applications. Shipbuilding techniques advanced dramatically with the synthesis of various local traditions.

---

[3] Climate change elicited no systematic or even conscious reaction from medieval societies: it happened too slowly and imperceptibly except for sudden crises, which appeared simply as "weather events," not as part of deep systemic change. The environmental background was taken as constant. Even in our modern scientific cultures, climate change has had to reach the proportions of a looming and immediate catastrophe to gain widespread (but sadly not universal!) acceptance in popular consciousness.

In China, northern and southern shipbuilding traditions merged in the form of the huge treasure ships of the beginning of the 1400s; the eunuch admiral Zheng He led fleets of these ships on trade-and-diplomacy missions to India, Persia, and as far as the east coast of Africa. In Europe, North Sea and Baltic shipbuilding techniques began to merge with Mediterranean ones, affecting hull construction and sail plans in ways that by the late 1400s produced the so-called "full-rigged ship" that carried explorers and conquistadors around the world. Ottoman shipwrights operated in both Indian Ocean and Mediterranean environments, though the two worlds did not interact or merge as much as Chinese and European traditions did. Better and more plentiful shipping stimulated (and also depended on) improvements in navigational technology – the Chinese magnetic compass, the Arabian astrolabe, and the general diffusion of more detailed and accurate maps and charts all spread through growing networks. All these innovations gradually became more and more relevant to the projection of military force through the world.

Second, of course, was the continued spread and improvement of gunpowder technology. Invented in China, probably in the late 900s, perhaps by accident as a result of a very traditional Taoist search for an elixir of immortality,[4] it spread across the same network of trade and intellectual connections that carried maritime knowledge. It affected warfare by adding a new source of power for getting destructive work done, as we discussed in chapter 4. When gunpowder weapons were put on oceangoing ships, a new realm of military possibility emerged.

Events

Renewed Crisis

The sudden conquests of the Mongols, as we have said, both typified the wars of encounter and cross-cultural conflict in the high Middle Ages, and marked a visible starting point for the age of crises that would shape the late Middle Ages. Climate change and pandemic followed the Mongols.

The dawn of the Little Ice Age The term "Little Ice Age" was coined only in 1939, as histories of global climate began to be possible.

---

[4] See above, ch. 4, note 7.

Its starting points and ending points, befitting a phenomenon as widespread, regionally variable, and diffuse as global climate, are not universally agreed on, but its existence is certain. Although evidence from glacial maxima and dendrochronology may indicate the beginnings of cooling as early as the 1280s in western Europe, the first real sign, as noted above, was the disastrously cool, wet summers of 1315 and 1316, which led to widespread famines and decisively ended a long period of population growth. For centuries thereafter, the world's people simply had to deal with somewhat shorter growing seasons for cereal production in particular, and in some areas, such as the north Atlantic, with seaways that became more treacherous because of more ice. Climate change thus constituted not an immediate and urgent crisis, but a general degradation of the conditions in which resources for supporting people and their polities could be generated and moved.

The second plague pandemic Far more instant and critical in its impact was the Black Death, or the second plague pandemic, as it is known among historians of disease and medicine. Bubonic plague, caused by the *Yersinia pestis* bacterium and usually transmitted by fleabites, was endemic among rodent (especially marmot) populations of the northern side of the Himalayas, adjacent to central Asian trade routes. The expansion of trade activity that followed on the creation of the Mongol Empire made it possible for the plague to spread from there to where it broke out in epidemic form. Outbreaks of plague at the Mongol siege of Baghdad in 1258 were probably the first sign of this effect, as we have noted. But major outbreaks erupted in China in the 1330s and among Mongol armies in the 1340s. One of those armies, besieging the port of Caffa on the Black Sea in 1347, catapulted plague casualties into the city in a pre-scientific use of germ warfare. A Genoese trade galley left the city shortly afterwards, making stops in Constantinople and Palestine on its way home to Italy. The plague broke out in each port of call. Egypt and Syria saw massive death tolls. The outbreak that began in 1348 in Italy spread throughout Europe in the course of three years, sparing only small regions in the Netherlands, the Pyrenees, and eastern Europe, for reasons that are not fully understood but that probably included a combination of nutrition, sanitation, and settlement density. Death totals that reached a third of the population certainly constituted a serious and noticed crisis.

The wars of 1300–1500 constituted a significant aspect of the way the world of medieval societies responded to the age of crises.

East Asian Worlds

Disruption and instability came to the worlds of east Asia in various forms, and led to wars that aimed in various ways at "returning to virtue" and restoring or maintaining stability.

Ming China: Mongols and Manifestations

The outbreak of plague in China in the 1330s, concentrated in major cities, destabilized the rule of the Mongol Yuan dynasty founded by Kubilai Khan. Growing peasant unrest gained intellectual shape and support from bureaucrats dissatisfied with foreign rule, no matter how Sinicized the Yuan became. Weakened by plague themselves, the Yuan succumbed to the new Ming dynasty, founded by a Buddhist monk peasant who overcame both the Yuan and other contenders for the throne, in 1368. The Ming founder's chosen reign name, Hongwu, meant "Vastly Martial," indicating the importance of military success in the reconstruction of Chinese power and order, though the emperor's peasant origins, not surprisingly, had no real positive effect on the power structure in favor of the agricultural labor base.

The Ming dynasty pursued two alternative paths of "returning to virtue" over the course of its existence. Although the second Ming ruler, Hongwu's son Yongle, reversed many of his father's specific policies after seizing the throne in a coup and civil war with his nephew that ended in 1402, Hongwu and Yongle generally took their model of virtue to be the Tang dynasty. They pursued aggressive, sometimes expansionist wars around the perimeter of the empire against Vietnam, the Uighurs, and Tibet, as well as Mongolia. And Yongle is best known for sending out the treasure fleets under the command of the eunuch admiral Zheng He. These armadas of humongous ships carried thousands of soldiers and sailors and vast quantities of trade goods to southeast Asia and Indonesia, India, Persia, and Africa. They therefore carried the image of China's power, prestige, and magnanimity to the known world, something of a discourse about tradition projected by megaphone.

But this stage of Ming imitation of Tang models did not last long. Yongle's successors proved both less interested in and less adept at engaging with the world beyond the Middle Kingdom. The expense of the treasure fleets, on top of Yongle's construction of a new capital in the north at Beijing, proved unsustainable in an economically restricted environment, and in 1449 the reigning emperor was captured in battle against the resurgent Mongols. The Ming turned to the virtues of the more self-contained, Sinocentric Han model, not only permanently suspending the treasure fleet expeditions, but prohibiting Chinese merchants from sailing abroad. Attempts to tame the Mongol threat offensively, as Yongle had done, gave way to the reconstruction of the Qin–Han era rammed earth walls facing Mongolia in brick, stone, and mortar, producing the Great Wall that has since symbolized Chinese defensiveness.

Yet the underlying grand strategy of Ming military activity remained relatively constant throughout. Chinese campaigns aimed to, as historian Ken Swope translates the concept, "manifest awe."[5] Military expeditions, in other words, aimed to demonstrate, visibly and symbolically, the strength and grandeur of the empire, with the aim of drawing foreigners under Chinese influence and intimidating those who would not be convinced. This was an imperial grand strategic style that would have been recognizable to the Achaemenid Persians, the Indian Guptas, and even the Aztecs: it maximized the wealth of great empires as a tool of diplomacy while usually minimizing the chance of a disaster in combat.

The Ming also developed and deployed increasing numbers of gunpowder weapons, which as they gradually improved proved effective in defense against both Mongol raiders and coastal pirates, domestic and Japanese, who filled the vacuum left by China's abandonment of the high seas. The great Ming general Qi Jiguang developed ways to counteract the pirates and invented, independently of European innovators, the technique of ranked volley fire for his gunners.[6] The Ming combination of strategic caution and tactical innovation usually worked, and the Ming survived until they fell in 1644 to a combination of Manchu attacks and economic crises brought about by the cooling climate that led to constant peasant unrest and internal strife.[7]

In sum, in this period (and beyond, at least to 1644) China dealt with the challenges of Mongols, plague, and climate change. Chinese imperial responses, whether aggressive or defensive, deployed a combination of military and non-military techniques to create a discourse that reaffirmed and constantly reconstructed Chinese tradition and identity even as it incorporated (and generated) the innovations it

---

[5] Swope, "Manifesting Awe."
[6] Andrade, "Arquebus Volley Technique in China."
[7] Brook, *Troubled Empire*.

found necessary to survive. It is probably as close as we can come to a paradigmatic case for this era.

Japan from Kamakura to Tokugawa

Although the samurai successfully resisted the Mongol invasions of 1274 (figure 19) and 1281 (with some help from the gods of the winds), the effort destabilized the Kamakura shogunate. As defensive campaigns, the victories gained the shogunate no lands with which they could reward their followers. Unrest grew, and the emperor Go-Daigo, who was supposed to be a figurehead, overthrew the shogunate and reestablished direct imperial rule.

The complicated nature of the medieval Japanese state needs some explanation here. The shogunate, or *bakafu* ("tent government"), in Kamakura was a military government that shared power with the civil government in Kyoto. The *bushi*, or warrior class over whom the shogunate exercised authority, had arisen as a sort of internal police force in the service of the civil court (the root of the word "samurai" is the verb *saburu*, "to serve").[8] But the power-sharing arrangement proved unstable. The imperial state assigned both warriors and civil aristocrats income from designated landed estates, a system overseen by both sides of the government. But when there were disputes, the side with the swords predictably had the upper hand.

Go-Daigo's attempt to restore direct imperial rule aimed to reverse that tide flowing toward the warriors. But to pursue that aim, he needed warriors, and drew followers from among the samurai disaffected by the post-Mongol settlement of debts. Those warriors, led by Ashikaga Takauji, a member of the family for whom the shogunate was a hereditary possession as much as the imperial throne belonged to the family that still holds it today, established a new shogunate in 1336, relegating Go-Daigo and his heirs back to figurehead status. But one side of Go-Daigo's clan refused to accept this coup, and until 1392 a complicated civil war raged between two imperial courts and their respective warrior supporters. The Ashikaga shogunate, also known as the Muromachi shogunate after the district in Kyoto where the government was based, therefore suffered from seriously weakened legitimacy (which derived from the imperial family, even

---

[8] The existence and long history of an extensive and powerful warrior class in a country that faced almost no threat of external invasion before or after the Mongol incursions (at least until 1945) is proof that Job 1 of agrarian-era warriors was to defend the power structure itself, as discussed in ch. 3.

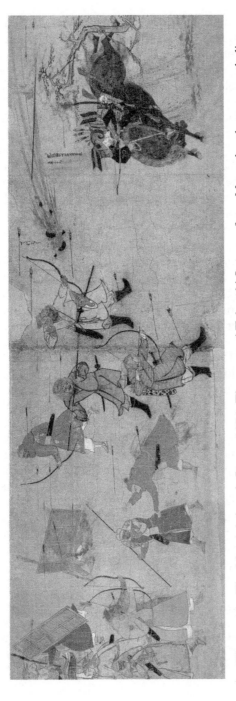

Figure 19 The Mongols invade Japan, 1274. The samurai Takezaki Suenaga faces Mongol archery, an exploding gunpowder bomb, and a culturally unfamiliar opponent during the Kamakura shogunate's defense of Japan against the Mongol invasion of 1274, the first of two that would fail in the face of fleet-destroying storms.

Source: Wikimedia Commons.

as figureheads; the division of that family essentially cancelled the authority of both sides). The shogun's control over the lucrative foreign trade that came through Kyoto made him first among equals with the military governors of the districts into which the country was divided, but the whole system was essentially just a military dictatorship with weak ties to the rural peasant base of society.

Still, the Muromachi arrangement lasted in a precarious balance through the settlement of the imperial civil war in 1392 and down to 1467, when factional disputes escalated into an open civil war called the Onin War. By the end of the war in 1477, the upper echelon of the warrior class, the military governors, had wiped each other out, the shogunate had been reduced to a second level of figurehead status, and the country broke up into essentially independent statelets led by the next level down of warrior families, the daimyo. It was the conflicts between these daimyo domains that shaped the development of Japan from 1477 until the wars led to the reunification of the country near the end of the 1500s. It was during this *sengoku jidai*, or "age of the country at war," that daimyo rulers forged new, more effective state ties to peasant production and economic activity, began to raise larger, infantry-based armies that adopted gunpowder weapons effectively when a Portuguese shipwreck accidentally introduced them in 1542, and laid the foundations for the Tokugawa shogunate that would rule Japan from 1603 until 1868.[9]

In sum, the disruption of the Mongol invasions led Japan into three centuries of constant armed conflict that was almost exclusively internal and was aimed at (re)establishing a stable order and cultural identity. The wars of 1333–1603 stimulated social change, drew on global trade connections, and spawned many of the features of "classic" samurai-centered Japanese culture as it is known even today. The wars introduced guns to the island, where their impact was shaped by the preexisting political and cultural environment created by the wars (as opposed to shaping that environment, as technological determinist arguments would have it). Too specifically Japanese to be paradigmatic, Japanese warfare in this period is nonetheless a classic case of adjustment to crisis via armed discourse.

---

[9] For a thorough examination of the *sengoku jidai* with an emphasis on understanding the impact of gunpowder in the context of the so-called "Military Revolution," see Morillo, "Guns and Government." The article also shows how it is the fragile political structure of the Tokugawa settlement that accounts for the Japanese "giving up the gun" in the early 1600s, rather than a (mythical) samurai cultural attachment to the sword.

Finally, the Japanese case cannot be paradigmatic of the world of late medieval conflict because we have no evidence of plague coming to Japan (its isolation apparently sparing it that crisis), and the effects of climate change on the island are unstudied for this period. Not that these factors necessarily had no effect – we simply cannot say anything about them. We'll let this limitation stand as a lesson in not trying to shoehorn too much into an overly restrictive schema.

Russia: The Fur World

At the other end of the steppes from China, the Rus principalities centered on Kiev had been conquered by the Mongols, suffered outbreaks of the plague, and certainly felt the cooling climate, though abundant land and the underdeveloped nature of Russian agriculture meant it had more room for adjustment than regions that were already at the edge of their capacity. Under Mongol rule, the Dukes of Muscovy rose to prominence among the local rulers deputized to collect and forward tribute payments. The dukes used this position to build their own power and military forces, allied with the Mongols to eliminate their rivals, and by the mid–1300s, having become Grand Princes of Muscovy, were looking to throw off Mongol overlordship. They defeated the Golden Horde at the Battle of Kulikovo in 1380, but did not free all Rus territory from Mongol rule until Ivan III faced down a Great Horde army at the Ugra River in 1480.

During their rise to prominence, Muscovy had tied itself closely to the Orthodox Church as its defender, and gained the legitimacy of church backing. This alliance became foundational to the Russian identity that emerged by the 1500s: the rulers called themselves czars, or caesars, and in the Russian view of history Moscow was the Third Rome (after Rome and Constantinople). This identity contributed to a cultural distance between Russia and Catholic western Europe that (again in the view of much Russian historiography) originated with their time of isolation under "the Tatar yoke," though this concept is as much a construct that contributed to the building of Russian identity as it was an historical reality.

In fact, the Russians inherited much and learned more from the Mongols, and for centuries after driving out the Mongols faced east into Asia as much as west into Europe. The vast expansion of Russian territory went east, across the forests of Siberia where a rich network of fur trapping and trading developed. The Russian colonization of the fur network in Siberia after 1500, accomplished in part through Moscow's successful co-opting of steppe-nomadic-style forces in the

form of the Cossacks, is a striking overland analogue to the colonization of maritime trade routes into the Indian Ocean undertaken by
the Portuguese at the same time.

The depth of the challenge that faced the Rus principalities in this
period is more like the depth of the challenges that faced the classical
world in the 500s than elsewhere. Thus, Russian development in this
period looks like developments in the early Middle Ages elsewhere:
a complete reconstruction of society, economy, and state structures
accompanied by a construction virtually *ex nihilo* of a new cultural
identity. One can see Russian development in this period as a forced
march through the medievalization that their Byzantine progenitors
never accomplished, after which a newly rich and resilient society
expanded into encounters and armed conflicts with other cultures:
indigenous tribes in Siberia, and, at either end of their expansion,
China and western Europe.

Continuity

The stories of east Asian warfare in this period not only illustrate the
themes of rebuilding and maintaining stability that are central to this
chapter, but also demonstrate unequivocally that placing the end of
the Middle Ages at roughly 1500 is artificial and Eurocentric. Across
east Asia, continuity across that chronological divide is obvious. The
Ming dynasty crossed that divide with no appreciable difference
between its pre- and post-1500 existence. One might place a divide
at 1450, but that works only for China. Japan's Onin War, from
1467 to 1477, might also mark a Japan-centered division, but in both
China and Japan the continuities and developments across the supposed divides are vastly more important than any changes marked by
the divides. Russian history can plausibly be divided at 1480 when
Mongol rule was finally ended, but continuities between pre- and
post–1480 Russian history are arguably far more important than
changes across that divide. We will return to this question throughout the chapter.

The Ottoman World

In 1300, the Ottoman "state" was one of a number of small *beyliks*,
or independent Turkish principalities into which the Seljuk Empire
had fragmented, in Asia Minor in particular; it was led by the "tribal"
leader Osman (d. 1323/4), who gave his name to the political (not

ethnic) identity "Ottoman." By 1500, the Ottoman state was the most powerful polity in the eastern Mediterranean world, a major player in Eurasian trade, politics, and culture, and the center of an entire region of the Eurasian world. But while the Ottoman story of expansion, encounter and conflict, and identity construction fits the broader themes of this chapter (and its echoes of the early Middle Ages in chapter 5), the Ottoman relationship to the larger environmental and disease challenges that shaped the late medieval world is, as far as it can be seen, strikingly different.

Expansion to 1500

Osman's small beylik was at its founding in 1299 far from an established state, though it shared the established medieval culture and political structure of the post-Abbasid Islamic world, including a military built around a small core of slave soldiers and a larger set of semi-nomadic *iqta* holders operating in the classic style of steppe horse archers. And it benefited, compared to its many rival beyliks, from its position at the frontier of remaining Byzantine territory, so it had room to expand without having to go to war with other Islamic states. Thus, it could attract *ghazis*, or frontier warriors inspired to carry *jihad* against the infidels. By the mid–1300s, this expansion into Byzantine territories carried the Ottomans across the Bosporus into the southern Balkans, where further Christian lands invited continued expansion.

In its early expansion, it seems not to have suffered badly from the spread of the plague. The pandemic did strike Constantinople, but the hostility between Ottoman-held rural areas outside the city and the Christian city may well have limited the spread of the plague beyond the city walls. As for the gradually cooling climate, the somewhat arid Ottoman possessions in Anatolia could in fact have benefited from the cooling climate, especially in terms of an increase in scrub vegetation on which horses could feed, much as the LALIA had benefited the Arabs of Muhammad's time. In short, the challenges that affected others probably provided the early Ottomans with opportunities instead. The only version of the challenges that slowed Ottoman expansion, though only temporarily, was the conquests of Timur the Lame, who led an echo of the original Mongol conquests in the late 1300s. At the Battle of Ankara in 1402, Timur crushed an Ottoman army and captured Sultan Bayezid I, provoking a succession crisis and civil war. Mehmed I, the son of Bayezid who emerged victorious, restored Ottoman power and restarted expansion. Sultan

Figure 20   Ottoman siege cannon. Gigantic Ottoman bronze cannons,
such as these trophies on the grounds of Les Invalides in Paris, provided
enough concentrated destructive power to breach even the great walls of
Constantinople.
Source: Guilhem Vellut, via Wikimedia Commons.

Suleiman the Magnificent, deploying a train of gigantic cannons,
captured Constantinople in 1453, providing a marker of ongoing
Ottoman expansion (figure 20).

The complexities of Ottoman identity emerged from the varied
contexts they encountered around them. As their empire grew, their
military system increasingly came to be a synthesis of traditional
Turkish steppe-nomadic cavalry and the gunpowder-armed infantry
and siege cannon of a sedentary power. The combination is displayed symbolically in items such as a jewel-encrusted canteen that
proclaims, simultaneously, the horse-riding origins of the Turks and
the wealth of an imperial state: the Ottomans consciously saw themselves as both nomadic conquerors and successors of Byzantium.
Expansion at the expense of Byzantium allowed the Ottomans to
cast themselves as Defenders of the Faith, a title they reinforced by
defeating and driving back the Shi'a forces of Safavid Persia at the
Battle of Chaldiran in 1514, and with their conquest of Mamluk
Egypt in 1517 (the Mamluks having claimed that title since defeating the Mongols in 1260). All of this gave the Ottomans an unusual

level of legitimacy within the Islamic world. But they never solved the problem of orderly succession (a legacy of their Turkish identity), and slave soldiers – the Janissary Corps – remained a central and politically volatile component of the military establishment, a legacy of their medieval Islamic ancestry. Tellingly, the Janissaries were recruited (or conscripted) from the Christian Balkan territories of the empire, where Islamic rule could not be legitimized effectively.

Thus, by the early 1500s, the Ottomans were in the midst of a world for which they were the center of gravity, but that put them astride a number of cultural, political, and military boundaries that continued to shape their history.

The Ottomans beyond 1500

The Ottomans in Europe The Ottoman conquest of the Balkan Peninsula carried them to the gates of Vienna, which they besieged in 1529. This made them a major player in European politics, a role in which their religious affiliation became secondary: as enemies of the Austrian Hapsburg dynasty, the Ottomans found common interest with the French, and Franco-Ottoman alliances became a regular feature of European diplomacy. But after the high tide at Vienna, the Ottoman frontier in Hungary and the Balkans became less active. Ottoman military interests instead focused, in European terms, on two fronts. First, Ottoman power in the eastern Balkans and the Caucasus region faced the rising power of Russia. Second, Ottoman offensives focused on naval expansion in the Mediterranean, where expanding Ottoman power ran up against various combinations of Venice, Spain, and the papacy as naval powers. This naval warfare was based on the classic Mediterranean warship, the oared galley, now armed with cannon mounted at the bow. At the small-arms level, it also increasingly pitted Ottoman bowmen against European (especially Spanish) arquebusiers. While these two were relatively evenly matched in term of effectiveness in battle, the longer-term advantage lay with the arquebusiers, who were far easier to train (rough and ready in a matter of weeks) and thus replace than the archers (who needed years to decades of practice), as the aftermath of the great Battle of Lepanto in 1571 showed. There, significant Ottoman losses in ships were fairly quickly replaced, but losses in trained archers were not, hindering Ottoman naval efforts thereafter. (Note that the Janissaries, as arquebusiers, had some of the same advantages as Spanish arquebusiers, but by tradition did not serve much on shipboard.) In both land combat and naval warfare,

Ottoman involvement in Europe tied them into the military developments happening among the western European countries, developments that usually go under the rubric of the "early modern Military
Revolution." In this book's view, this "revolution" constitutes a false
event set in a false era, as the continuities of Ottoman military history
across 1500 attest.

The Safavid Other On its eastern frontier, the Ottoman Empire faced,
after 1501, the newly established Safavid dynasty of Persia. Of native
Iranian origin, the Safavids established Shi'a Islam as the official
religion of the state; this became the cornerstone for a construction
of Iranian national identity that has lasted to the present day and
pitted them openly against the authority of the Sunni Ottomans.
The Safavid military was a mixed bag: indigenous tribal warriors
who were largely cavalrymen; slave soldiers from various regions
beyond Iran, especially the Caucasus, also largely cavalry; and later
both infantry armed with muskets and an artillery train, both established with European assistance under Shah Abbas I (1571–1629),
the greatest of the Safavids. Though the frontier between the Safavids
and the Ottomans shifted back and forth across Iraq and in the
Caucasus depending on circumstances, the Ottomans generally had
the advantage, especially in pitched battles, because of their superior
gunpowder infantry, the Janissaries, and artillery. It was this deficit
that Abbas worked successfully to reduce.
    Ottoman wars against Persia periodically brought them access to
the Persian Gulf, which combined with their control of the Red Sea
to create the basis for an Ottoman maritime presence in the Indian
Ocean. After 1498, this brought them into increasing conflict with
the Portuguese, who were attempting to bypass Ottoman control
of the trade routes to south and east Asia. This was a very different
arena of naval warfare from the Mediterranean, as outside the Red
Sea the Indian Ocean was unsuited to oared galleys. This forced
the Ottomans to maintain what were essentially two separate naval
establishments.

The Mughal echo The final significant power in the Ottoman-centered
Islamic world after 1500 was the Mughal Empire of the Indian subcontinent. It can count as another of the ripple effects of the Mongol
conquests (though plague and climate change seem not to have
played a major role here). Mongol incursions had already destabilized
the Delhi sultanate in the early 1300s. Babur, a warrior of central
Asian origin who descended from both Timur and Chinggis Khan,

founded the empire by defeating the last Delhi sultan in 1526 at the Battle of Panipat. The Ottomans assisted Babur through gifts of guns and cannon, though Mughal cavalry was the key to his victory. The Ottomans may have viewed Babur's rise as a chance to establish an allied power on the other side of the Safavids, though Mughal art and architecture ended up as a brilliant synthesis of Persian and Indian traditions. It was under Babur's grandson Akbar, a contemporary of Shah Abbas, that the Mughals reached their pinnacle.

The Closing of the Steppes

We may note one final development connected, though not exclusively, to the rise of the Ottomans. We noted above that the effectiveness of the Ottoman military establishment was partly a product of how the Ottomans managed to synthesize the strengths of steppe-nomadic cavalry warfare and sedentary infantry-and-siege warfare, including the use of cannons. This was also characteristic, in various degrees, of the military establishments of the Mughals, czarist Russia, and the Manchu Qing dynasty that took China from the Ming in 1644. These synthetic forces proved effective not just against rival sedentary states, but also against the remaining purely steppe powers. By 1700 or so, the rise of these synthetic powers had closed and tamed the steppes, which afterwards no longer acted as a source of disruption for the worlds around them.

The combat effectiveness of the synthetic polities was not the only factor behind the decline of steppe power. The encroachment on steppe mobility made possible by advancing systems of gunpowder-armed fortifications played a large role. This in turn was grounded in very long-term trends, mostly demographic and economic, that steadily ran against the pastoralists and in favor of the agricultural-ists. Farming supported far more people than herding, and gradually advanced, sometimes via irrigation, into steppe lands. And manufac-turing and metallurgy, always a sedentary area of advantage, gained new importance with the spread of gunpowder weaponry.

More Continuity

Given the central role steppe military power had held in agrarian-era political, economic, and cultural relationships since the domestica-tion of horses and the associated use of wheeled vehicles such as carts and chariots, the closing of the steppes was truly a significant historical divide. That the process of "taming" the steppes concluded around 1700 is further evidence that 1500 makes a poor and arbitrary dividing line in military history, in southwest, south, and central Asia as much as in east Asia.

Europe at Sea

The Mongols threatened western Europe in 1240, causing widespread panic, but never made it back after withdrawing to elect a new Great Khan. But climate change hit Europe hard, with the impact showing up as early as the cold, wet summers of 1315 and 1316, and the Black Death killed a huge percentage of the region's population between 1348 and 1351. In short, western Europe certainly faced the challenges common to the medieval world in the 1300s.

But it faced them from a position that was disadvantageous, or at least unusual, in one important way. When crisis came to response, Europeans faced a cultural crisis of tradition, and therefore found that it lacked agreed-on "virtues" to return to, in the way that most of Eurasia had looked back to earlier models for guidance on rebuilding their societies. As a result, Europe found itself "at sea," both figuratively in terms of lacking a clear path forward and literally because the most important path it found took Europeans across the world's oceans.

Traditions? Virtues?

In terms of political organization, kingdoms and principalities competed with city-states and other local forms of governance, with no one model predominating or even having undisputed prestige. (The old Roman imperial model of unity was theoretically the ideal, but no one wanted *that particular* emperor or king to assume universal suzerainty, a contradiction that would persist in European politics until the ideal died with Napoleon's empire.[10]) And states collectively continued to dispute sovereignty with the Catholic Church. The church itself moved the papacy to Avignon in southern France in 1305 as a result of the pressures of this dispute, which alienated both common folk who saw a rich papal palace arise in a poverty-ridden town, and countries such as England and Germany who were not politically

---

[10] The ideal revived briefly with the European Union, but currently looks to have been dealt a mortal blow by Brexit and the resurgence of right-wing ethnic nationalism.

friendly to France. By 1360, this resulted in a disputed papal election and a schism, with a pope and an anti-pope supporting an anti-emperor and an emperor respectively, each excommunicating each other's followers in the midst of the aftermath of the Black Death. Thus, if the theology of the day was right, life sucked and everyone was going to hell.

The plague exposed one other problem: western Europe's divided political hierarchy had been unable to contain or tame the region's growing merchant class, whose network-based values began to undermine the hierarchy values common to agrarian states. A key piece of evidence: in England, the labor shortage created by the plague led Parliament to meet and pass the Statute of Labourers in 1351, which (in a perfectly traditional agrarian hierarchy way) restricted labor freedom: it limited wages to those prevalent before the plague and said farmers must remain on their family lands. But the money-based logic of networks and markets overrode the law, and labor shortage led to higher wages, lower rents, and increased peasant freedom as the lords who passed the laws cheated on each other relentlessly.

With no "traditional virtues" to return to, innovative solutions to challenges not only happened as they did elsewhere, but gained prestige *as innovations*, and innovation grew as a respected cultural value, especially in conjunction with the growth of network-based merchant capitalism as an organizing force in society.[11] This was the force behind the entrepreneurial activity that produced, for instance, Gutenberg's printing press and its expanding effects on intellectual culture, including, in many accounts, the Renaissance. Indeed, the prestige of novelty and innovation, married to the remains of classical cultural prestige, led to the invention of both the Renaissance and the static "Middle Ages" that made Renaissance innovation necessary.

For our purposes, innovation, experimentation, and entrepreneurship came to characterize much of the military activity of the period after 1300 in Europe. Mercenary service, in particular, often organized through some form of partnership between state employment and private contractors, increased steadily in importance after 1300. And there was plenty of opportunity for the development of such systems, as armed conflict, both within Europe and beyond it, remained the most prevalent form of discourse about the directions and values of this civilization, including how it dealt with crises.

---

[11] See Morillo, *Frameworks*, ch. 14, for a detailed survey and explanation of these topics.

Conflict Within Europe: Let's Take This Inside and Settle It

European warfare after 1300 shows that the cultural emphasis on novelty, invention, and innovation can obscure the fact that there was as much "disguised" continuity in Europe as there was "disguised" innovation elsewhere. This is especially visible in the warfare of late medieval Europe, starting with the fact that the disruptions of climate and disease and their dire effects on demography had a much less catastrophic effect on the waging of war than might be expected. The greatest conflict of the age, the Hundred Years War between England and France, probably the two most organized kingdoms on the continent in 1300, demonstrates this. The first phase of the war from 1337 to 1360 saw Edward III of England pursue his (real but dubious) claim to the French throne via "chevauchées," pillaging rides through French territory designed to show that the French king could not protect his realm and thus did not deserve to rule it. The chevauchée of 1347 ended in the Battle of Crécy, where the devastating effect of English longbow archery cut down the finest knightly cavalry in Europe. (Longbowmen had already, in 1340, been central to the English naval victory at the Battle of Sluys in the English Channel.) Then, the Black Death hit and 30 percent of Europe died, and the war paused. For all of eight years.

In 1356, England and France, being rich, resilient, complex medievalized societies, shrugged off the plague and went back at it. A new chevauchée – somewhat smaller than the Crécy army, admittedly, but still destructive – under Edward's son Edward the Black Prince rode through France, culminating in another stunning longbow victory at Poitiers, where King John of France was captured. The countries agreed to a peace in 1360 that lasted nine years before hostilities resumed. These turned in favor of the French and led to a second peace from 1389 to 1415.

During the two periods of "peace" neither side proved as capable of ending a war as they had of starting it, especially in terms of demobilizing troops. Mercenary companies spawned by the war sought employment in Iberia and Italy, inflaming new wars in those places, and the combined destructiveness of the war and the plague led to increased class conflict across Europe. The Jacquerie, a French peasant revolt, broke out in 1358 and was mercilessly crushed by the French knights who had been losing to the English. A poll tax imposed by the English crown in 1380 to fund the war led to a peasant revolt that ended with the execution of a few leaders, illustrating important differences between the French and English states that are beyond our scope here to explore. And in 1378 the revolt of the Ciompi, Italian wool weavers, broke out in a precocious example of industrial class warfare.

The Hundred Years War resumed in 1415, when Henry V of England launched a new invasion and chevauchée that ended at the Battle of Agincourt, the last of the great English longbow victories. Using gunpowder artillery, Henry rapidly reconquered Normandy from the French and came within one event – his own premature death – of gaining the crown of both countries, but after his death the French, making increasing use of artillery in sieges and even in combat, regained what had been lost and ended the war in 1453, the same year that Constantinople fell to the Turks and Gutenberg perfected his printing press. Which would seem to make a fine date, at least symbolically, for the end of the Middle Ages, except that none of those three events really marked a turning point (except symbolically), and the date has no significance outside of the lands between the newly named Istanbul and London. Within Europe, wars between competing systems, classes, and ideologies continued, with the Battle of Morat from chapter 1 illustrating many aspects of the period's warfare.

Conflict Beyond Europe: Maybe We Should Take This Outside

All of Europe's internal conflict coexisted with, fueled, and helped disguise the continuity of growing European adventurism beyond the continent. The continuities were in the motivations for overseas exploration and conquest, often summed up, not inaccurately, as God, gold, and glory. The Crusading culture of high medieval Europe carried on. For example, when the Portuguese successfully circumnavigated Africa and entered the Indian Ocean trading world, they saw it as part of a crusade against the Ottomans who monopolized the routes through the eastern Mediterranean. But the trade routes also promised wealth to rulers and merchants alike, and Portuguese journeys around Africa had begun with stops on what became known as the Gold Coast, where the precious metal rewarded the explorers and encouraged them to reach farther. And explorations opened potential new avenues for the military classes of Europe to seek reputations.

Viewed as a murder mystery (and the slave trade that grew alongside the trade in spices and metals provided murders aplenty over the next four centuries), these motives had to be joined with means and opportunity. The means were the oceangoing ships that European shipwrights had been developing over the course of the 1400s, increasingly armed with gunpowder cannon to create a new realm of armed conflict on the high seas. The opportunity, especially in terms of the Asian trade in the Indian Ocean and beyond to east Asia, was the fact that the Chinese, with their gigantic treasure ships carrying tens of thousands of marines, had abandoned the playing field before 1450, as we discussed above, leaving the sea lanes uncontested to European fleets.

The Americas

In the long run, the most consequential of the explorations launched out of Iberia in the late 1400s was, of course, Columbus' attempt to reach Asia by sailing west, which resulted in the accidental discovery of two entire continents previously unknown to the inhabitants of the Afro-Eurasian world. Here, at last, we can bring the Americas into the global medieval world. But doing so raises again some of the questions with which we began this exploration in chapter 2.

"Medieval America"?

In histories of the Americas, the long era between the peopling of the continents during the last Ice Age and 1492 is usually simply referred to as "Pre-Columbian," with no significant subdivisions. If there were no breaks, how could any American society be in a "Middle Age"?

In chapter 5, we did establish Teotihuacan as an American version of a "classical" society, and saw that the volcanic eruptions that brought on the LALIA brought classical Teotihuacan to an end. But the limitations of the comparative factors noted in chapter 5, and the restricted geographical reach of Teotihuacan as a model for its successors, mean that we are not exactly dealing with a post-Teotihuacan medieval America, despite the same Common Rules applying and similar functions for warfare holding in some places.

It is even clearer that societies that had not been "medievalized" in the Eurasian manner in the period 540–850 did not face the same challenges beginning in 1300 that the Eurasian world faced. Climate change was global: the decline of the pueblo cultures of the North American southwest seems to have been brought on by droughts as the climate cooled. But the Mongols, world-conquering though they were, never reached the Americas. Nor did the bubonic plague pandemic. On the other hand, in 1492 American societies entered into medieval processes catastrophically. They faced Spanish invaders who seemed, as the Mongols had to the eyes of their victims, to come from another world or even plane of existence. The entire Eurasian disease pool crossed the Atlantic with the Spanish, killing a far higher proportion of the indigenous population (upward of 90 percent in some cases) than the bubonic plague ever did anywhere. And again, the Little Ice Age was global.

Next question: was the world still medieval after the globalization of the world network? The year 1500 (effectively 1492) is usually taken as a major dividing line in world history.[12] In the face of a vast historiographical consensus that a new era began in 1500, let us simply remind ourselves of the major continuities that crossed that divide. First, the fundamental economic – that is, agrarian – foundations of the world continued.[13] One sure sign of this is that the agrarian rule that labor shortage led to lower labor freedom operated in full force in the Atlantic slave trade. Second, the Common Rules of medieval armed conflict still applied. Finally, the dynamics of late medieval expansion, encounter, and conflict that have underpinned this chapter certainly continued.

Whether all this means that the world was still "medieval" or not probably comes down to a judgment call. The answer here is "yes." A "no" answer for purposes of chronological clarity is not indefensible. What is indisputable is that at least the major American civilizations, the Aztecs and Incas, *met* the medieval world and became part of it.

The Aztecs

The Aztecs had settled in the Valley of Mexico around 1300, founding their capital at Tenochtitlan in 1345. They went on to create, in less than a hundred years, the biggest Mesoamerican empire to that time.

The empire was held together not by armies of occupation and Aztec administrators, but by the perception of Aztec power – that is, Aztec ability to punish non-cooperation by reconquest and imposition of heavier tribute. The Aztecs' need to periodically renew the image of their power reinforced a tendency to expansionism that arose from the benefits in tribute, wider trade networks, and prisoners for ritual sacrifice that an expanding empire brought. Periodic

---

[12] Including in my own world history textbook, *Frameworks of World History*.

[13] Emphasized in Morillo, *Frameworks*, where the period 1500–1800 is presented as "the Late Agrarian Era," *not* "the Early Modern Age."

revolts by subject city-states were thus an inevitable aspect of the empire.

The Aztec army that projected imperial power had at its core a military aristocracy that formed a professional standing force. This elite was backed by commoner warriors in great numbers drawn from the urban and farm populations. The usual campaign season was December to April, the dry season after the harvest, when roads were passable, supplies were plentiful, and farmers were available for duty. Aztec warriors used bows with bronze-tipped arrows, slings, spear throwers, and obsidian-bladed broad swords and spears. Both missile and bladed weapons were effective, the latter's chief disadvantages compared to steel swords being weight and fragility. The elites wore padded cotton armor that provided good protection for light weight (figure 21).

The chief limit on Aztec armies was logistical. With no pack animals or wheeled transport, all supplies had to be carried by porters, generally one for every two soldiers. This meant that Aztec armies could only march about three days beyond friendly territory to fight a battle, and that sieges were very rare. Conquests of larger polities larger therefore had to be piecemeal, chipping away at the edges or surrounding them, cutting them off from allies, and wearing them down. The strategy against a powerful foe could also include a "flower war," a form of ritual combat between elite soldiers that tied up the enemy army at small cost while conquests of encirclement were pursued. It could also escalate into a war of attrition and full conquest: the overall ritual nature of Mesoamerican war has been much exaggerated, and killing of foes was as much a part of Aztec war as capture of prisoners.

The Spanish conquest of the Aztec Empire was not a triumph of European arms as much as a story of Indian division. Head to head, the Aztecs had the military ability to defeat the invaders. But the political structure of the Aztec Empire made it vulnerable: revolts were built into the system, creating the openings and allies that Cortes could not have succeeded without. Better luck could have led to the defeat of the invasion (which ran against official Spanish policy and was only justified post hoc by its success) and the establishment of more "normal" diplomatic contacts between Spain and Mexico. But making such resistance work was always going to be a difficult management problem for the Aztecs, because their empire by its nature harbored so many potential enemies.

Figure 21   Aztec warriors. The costumes of elite Aztec warriors (here two Eagle warriors and a Jaguar warrior) acted as padded armor. Each warrior bears a macuahuitl, a wooden "sword" whose blade was composed of embedded shards of obsidian.

Source: Wikimedia Commons.

The Incas

Like the Aztecs, the Incas had risen to dominance in their world fairly recently before the Spanish invasion, initiating their expansion in the mid-fourteenth century. By 1530 they controlled a vast empire stretching down the Andes from present-day Colombia to Chile and including all or part of Bolivia, Peru, and Ecuador. Given the limited trade contacts the Peruvian world had even with Mesoamerica, the Incas had come to dominate most of civilization as they knew it.

Despite their isolation, the Incas developed a sophisticated political and military apparatus. Unlike the Aztec Empire, the Inca Empire incorporated newly conquered areas into the existing administrative structure of the state, headed by Inca local and regional administrators. Conquered tribes were sometimes resettled to distant parts of the empire to reduce their ability to revolt. Local elites were separated from their people and "invited" to the Inca capital, essentially as hostages, to be integrated into the Inca ruling elite; offspring of local elites were given an Inca education and instructed in the Inca religion, which was imposed on top of or instead of local religions throughout the empire. The ruling family was integral to the religion, as, like the Japanese royal house, they claimed descent from the sun god. The only weakness in Inca administration was their lack of a true written language, though a system of knotted ropes and official record keepers mitigated this deficiency.

The geographic range of the empire included a vast horizontal expanse of land and a wide variety of altitude divisions. Tying the whole empire together and facilitating economic exchange was a system of royal roads that were as well built as Roman roads and similarly carried both armies and goods. Universal conscription produced an army wielding a variety of regional weapons, led by a professional officer corps. Spearheading Inca forces was a full-time professional army of military aristocrats tens of thousands strong that included an imperial body guard of several thousand. The Incas' effective military mobilization of their population certainly exceeded the Aztecs', and rivaled any state's in the world. They could maintain in the 1500s three independently operating armies of over 30,000 men at the same time. And the terrain itself was an ally of the Incas. Not only were the steep mountains and narrow passes easily defensible, the sheer altitude of much of the empire could be debilitating to lowlanders who lacked the greater lung capacity highland peoples had acquired through evolution. Finally, Inca warfare was deadly in intent and execution, with no culture of taking prisoners as in Mesoamerica.

The great Inca weakness in the face of the Spanish, however, was their weaponry. Though they knew the use of bronze, almost all their weapons were of stone, wood, and bone, and were designed for crushing blows, delivered by club or sling. They lacked slashing and cutting weapons such as the Aztec obsidian swords, and underutilized the archery skills of jungle peoples on the fringes of the empire. Shortages of good wood, another consequence of high elevation, also kept the length of Inca spears down. The result was that Inca armies were far more vulnerable to Spanish weaponry, especially cavalry charges, and less able to penetrate Spanish armor than were the Aztecs, and thus were at a severe disadvantage in head-on fights on open ground.

Like Cortes' conquest of the Aztecs, Pizarro's conquest of the Incas resulted from a combination of good luck (the Spanish arrived just at the end of a civil war brought on when the previous Inca ruler had died of a European disease), Inca incomprehension of what they faced versus Spanish experience, and tactical superiority. For if the political structure of their empire was always going to be the central problem for Aztec resistance to the Spanish, no matter when they came, military technology was the key problem for the Incas. In different circumstances, this might have been a more solvable problem. Given more time before contact, Inca success is easily imaginable. But the Incas didn't have any extra time, and alternative possibilities must remain purely speculative.

Finally, perhaps the decisive underlying factor in eventual Spanish domination of both the Aztec and Incan worlds, if not their immediate conquest of them (though epidemics played a role in both), was disease. The Eurasian disease pool, arriving in a world with no previous exposure, was epochally disastrous. The best estimates for the century after Spanish arrival are that the population of Mexico dropped from 19 million to 1 million; Peru's from 8 million or so to under 1 million. Depopulated continents lay behind the slave trade that became a central feature of the relationship between the Old and New worlds.

Conclusions

The stories of warfare in the period after 1300 are, as this chapter has shown, largely stories of resiliency in the face of challenges and thus of continuity despite disruption. The high medieval discourses of 850–1300 about expansion, encounter, and identity continued through new conflicts as the societies that met negotiated, via armed conflict, the shape of the new medieval world they were constructing. As a result, far from crashing to a halt as the classical world had done when faced with similar challenges in the 500s, the medieval world of 1300 continued to expand through its crises. By 1500 that expansion had brought the Americas into the medieval world's violent conversations and began to construct a truly global network of connections.

Whether this expansion, by reaching global proportions, transformed the medieval world into something different after 1500 is clearly a matter of debate, though the long-standing conventions of periodization in historiography have tended to mute that debate in favor of an accepted status quo. But as this chapter has also shown, the conventional stands on shaky foundations. We shall return to this question in more detail in the concluding chapter of this book.

8

Conclusions

Making the Medieval World

When the Late Antique Little Ice Age descended from the ash of massive volcanic eruptions to cool the earth from roughly the year 540 for over a hundred years, not just bringing disruptions to agriculture but also triggering (or at least coinciding with) the pandemic spread of deadly diseases, the structures of "classical civilizations" came apart. Even if the major state centers of classical societies represented only the anomalous high points of social and cultural complexity at that point in world history, they nevertheless were already home to a majority of the world's population. And the networks of economic, cultural, and political exchange that connected them to each other and the widespread non-state regions of the world carried the effects of the LALIA-based nexus of crises across the globe.

The great classical states and empires did not, of course, simply disappear off the face of the earth. Some survived, adapting and transforming as they could. Even those that fragmented into smaller local pieces left memories of their existence and models of social, political, and administrative organization to the peoples who inhabited a world newly full of opportunities and options, a reminder that "collapse" casts the processes that began with the LALIA far too much in terms set by the rulers of the classical world. Disaster for them was freedom for many. Thus, the successors of the classical world set about to rebuild and reshape their world.

It is the argument of this book that war and conflict were central to the process of rebuilding the world and redefining what it meant that ensued after 540, a process that created the medieval world. To understand the dynamics and contributions of war to this process, we examined first what I call the "Common Rules" of armed conflict. These include the physical and structural limits on warfare: where it could take place, and how that limit was inextricably tied to where the political structures (states) that could generate the large-scale elements of warfare (armies and major military infrastructure such as fortifications) could exist. They also include the physics of armed conflict in an age when all "work" had to be performed with the limited power sources available in a preindustrial world. These are "Common Rules" because they applied to all armed conflicts across the world in this period, regardless of scale – that is, no matter how many or few people were involved. The Common Rules therefore also serve as a reminder that war and conflict were not activities monopolized by states and formal state armies. Sub-state and non-state fighting happened so frequently in so many places that, although the scale of major wars could have significant historical impacts, the sheer volume of sub- and non-state armed conflict shaped the course of history constantly. The Common Rules therefore also help us see the parameters of this constant tide of war and conflict.

The construction of the medieval world, however, took place in culturally and chronologically specific circumstances within the confines of the Common Rules, and so the second part of this book examined the "scenarios" of medieval warfare. The argument there is that we can see medieval war as falling into three periods. In the first, from 540 to 850, warfare appeared as central to the processes, largely internal to different societies, that "medievalized" those societies. This involved conflicts that spread militarized forms of social-political organization more deeply into societies, which in turn stimulated economic development literally "from the ground up" in many places. Military activity was also closely associated with the spread of what world historians call the salvation religions. Religiously motivated forms of social and cultural organization, as well as religious interpretations of the meaning of the world, acted hand in hand with military structures and military cultural discourses to lay medieval foundations that would shape the world in lasting ways.

In the second period, from 850 to 1300, the expansive, culturally self-confident worlds that emerged from the early period of medieval development increasingly encountered each other, often violently even as they also traded and exchanged ideas. Indeed, as in the first period, we viewed military activity acting as a form of discourse through which ideas, ideologies, and forms of social and political organization were "discussed" – argued over, promoted, and resisted, with the result that a larger, ever-spreading "conversation" is what created a coherent medieval world from a set of emergent medieval worlds.

Finally, the period that began in 1300 saw the richer, more complex, medieval world face a new period of challenges similar to those that ended the classical world: a cooling climate and a vast, deadly pandemic, piled on top of the shock provided by the conquests of the Mongols, whose wars typified the conflicts of the second of our periods. But instead of breaking apart as the classical world had done, the medievalized societies of the 1300s and beyond showed their resiliency. They did not collapse, but met the challenges, reaffirmed their cultural identities, and carried on with the expansive, interactive trajectories they'd established already, ultimately bringing the entire world into their violent discourses.

It is this "carrying on" in the last period of medieval wars we examined that raised the question of when the Middle Ages ended, because as we saw in chapter 7, 1500 does not make a good breaking point across most of the world. When did the Middle Ages end?

The End of the Middle Ages?

Transformations and Globalizations

Having taken a global perspective throughout, we can ignore the phenomena usually cited as marking the end of the Middle Ages (especially, for example, the Renaissance) as too Eurocentric to justify a global periodization change. From a global perspective, there are two developments that can justify a period change around 1500. First, the increasing importance of gunpowder weaponry, which in the view of some historians is an aspect of the so-called "Military Revolution" of the period 1500–1800. Since the very existence of a "Military Revolution" is disputed, let us focus on gunpowder weaponry in its own right.

There is no denying that gunpowder brought change to warfare. It was, as we discussed in chapter 4, the first sort of weaponry that transcended the limits of wind, water, and muscle power for getting the destructive work of warfare done. In its earliest forms, however, it was not much more powerful than the best of the traditional weapons – counterweight trebuchets were more powerful siege weapons than any early guns, for example. And even after centuries of development, gunpowder weaponry remained comparable to, rather than worlds apart from, traditional weapons in terms of physics. Even eighteenth-century artillery was largely a line-of-sight weapon with a range of a few hundred yards. Admittedly, the gradual development of cannon had created a new (or at least newly effective) combat arm: field artillery. But "gradual development" raises a question that has dogged debates about the "Military Revolution": was there a decisive "revolutionary" moment in the long evolutionary history of gunpowder when we can say "There! That's when things changed!"? It's hard to find one, and so gunpowder becomes an example of a medieval technology whose development extended from Song China in the 1000s into the 1800s and beyond. The one exception, arguably, is that when medieval trends in shipbuilding intersected with medieval trends in gunpowder weapons development, the result was not medieval.

The second development that can justify a periodization moment in global perspective is the true globalization of the world's network of exchanges after 1492. The Columbian Exchange of foodstuffs and other primary agricultural products was undeniably significant, as was the associated movement of populations, especially the emergence of the Atlantic slave trade in the wake of the epidemic-induced depopulation of two continents. It is hard to say that with the addition of the New Worlds of the Americas, there was not a New World globally.

The question then becomes, however, what kind of New World was created by the incorporation of the Americas into the Eurasian-centered world that existed before 1500? The answer to this question brings continuity to the fore again.

An Extended Medieval World, to 1800?

Continuities

Let us take this back to the fundamentals that we first discussed in chapter 3. Demographically, the period 1500 to 1800 fits on the second relatively flat part of the graph of total human population that we presented there (figure 4, repeated here as figure 22).

That is, there was no population explosion after 1500, despite the benefits of the Columbian Exchange in some areas – not surprisingly, given that the period began with the depopulating of the Americas and continued with the deaths and dislocations of the slave trade. Moreover, the essential contexts of economic activity underwent no change in 1500. Technologically, low productivity and slow communications were still the basic constraints on wealth creation and distribution. And the Little Ice Age that began around 1300 continued

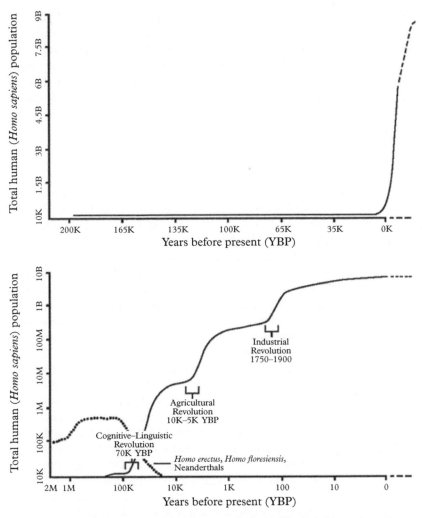

Figure 22   Graph of total human population. (Top) Arithmetic scale. (Bottom) Logarithmic scale for time and population.

Source: Author.

unabated into the 1800s. Thus, despite the extension of maritime trade routes and connections, global economic activity can easily be seen as a continued slow expansion of medieval economics.

Since nothing transformed the economic and demographic bases of social organization, it is even more obvious that the political structures of the world after 1500 were similar to – indeed usually the same as, in direct survival or succession from – medieval polities. Thus, monarchies dominated global politics, to the extent that they were everywhere still taken as the "natural" form of governance.

Finally, in terms of the military patterns of activity that have been the focus of this book, the Common Rules constraining and shaping combat and campaigns – constraints of geography, political structure, and technology – remained the same, with the above discussion about gunpowder kept in mind.

The Industrial Transformation

All these points about continuity are highlighted and emphasized when they are viewed in terms of the true change in global history: the Industrial Revolution. The demographic chart (figure 22) shows the drastic effect the coming of industrial economics had on world population, initiating a period of explosive growth that is only today beginning to abate worldwide. The onset of industrialization also roughly coincided with (and even preceded) the ending of the Little Ice Age, and although early industrialization was limited enough that it probably did not bring the cool period to an end itself, by now the drastic and potentially catastrophic warming of the world from industrial-era fossil-fuel energy use has guaranteed that the cold won't return. Industrialization put an end to the constraints of low productivity and slow communications, revolutionizing economic activity globally. Mass production (and mass consumption, and mass culture – "mass" is the keyword, obviously) inevitably transformed politics. The revolutionary political changes in parts of the Atlantic world in the second half of the eighteenth century gained permanence and were amplified by these changes. Democracy was not the inevitable result, but mass politics of various sorts was, increasingly, organized around mass political-cultural ideologies such as nationalism and capitalism, as well as the more explicitly political schools of liberalism, fascism, and so forth. And international relations were certainly revolutionized, recasting old isms such as colonialism and imperialism in new forms.

The revolutionizing of international relations depended crucially on the real "revolution," the one that flowed from industrialization. Steam power, mass production, and political transformation changed the Common Rules of warfare radically and continually – rapid technological change became one of the constants of military activity and everyday life.

The result, summing over all these categories, was the creation of the "modern" world, where "modern" is basically a sloppy synonym for "industrial." Compared to truly revolutionary transformations such as these, the differences between the world of 540–1500 and the world of 1500–1800 appear gradual, incremental, and, thus, characterizable as a species of continuity.

Extended Middle Ages versus Late Agrarian

The conclusion that flows from this discussion, it seems to me, is that there is no light cast, and indeed much confusion sown, by calling the period 1500–1800 "early modern." If we accept the synonym just proposed, it was clearly not an "early industrial" era. That name might best describe the nineteenth century as a whole. Nor are the markers of "early modernism" that are common in historiography especially modern looking. The increasing sophistication and bureaucratization of states, to take just one example, in the context of continued monarchical government can be seen simply as part of the maturing of medieval systems of governance. Basically, the farther we move from the onset of industrialization, the less "modern" the world of 1500–1800 looks. To call upon a military example, the Duke of Marlborough's Blenheim campaign of 1704 bears far more resemblance to the campaigns of King Henry V in Normandy in 1415 than to the campaigns of Norman Schwarzkopf in Iraq in 2003–4. Jacques Louis David knew this in 1803 (figure 23).

So what do we call the period? Historiography abhors a vacuum as much as nature supposedly does, so we can't just tear down "early modern"; we must replace it with something that emphasizes the essential continuity of the period. I see two choices. In the context of this book, referring to 1500–1800 as "the extended Middle Ages" certainly makes sense. But as a military historian I recognize that this label may give more weight to military history than it can bear in the wider historical profession. The second option is the one I deployed in *Frameworks of World History*: 1500–1800 is "the late agrarian era," the age when the agrarian world reached maturity in every way, not just militarily. This also has the advantage of emphasizing continuity while recognizing the shifts in globalization and network connectedness that suggest a periodization marker in 1500.

But militarily, one of the conclusions this book shows is that the fundamentals of "medieval" warfare continued well into the eighteenth century. This strikes me as a conclusion worth emphasizing, even if not through the imposition of the label "extended Middle Ages" on the late agrarian world.

Figure 23 (Very) late medieval warrior. *Napoleon Crossing the Alps*, by Jacques Louis David, c.1803. Note that David groups Bonaparte's name at the bottom of the painting with those of Hannibal (Annibal) and Charlemagne (Karolus Magnus), showing that the continuities of the agrarian era made such comparisons plausible.

Source: Wikimedia Commons.

Lessons?

Finally, with respect to conclusions, we may ask what lessons our current world might draw from the history of medieval war and conflict in global perspective. We will tread carefully in this question, as the usefulness of history sits in a fine and tense balance between its relevance to today (that is, the day of the historian, a constantly moving target) and what can be learned from experiencing the past on its own terms, as an explicitly *different* place from the present. Our distance from John Churchill, 1st Duke of Marlborough and victor at Blenheim, should remind us forcefully of the latter.

That distance indicates that explicitly military lessons from the history of medieval warfare are probably few and far between. The contexts of war and conflict are so different that details – "Gosh, what's the best battlefield plan when facing a horde of Mongol invaders?" – almost certainly won't apply. Lessons are more likely to come at a higher, somewhat more abstract level of analysis.

That lessons might be available looks possible from one unfortunate set of contexts. We have defined the Middle Ages, in a global perspective, as the period defined by its emergence and eclipse in eras of climate change and pandemics (letting the end point retain some ambiguity in these terms). The world today, in the year 2021 as I write this sentence, faces potentially catastrophic climate change and is living through a major pandemic. Do the dynamics of the emergence of the medieval world from similar circumstances tell us anything about our potential paths forward?

The medieval world was constructed, as we have seen, in large part from wars and armed conflicts at every social level that we analyzed as forms of discourse: ways that human communities (and those communities' subsections) staked out positions, claimed power, and performed identities. This process proved successful in establishing both communal identities and power structures and in negotiating what the world meant to its inhabitants. In short, war and conflict in the Middle Ages built societies with cultural traditions that have shown tremendous resilience and lasting power ever since – the outlines of the medieval world's cultures are still clearly visible even after the industrial transformation.

But the history of war and conflict in the Middle Ages is also full of death, destruction, and the building of power structures that (perhaps inevitably in conditions of low productivity and slow communications) were oppressive and unfair to the vast majority of the humans who occupied them. And that was when war and conflict were played by Common Rules that were very constraining geographically and in terms of basic physics. Carrying on global discourses about the shape of the future through armed conflicts powered by nuclear weaponry does not sound, to me, like a good idea, perhaps seriously limiting what we can learn from that past. Or the lesson is negative: if our main forms of discourse rely on armed force, the likely result will be inequality, oppression, and more damage than construction. War and conflict in the Middle Ages, from this perspective, can stand as an example of what my son Robin said when he was about five years old: "That's how you *don't* do it."

On the other hand, the larger shape of the conflicts of the medieval world may hold a few useful lessons. For one, we have arrived at a world that, in its multipolarity, resembles the medieval world more than it does recent histories of nineteenth-century British dominance and twentieth-century US dominance (or at least Cold War bipolarity). Adapting to our changing and challenging world, a world once again beset by climate change and pandemics, might well benefit from medieval lessons in the dangers of a world-dominating power like the Mongols and in tolerance for multiplicity, contradiction, and answers that need not be final.

Works Cited

Allsen, Thomas T. *Commodity and Exchange in the Mongol Empire: A Cultural History of Islamic Textiles.* Cambridge Studies in Islamic Civilization. Cambridge University Press, 1997.

Andrade, Tonio. "The Arquebus Volley Technique in China, c. 1560: Evidence from the Writings of Qi Jiguang." In Y. Sim (ed.), *The Maritime Defence of China.* Springer, 2017.

Andrade, Tonio. *The Gunpowder Age: China, Military Innovation, and the Rise of the West in World History.* Princeton University Press, 2017.

Anthony, David. *The Horse, the Wheel, and Language: How Bronze Age Riders from the Eurasian Steppes Shaped the Modern World.* Princeton University Press, 2007.

Avari, Burjor. *India: The Ancient Past: A History of the Indian Subcontinent from c. 7000 BCE to CE 1200,* 2nd edition. Routledge, 2016.

Bartlett, Robert. *The Making of Europe: Conquest, Colonization and Cultural Change, 950–1350.* Princeton University Press, 1994.

Beckwith, Christopher I. *Greek Buddha: Pyrrho's Encounter with Early Buddhism in Central Asia.* Princeton University Press, 2015.

Black, Jeremy. *European Warfare, 1494–1660.* Routledge 2002.

Black, Jeremy. *European Warfare, 1660–1815.* Routledge, 1994.

Black, Jeremy. *Rethinking Military History.* Routledge, 2004.

Black, Jeremy. *War and Technology.* Indiana University Press, 2013.

Braasch, Ronald. "The Skirmish: A Statistical Analysis of Minor Combats During the Hundred Years' War, 1337–1453." *Journal of Medieval Military History* XVI (June 2018), 123–57.

Brook, Timothy. *The Troubled Empire: China in the Yüan and Ming Dynasties.* Harvard University Press, 2013.

Büntgen, Ulf, Vladimir S. Myglan, Fredrik Charpentier Ljungqvist, et al. "Cooling and Societal Change during the Late Antique Little Ice Age from 536 to around 660 AD." *Nature Geoscience* Advance Online Publication (8 February 2016).

Campbell, Bruce M. S. *The Great Transition: Climate, Disease, and Society in the Late-Medieval World*. Cambridge University Press, 2016.

Chase, Kenneth. *Firearms: A Global History to 1700*. Cambridge University Press, 2003.

Crone, Patricia. *Preindustrial Societies: Anatomy of the Pre-Modern World*. Blackwell, 1991.

Crone, Patricia. *Slaves on Horses: The Evolution of the Islamic Polity*. Cambridge University Press, 1980.

Curry, Anne and David A. Graff, eds. *The Cambridge History of War. Vol. II: War and the Medieval World*. Cambridge University Press, 2020.

Davis, Kathleen and Michael Puett. "Periodization and 'The Medieval Globe': A Conversation." *The Medieval Globe* 2.1 (2015), 1–14.

DeVries, Kelly. "Catapults are not Atomic Bombs: Towards a Redefinition of Effectiveness in Premodern Military Technology." *War in History* 4 (1997), 454–70.

DeVries, Kelly and Michael Livingston. *Medieval Warfare: A Reader*. University of Toronto Press, 2019.

Diamond, Jared. *Guns, Germs, and Steel*. W. W. Norton, 1999.

Donner, Fred McGraw. *The Early Islamic Conquests*. Princeton University Press, 1981.

Dupuy, R. Ernest and Trevor N. Dupuy. *The Encyclopedia of Military History from 3500 B.C. to the Present*. Rev. 2nd edition. Harper and Row, 1986.

Fancy, Nahyan and Monica Green. "Plague and the Fall of Baghdad (1258)." *Medical History* 65.2 (2021), 157–77.

Fang, Cheng-Hua. "Military Families and the Southern Song Court: The Lü Case," In P. Lorge (ed.), *Warfare in China to 1600*. Routledge, 2016.

Ferguson, Brian. "Archaeology, Cultural Anthropology, and the Origins and Intensifications of War." In E. Arkush and M. Allen (eds.), *Violent Transformations: The Archaeology of Warfare and Long-Term Social Change*. University of Florida Press, 2005.

Ferguson, Brian. "Violence and War in Prehistory." In D. L. Martin and D. W. Frayer (eds.), *Troubled Times: Violence and Warfare in the Past*. Gordon and Breach, 1997.

France, John. *Victory in the East: A Military History of the First Crusade*. Cambridge University Press, 1994.

Golden, Peter B. *Central Asia in World History*. Oxford University Press, 2010.

Gordon, Matthew. "The Early Islamic Empire and the Introduction of Military Slavery." In A. Curry and D. A. Graff (eds.), *The Cambridge History of War. Vol. II: War and the Medieval World*. Cambridge University Press, 2020.

Graff, David A. "The Battle of Huo-I." *Asia Major*, 3rd series, 5.1 (1992), 33–55.

Graff, David A. "China: The Tang, 600–900." In A. Curry and D. A. Graff (eds.), *The Cambridge History of War. Vol. II: War and the Medieval World.* Cambridge University Press, 2020.

Graff, David A. *Medieval Chinese Warfare, 300–900.* Routledge, 2001.

Green, Monica. "Black as Death" [review of Campbell, *Great Transition*]. *Inference: International Review of Science* 4.1 (May 31, 2018). https://inference-review.com/article/black-as-death.

Green, Monica. "When Numbers Don't Count: Changing Perspectives on the Justinianic Plague." *Eidolon* (November 18, 2019).

Guilmartin, John. "The Cutting Edge: An Analysis of the Spanish Invasion and Overthrow of the Inca Empire, 1532–1539." In K. Andrien and R. Adorno (eds.), *Transatlantic Encounters.* Berkeley, 1992.

Haldon, John. "Byzantium to the Twelfth Century." In A. Curry and D. A. Graff (eds.), *The Cambridge History of War. Vol. II: War and the Medieval World.* Cambridge University Press, 2020.

Halsall, Guy. "Reflections on Early Medieval Violence: The Example of the 'Blood Feud'." *Memoria y Civilización* 2 (1999), 7–29.

Halsall, Guy. *War and Society in the Barbarian West.* Routledge, 2003.

Halsall, Guy. "The Western European Kingdoms, 600–1000." In A. Curry and D. A. Graff (eds.), *The Cambridge History of War. Vol. II: War and the Medieval World.* Cambridge University Press, 2020.

Hanson, Chris. "The Mongol Siege of Xiangyang and Fan-ch'eng and the Song Military." *De Re Militari* (May 11, 2014). https://deremilitari.org/2014/05/the-mongol-siege-of-xiangyang-and-fan-cheng-and-the-song-military.

Hassig, Ross. *Aztec Warfare: Imperial Expansion and Political Control.* University of Oklahoma Press, 1988.

Hemming, John. *The Conquest of the Incas.* Pan Macmillan, 1993.

Hogan, William. "The Great Staring Contest: 200 Years of Crusading and Cultural Exchange in the Baltics". Unpublished research paper, 2020.

Howard-Johnston, James. *Witnesses to a World Crisis: Historians and Histories of the Middle East in the Seventh Century.* Oxford University Press, 2010.

Jackson, Peter. *The Delhi Sultanate: A Political and Military History.* Cambridge University Press, 1999.

Keegan, John. *The Mask of Command.* Penguin, 1988.

Kennedy, Hugh. *The Great Arab Conquests: How the Spread of Islam Changed the World We Live In.* Hachette Books, 2007.

Knox, MacGregor and Williamson Murray, eds. *The Dynamics of Military Revolution, 1300–2050.* Cambridge University Press, 2001.

LeDonne, John P. *The Grand Strategy of the Russian Empire, 1650–1831.* Oxford University Press, 2004.

Lee, Wayne E. "Conquer, Extract, and Perhaps Govern: Organic Economies, Logistics, and Violence in the Preindustrial World." In E. Charters, M. Houllemare, and P. H. Wilson (eds.), *A Violent World? A Global History of Early Modern Violence and its Restraint.* Manchester University Press, 2020.

Lee, Wayne E. *Waging War: Conflict, Culture, and Innovation in World History.* Oxford University Press, 2015.

Lewis, Bernard. *Islam, from the Prophet Muhammad to the Capture of Constantinople. Vol. 2: Religion and Society.* Walker, 1976.

Lieberman, Benjamin and Elizabeth Gordon. *Climate Change in Human History: Prehistory to the Present.* Bloomsbury, 2018.

Lorge, Peter. *The Asian Military Revolution: From Gunpowder to the Bomb.* Cambridge University Press, 2008.

Lorge, Peter. "The Northern Song Military Aristocracy and the Royal Family." In P. Lorge (ed.), *Warfare in China to 1600.* Routledge, 2016.

Lorge, Peter. *War, Politics, and Society in Early Modern China, 900–1795.* Routledge, 2005.

Lorge, Peter, ed. *Warfare in China to 1600.* Routledge, 2016.

Luttwak, Edward. *The Grand Strategy of the Roman Empire.* Johns Hopkins University Press, 1976.

Lynn, John, ed. *Tools of War.* University of Illinois Press, 1990.

Marshal, Christopher. *Warfare in the Latin East, 1192–1291.* Cambridge University Press, 1992.

Marvin, Laurence W. *The Occitan War: A Military and Political History of the Albigensian Crusade, 1209–1218.* Cambridge University Press, 2009.

May, Timothy. *The Mongol Art of War: Chinggis Khan and the Mongol Military System.* Westholme, 2007.

Morillo, Stephen. "The 'Age of Cavalry' Revisited." In D. Kagay (ed.), *The Circle of War.* Boydell and Brewer, 1999.

Morillo, Stephen. "Battle Seeking: The Contexts and Limits of Vegetian Strategy." *The Journal of Medieval Military History* 1 (2002), 21–41.

Morillo, Stephen. "Contrary Winds: Theories of History and the Limits of *Sachkritik*." In G. I. Halfond (ed.), *The Medieval Way of War: Studies in Medieval Military History in Honor of Bernard S. Bachrach.* Ashgate, 2015.

Morillo, Stephen. *Frameworks of World History: Networks, Hierarchies, Culture.* Oxford University Press, 2014.

Morillo, Stephen. "A General Typology of Transcultural Wars: The Early Middle Ages and Beyond." In H.-H. Kortüm (ed.), *Transcultural Wars from the Middle Ages to the 21st Century.* Akademie, 2006.

Morillo, Stephen. "Guns and Government: A Comparative Study of Europe and Japan." *Journal of World History* 6 (1995), 75–106.

Morillo, Stephen. "Ibn Khaldun Views Olitski." The 32nd LaFollette Lecture (October 7, 2011). https://www.academia.edu/15037495/Ibn_Kh aldun_Views_Olitski.

Morillo, Stephen. "Kings and Fortuna: The Meanings of Brémule." In J. D. Hosler and S. Isaac (eds.), *Military Cultures and Martial Enterprises in the Middle Ages: Essays in Honour of Richard P. Abels.* Boydell Press, 2020.

Morillo, Stephen. "Mercenaries, Mamluks and Militia: Towards a Cross-Cultural Typology of Military Service." In J. France (ed.), *The Mercenary Identity in the Middle Ages.* Brill, 2007.

Morillo, Stephen. "Milites, Knights and Samurai: Military Terminology, Comparative History, and the Problem of Translation." In B. Bachrach and R. Abels (eds.), *The Normans and their Adversaries at War: Essays in Honor of C. Warren Hollister*. Boydell and Brewer, 2001.

Morillo, Stephen. "The Sword of Justice: War and State Formation in Comparative Perspective." *Journal of Medieval Military History* 4 (2006), 1–17.

Morillo, Stephen. *Warfare under the Anglo-Norman Kings*. Boydell and Brewer, 1994.

Morillo, Stephen, Jeremy Black, and Paul Lococo. *War in World History: Society, Technology, and War from Ancient Times to the Present*. McGraw Hill, 2008.

Newfield, Tim. "The Global Cooling Event of the Sixth Century: Mystery No Longer?" *Historical Climatology* (May 1, 2016). https://www.historical climatology.com/features/something-cooled-the-world-in-the-sixth-centu ry-what-was-it.

Ohlén, Carl-Eric, Dag W. Scharp,, and Mats Rehnberg, eds. *Från fars och to ffarfars tid*. 2nd edition. Gotlandskonst, 1973.

Parker, Geoffrey, ed. *The Cambridge History of Warfare*. Cambridge University Press, 2005.

Parker, Geoffrey. *The Military Revolution*. Cambridge University Press, 1988.

Pegg, Mark Gregory. *A Most Holy War: The Albigensian Crusade and the Battle for Christendom*. Oxford University Press, 2008.

Peters, Edward, ed. *The First Crusade: The Chronicle of Fulcher of Chartres and Other Source Materials*. 2nd edition. University of Pennsylvania Press, 1998.

Pongratz, Julia, Ken Caldeira, Christian H. Reick, et al. "Coupled Climate–Carbon Simulations Indicate Minor Global Effects of Wars and Epidemics on Atmospheric CO_2 between AD 800 and 1850." *Holocene* 21.5 (2011), 843–51.

Powers, James. *A Society Organized for War: The Iberian Municipal Militias in the Central Middle Ages, 1000–1284*. Berkeley, 1988.

Rogers, Clifford. "'As if a new sun had arisen': England's Fourteenth Century RMA." In M. Knox and W. Murray, *The Dynamics of Military Revolution, 1300–2050*. Cambridge University Press, 2001.

Rogers, Clifford, ed. *The Military Revolution Debate*. Westview Press, 1995.

Rogers, Clifford. "The Offensive/Defensive in Medieval Strategy." In *From Crécy to Mohács: Warfare in the Late Middle Ages (1346–1526). Acta of the XXIInd Colloquium of the International Commission of Military History (Vienna, 1996)*. Heeresgeschichtliches Museum/Militärhistorisches Institut, 1997.

Rogers, Clifford. "The Role of Cavalry in Medieval Warfare." *Journal of Military History* (forthcoming).

Rogers, Clifford. *Soldiers' Lives through the Ages: The Middle Ages.* Greenwood, 2007.

Rogers, Clifford. "The Vegetian 'Science of Warfare' in the Middle Ages." *Journal of Medieval Military History* 1 (2002), 1–19.

Rossabi, Morris. *The Mongols and Global History.* W. W. Norton, 2010.

Scott, James C. *Against the Grain: A Deep History of the Earliest States.* Yale University Press, 2017.

Smail, R. C. *Crusading Warfare, 1097–1193.* 2nd edition. Cambridge University Press, 1995.

Sumption, Jonathan. *The Albigensian Crusade.* Faber, 1978.

Swope, Kenneth. "Manifesting Awe: Grand Strategy and Imperial Leadership in the Ming Dynasty." *The Journal of Military History* 79 (2015), 597–634.

Telegraph Online. "Deluge Drowned Mighty Guptas: Study." *The Telegraph Online* (February 24, 2019). https://www.telegraphindia.com/india/deluge -drowned-mighty-guptas-study/cid/1685500.

Tibble, Steven. *The Crusader Armies.* Yale University Press, 2018.

Turnbull, Stephen. "Biting the Bullet: A Reassessment of the Development, Use and Impact of Early Firearms in Japan." *Vulcan* 8 (2020), 25–53.

Turney-High, Harry Holbert. *Primitive War: Its Practice and Concepts.* University of South Carolina Press, 1949.

Urban, William L. *The Teutonic Knights: A Military History.* Greenhill, 2003.

Wagoner, Phillip B. "India, c. 1200–1500." In A. Curry and D. A. Graff (eds.), *The Cambridge History of War. Vol. II: War and the Medieval World.* Cambridge University Press, 2020.

Wallacker, Benjamin. "The Siege of Yu-pi, A.D. 546." *The Journal of Asian Studies* 28 (1969), 789–802.

Watson, Andrew. *Agricultural Innovation in the Early Islamic World: The Diffusion of Crops and Farming Techniques 700–1100.* Cambridge University Press, 1983.

White, Sam, Christian Pfister, and Franz Maulshagen, eds. *The Palgrave Handbook of Climate History.* Palgrave Macmillan, 2018.

Whittow, Mark. *The Making of Orthodox Byzantium, 600–1025.* Macmillan, 1996.

Wink, André. *Al Hind: The Making of the Indo-Islamic World. Vol. 1: Early Medieval India and the Expansion of Islam, 7th–11th Centuries.* Brill, 1990.

Winkler, Albert. "The Battle of Murten: The Invasion of Charles the Bold and the Survival of the Swiss States." *Swiss American Historical Society Review* 46 (1), 8–34.

Woosnam-Savage, Robert and Kelly DeVries. "Battle Trauma in Medieval Warfare: Wounds, Weapons and Armor." In L. Tracy and K. DeVries (eds.), *Wounds and Wound Repair in Medieval Culture.* Brill, 2015.

Wright, David. "The Northern Frontier." In David Graff and Robin Higham (eds.), *A Military History of China.* 2nd edition. University Press of Kentucky, 2012.

Index

Page numbers in *italics* refer to figures.